More Advance Praise for
How I Found God in Everyone and Everywhere:
An Anthology of Spiritual Memoirs

"This passionate and captivating book is a collection of inspiring spiritual memoirs told by many eminent scholars and spiritual leaders of our day. Capturing the many twists and turns of human experience, these memoirs movingly illuminate the many spiritual and intellectual questions which shape the journey to God, and beyond, in the 21st century. ... Scholars, religious leaders, students, and interested seekers will find inspiration and challenge in these narratives."
—The Rev. Dr. Sheryl A. Kujawa-Holbrook,
dean of the faculty, Claremont School of Theology;
and author of *God Beyond Borders: Interreligious Learning Among Congregations*

"What a world we live in—filled with believers, nonbelievers, and the vast majority who are somewhere in between. We in-betweeners ... yearn to find God—or something like God—in the here and now of daily life, in the garbage and, yes, the flowers. It helps if we have stories from others: people who likewise struggle and somehow find their way into a God of tenderness and creativity, of struggle and peace, of faith and doubt. They become our mentors, evoking and inspiring us with an invitation to seek God on our own terms, too, and in our own way. This marvelous anthology can do just that. Read carefully and freely, with a relaxed grasp, and let the stories take you on a journey well worth the walking."

—Jay McDaniel, founder of Open Horizons
and author of *Gandhi's Hope: Learning from the World's Religions as a Path to Peace*

"This is a book for people who, in spite of themselves, cannot stop dreaming about God. Unwilling to dismiss their dreams as mere wishes, to discount their imaginations as pure fantasy, they seek words and concepts by which they may begin to think and talk their way back to 'God after God.' In *How I Found God in Everyone and Everywhere*, readers get to meet a rich array of others on their own versions of this 'spiritual journey beyond the dead-end.'"

—Rabbi James Ponet, emeritus Jewish chaplain
and Divinity School lecturer, Yale University

"Davis and Clayton are ontological trail guides. They have gathered the stories of an impressive array of theological and spiritual leaders who discovered a living and credible God after the God of old had died for them. It turns out that God was not dead after all. God is hidden where we least expect it—in butterflies and hospital beds, waterfalls and embodied rage, in the messiness and mysteriousness of our own real life experience. These guides know. They point to and describe a God who is with us."

—Frank Rogers Jr., director of the Center for Engaged Compassion at the Claremont School of Theology,
and author of *Practicing Compassion*

how I found GOD in everyone and everywhere

An Anthology of Spiritual Memoirs

Andrew M. Davis *&* Philip Clayton

MONKFISH BOOK PUBLISHING COMPANY
RHINEBECK, NEW YORK

Cover design by Nita Ybarra
Interior design by Colin Rolfe

Paperback ISBN: 978-1-939681-88-1
eBook ISBN: 978-1-939681-89-8

Library of Congress Cataloging-in-Publication Data

Names: Davis, Andrew M., 1987- editor. | Clayton, Philip, 1956- editor.
Title: How I found God in everyone and everywhere : an anthology of spiritual
  memoirs / [edited by] Andrew M. Davis & Philip Clayton.
Description: Rhinebeck, New York : Monkfish Book Publishing Company, 2018.
Identifiers: LCCN 2018010751 (print) | LCCN 2018010938 (ebook) | ISBN
  9781939681898 (ebook) | ISBN 9781939681881 (pbk. : alk. paper)
Subjects: LCSH: Pantheism. | Panentheism. | Spiritual biography.
Classification: LCC BL220 (ebook) | LCC BL220 .H69 2018 (print) | DDC
  204--dc23
LC record available at https://lccn.loc.gov/2018010751

Monkfish Book Publishing Company
22 East Market Street, Suite 304
Rhinebeck, New York 12572
USA (845) 876-4861
www.monkfishpublishing.com

"'God is dead' or so it seems to us…until, round the next bend in the road, 'we find [God] again, alive'. Once again [God] makes [the Divine Self] known, in spite of all that we have left behind on the road, all that was only a viaticum for one stage of our journey, all that was only a temporary shelter till we had to make a fresh start…"

—*Henri de Lubac*

"To be on a journey is to be in movement. Moving from place to place—there is change in such a life. A journey is a process that involves our whole being. It involves our feet as well as our minds and our heads. A journey involves following a path or a way. To be on a journey is not to be wandering aimlessly, though there may be times when it feels like that; people have gone on this journey before us, and there is a trail, a path, a way that we are called to."

—*Marcus J. Borg*

Contents

Acknowledgments and Dedication

Two longstanding interests have converged in the emergence of this volume: a desire to both engage today's fresh and dynamic understandings of God and also peer into the personal, spiritual, and intellectual journeys which underlie their discovery. These two interests are grounded in the basic conviction that w*hat* one affirms about the divine and *how* they have come to this affirmation, are holistically entangled. The personal, albeit intellectual, approach of Marcus Borg, coupled with Richard Kearney's notion of "anatheism" ("returning to God after God"), formed the backdrop and initial stimulus for the project. I remain indebted to the influence of these men in the final arrival of this volume.

Grateful thanks are of course due to many:

To Philip Clayton, my advisor and co-editor, who received my initial idea and invitation to the volume with enthusiasm and encouragement. Partnership with Philip continues to be nothing short of inspirational. I remain grateful for his model scholarship and mentorship. Without his willingness and collaboration, this volume would have never been developed. To Stephanie Londono, whose encouragement to "stop reading and start writing" was well taken and whose hours of faithful conversation underlie the vision of these pages. To Malcom Oliver II, loyal conversation partner and valued friend. To the respected contributors, who welcomed the vision and themes of this volume and whose personal reflections and journeys comprise the flow of its chapters. To Paul Cohen and the skillful editorial team at Monkfish, for seeing both the potential and value of the volume for today's changing spiritual climate. To both my father, Reed C. Davis, and my brother, Ben C. Davis, whose support and love I have never doubted.

Finally: to my beloved mother, Bonnie J. Davis, whose humor, wonder and faith will always be the foundation of my own and whose encouragement and excitement for this volume made it worth pursuing, even if she were the only one to ever read it. Succumbing to breast cancer at age 63 took that opportunity from her. It is to her life and legacy that I lovingly dedicate this volume; and it is Whitehead's words which always bring her to mind: "It is characteristic of the learned mind to exalt words. Yet mothers can ponder many things in their hearts which their lips cannot express. These many things, which are thus known, constitute the ultimate religious evidence, beyond which there is no appeal."

Andrew M. Davis
Claremont School of Theology
August 2018

Introduction: The Journey Ahead

Andrew M. Davis

There is great value in taking a journey. Journeys not only beckon us to potential adventures that lie ahead, but they also bring with them personal transformations, allowing us to see things differently upon returning home. This is one of the principal reasons we take journeys: they change us and the way we view the world. The value of a journey does not exist only for the one who takes it, however. After all, what good are journeys if they cannot be shared? If you have ever returned from a series of travels, you know you will be met with an avalanche of questions: "Where have you been?" "How did you get there?" "What did you experience?" "What did you learn?" In a certain sense, we look forward to these questions and to sharing the nature of our journeys with others. In doing so, we find that they too are able to journey with us.

Life, of course, consists of all manner of journeys. There are those short journeys we anticipate beginning, those long journeys we look forward to ending, and those meandering journeys that always seem to begin again, over and over. For millions of people, the most important journey is their spiritual journey, their journey with—or to—God. And the journey with God is, to be sure, a meandering one, including ups and downs, stops and starts, U-turns and even dead-ends. As the philosopher and mathematician Alfred North Whitehead once commented, "The modern world has lost God and is seeking him." His claim seems to be true, for an increasing number of people find themselves doing a lot more seeking. As the biblical injunction goes, "seek and you will find." But many of these same people also feel the weight of wandering—a deep sense that while their "seeking" may have increased, their "finding" has actually decreased.

Nearly a century has passed since Whitehead commented on a seeking modern world; and today our postmodern world seeks God all the more. Like the Madman in Nietzsche's infamous parable, many internally cry, "I seek God! I seek God!" to no avail. Nietzsche would soberly remind us that our predicament today is not simply that God has lost his way "like a child" or "gone on a voyage" or "emigrated" to some distant region of the cosmos. Rather, "God is dead" and "we have killed him." Under heaps of criticism, running from science to the vexing problem of evil, God is not simply lost, but also irrelevant and dead. And for many, when God dies, so dies the theological and spiritual journey.

Nevertheless, the question still remains: Is there a way of returning to God *after* God, of (re)discovering a new God rising from the ashes of a dead one? If so, what might this spiritual and intellectual journey look like, and to what understanding of God does it lead?

Much can be gained from trailing the spiritual and theological narratives of those who have traveled ahead of us, for the God they have found we may have never considered. This volume is not only about *sharing* the meandering nature of that "seeking" as it crosses a fascinating variety of spiritual terrains, but is also about the *kind of God* that may be found. These are visions of God that, although ancient in origin, are reemerging and attracting the attention of an increasing number of people. They are notions neither of a king-like being of omnipotent rule, nor of an indifferent force indistinguishable from the world, but rather of something different—something that for many is allowing for a return to God *after* God and thus a continuation of the spiritual journey beyond the dead-end.

Of course, no two spiritual journeys are ever the same, nor should they be. And no traveler follows exactly the same path; rather, the terrain each maneuvers remains unique. This is something that is clearly seen in the dynamic and collaborative chapters which together form this volume. It is one thing to ask *what* these prominent contributors imagine of the divine in the 21st century, but quite another to ask *how* they have found their way. Indeed, to ask the *how* question of one's spiritual journey is to ready oneself to hear a tale. And that is what this anthology is all about.

While many of the contributors communicate deeply personal elements of their spiritual journeys—religious or mystical experiences, existential hardships and intellectual discoveries—others have chosen to broaden their focus, reflecting and commenting more generally on the evolving state of theology, religion, and spirituality. When you put all of these diverse narrative threads together, what emerges is a holistic spiritual tapestry, one that is woven together by a burgeoning theological vision.

This theological vision has come under the rather odd name of "panentheism." From the Greek meaning "All-in-God," panentheism is the view that the universe is *within* God, although God is *more than* the universe. The divine reality is *inclusive of* and also *immanent* ("dwelling in") within the universe, but it can never be reduced to the universe itself. God is thus the *immanent-transcendent* reality, in which we live and move and apart from which nothing at all can be. Rather than being somewhere else, God is right here; rather than being outside the world, God is "in, among, and through" the world as the intimate foundation of its being and the dynamic source of its becoming. And this relationship is often described in mutual ways: not only is God immanent in the becoming of the world, but the world is also immanent in the becoming of God—affecting God, sharing its own reality with that of the divine.

A deeply immanent and participatory conception of the God-world relationship can vastly reorient one's spiritual journey, transforming how one experiences the world. As these diverse spiritual memoirs testify, for many people today, the spiritual and intellectual journey has led to the discovery of a divine reality that, it turns out, we already inhabit, and that encompasses us all. This relational God—whether you want to call it "panentheism" or not—is the spiritual heartbeat found in the following pages. This heartbeat is not found in some people and some places, but in everyone and everywhere.

In sharing these journeys with readers, we hope to offer a vision of spiritual return and reenchantment. Relating one's own personal journey to that of others can offer new insight, inspiration and depth to one's life and to one's world. Opening this volume itself is the beginning of a journey. And while you never quite know where journeys will take you, you can be confident that you will not return home the same. Often it takes encountering the journey of another to help continue our own. The best journeys, after all, are those that are shared.

1. That of God in Every One

Philip Clayton

When, as a child, I lay down in the dry grass, it crunched against my back. The ground sloped up behind our house to the edge of the forest. From there I could see far out over the northern California hills, brown in the late summer sun. The tall blades of grass smelled like hay, and the thicker patches of it, rising overhead, almost blotted out the sky. Birds were busy in the oak trees. Sun warmed my entire body to contentment. I was absorbed by the meadow, and in that eternal moment it was as if the world held its breath.

"God *is* the flowers," I told my friend Linda Ross in elementary school. "God is the trees and the grass." No one in my house believed in God, so to use the word at all was a minor act of defiance. The idea that there were right and wrong ways to speak of God never occurred to me; I didn't even have a mental category for orthodoxy. But I knew I was grounded in those hills, related to those flowers and birds. That fact didn't need explaining. I didn't have to work at it, I knew; I just lived in it.

One summer my two sisters and I spent some weeks at an outdoor summer school, run by a couple who were, I later found out, Quakers. Their backyard also opened onto the rolling hills, and there also the sun warmed our backs as we painted, crafted, and listened to stories. Sitting on the hard adobe clay, I looked up above Mrs. Tappan's book at the gigantic oak that seemed to fill the sky. Its limbs were amazingly thick and strong, like the arms of a weightlifter; they stretched parallel to the ground for what seemed like forever. More than a dozen of us kids could slide along those limbs from the trunk to the small branches and leaves at their tips, and yet there would still be room for more of us. I didn't use the God-word—it would not have seemed necessary—but if Linda Ross had asked me again, I might have said, "Yes, look! If anything on earth is God, then it must be the giant oak."

Theologians say that your image of God defines your spirituality. Nothing could be more true. (Given all the theologies of a vengeful, distant, and disembodied God, this correlation is probably bad news for the planet.) The spirituality of an oak tree is grounded, stable, and nurturing; it radiates strength. An oak is not *in* a space; it defines a space, owns it. If I had any idea of eternity, it was that oak tree at the Tappans' house.

And eternity was also the ocean. After lunch on Fridays, we would all clatter into an ancient VW bus and the Tappans and some of our parents would drive us all out along the winding roads to a beach south of Jenner, to a place where the twisting coastal highway came right down to the water. We called it No Name Beach, and even stopping there somehow felt like a statement of political resistance, an act of peace. We slithered over the rocks and jumped into tidal pools and found little caverns in the steep cliffs where we could hide. Always we could hear the crashing surf and inhale the salt spray, and we would watch the fog as it canopied the sky.

When we finally wandered back from our explorations, the adults would have built a fire out of driftwood and water would be boiling in a huge kettle. To make Stone Soup, each child would find a rock to contribute, throw it in, and wait for the transubstantiation to happen. Sitting around the fire was my first experience of church, and Stone Soup was our sacrament of Communion. The fire and the stones were the ritual, and we immersed ourselves in the accompanying liturgy with all the attentiveness of high-church Anglicans:

"Once upon a time, many years ago, a stranger wandered into a village. The farmers, coming in from their fields, gathered around him on the village green. The stranger told them that he could make soup out of stones alone. Wanting to see the magic, the townspeople built a huge fire and placed on it a kettle large enough to feed the entire village. Each child was sent off to collect a stone and throw it into the boiling water. The stranger tasted the Stone Soup and noted that it would be perfect if it had just a little more spice. Four housewives ran off and brought back armfuls of spices to drop in. The stones are working, he proclaimed; just a touch of barley would balance out the taste. Potatoes, leeks, tomatoes followed, until the smell of the soup wafted out across the green. Bowls were brought, and the stranger distributed Stone Soup to each villager. The magic had worked, the soup was glorious, and the villagers feasted and sang and danced well into the night."

The mother officiating at our fire was our pastor and we were her congregants. We carried out each step of the sacrament as she recited it: Alison poured in the potatoes, Julie the tomatoes. Sitting on the sand, with the wind on our cheeks, we watched the steam rise from the soup, as amazed by that miracle as if we were witnessing Jesus distributing loaves and fishes. Holy Communion was not wafers and grape juice in a church building; it was communion with the gulls, the crabs, and the infinite ocean itself. Instead of hymns, we sang anti-war songs to the strong chords of the guitars, proclaiming our creed to the sound of the waves. Although the answer to the many questions posed in "Blowin' in the Wind" was, and remains, a mystery, the ocean breeze did indeed kiss us on the cheeks as we sang that the elusive answer was "blowin' in the wind."

Just before sunset, we walked slowly to the edge of the waves, silenced by the sacredness of the earth's first miracle. Holding hands, we stood motionless as the last flames of the sun sank into the ocean, and then softly sang our simple benediction:

Day is done, gone the sun,
From the lake, from the hills, from the sky;
All is well, safely rest, God is nigh.

Amen, and amen. God *was* nigh.

From time to time, kids from elementary school would invite my sisters and me to their churches. Deedee Milburn's parents took us to a Methodist church, I think, and Jane Bigelow brought us to the Catholic church in town. The latter was particularly frightening: I was always sitting down when they stood and standing when they knelt, failing to juggle the red book and the blue book, and dropping the instruction sheet. To me, as the offspring of heathen parents, it felt as if Catholics were all fluent in a language I could not speak. Grace at friends' houses was equally embarrassingly. I would dig happily into my plate of food, only to be glared at by the father across the table: "In *our* family, we pray before dinner." Apparently, his house was the moral norm, and we were the deviants.

Church and divine immanence first came together when I was 10. Jim Slater, a famous actor and member of the local Presbyterian church, invited my mother to perform Jesus' mother in *Family Portrait*, a play about Jesus' family during his last three years. I became the shepherd boy, wandering onto stage periodically, playing a wooden recorder. My first picture of Jesus, then, was a Christology of absence, since in this play all one sees are the effects on the family of their famous son, who never actually appears on stage. For me, also, Jesus was somehow hovering in the wings.

At the end of the production, the actors dismantled the set, and I was left alone for the first time in the silence of the darkened sanctuary. A huge cross hung down over the altar from the almost invisible ceiling above, illumined by a gentle light, radiating into the darkness. Its two conjoined pieces of wood pointed upward like an arrow. The Sacred, like the soft purple light, filled the sanctuary, around and within me. Motionless, in awe, skin tingling, I was drawn into an all-encompassing mystery.

At 14, in a dramatic conversion at a religious camp near Santa Cruz, I accepted Jesus as my Lord and Savior. No teenage rebellion could have been more effective. Sex, drugs, or a boyfriend would not have caught my parents' attention; but to proclaim to my English-professor father that all truth resides in one book alone was the greatest heresy imaginable. Sitting at the breakfast table, I formulated my first systemic theology—actually a *Heilsgeschichte*, a history of fall and redemption. My Christian worldview had all the sophistication of a two-day-old Christian:

"God is eternally Father, Son, and Holy Spirit. He created the heavens and the earth, and a bunch of animals and man. And then God took a rib out of Adam to make Eve, which is why women should submit themselves to men. God then had to find someplace to put them, so He created a garden. But they ate an apple off the Tree of Knowledge and, knowing, became ashamed of being naked. For their sin, God kicked them out and made them nomads, separated from Him. He sent them prophets to call them back to salvation; but when they continued to sin, he punished them by flooding them, turning them into pillars of salt, and having Israel be conquered by heathen nations. Fortunately, God finally sent His eternal Son, Jesus, to reveal the truth about God and to die for our sins. The church is now the Body of Christ, and accepting the living Jesus is the only path to salvation. The others will suffer eternally in hell. Jesus is coming back as conqueror; the sheep will be separated from the goats; and God will establish a new heaven and earth for all eternity."

This was a theology of the transcendent God in its strongest form. My father was too shocked to say a word, but I do remember my mother crying softly into her breakfast cereal.

During the following few years I moved even further to the right theologically. The college I chose held to the doctrine of plenary inspiration, which meant that God had dictated Scripture, which meant that the Bible could not contain any mistakes about any matters, scientific or historical or otherwise. To make things worse, by the time I arrived at college I had concluded that, if the Bible is the decisive revelation of God's eternal nature, then it must contain *all* truth, so we don't really need to read any other books to discover what is true—a great mindset for entering college!

My years as a fundamentalist faced a first challenge and a final collapse. Every verse of the Bible had to be true, so 1 Corinthians 11:10 also had to be true: "Therefore the woman ought to have a symbol of authority on her head, because of the angels." It puzzled me what a woman's head covering would have to do with angels. So I went to my youth minister for guidance. He thought for a moment and then announced that the head covering is for the sake of the angels because it keeps them from feeling sexual lust for the women while they're in church. Of course I trusted my youth minister, but as a hormone-charged adolescent male I *knew* that this one didn't make sense: the angels watch the women all the time, in bikinis and taking showers, but they can't handle observing the women's hair in church? That verse was just obviously wrong. But if even one verse wasn't true, then the Bible couldn't be inerrant in every respect. The long slide down the slippery slope had begun.

The final departure from fundamentalism came during my junior year. We were sitting in rapt attention as our favorite philosophy professor, Stan Obitts, was lecturing on the German philosopher Gottfried Wilhelm (von) Leibniz and Christian apologetics. The energy in the room grew and grew; we were approaching eternal verities. Suddenly, like a symphony conductor, he brought the discussion to a standstill with his hands, held us for a long dramatic pause, and then announced decisively, "*These* are the questions!" In that instant, as quickly as a snap of the fingers, I got it: in the end, it really *is* more about the questions than it is about the answers. I am certain that Dr. Obitts, of blessed memory, would never have agreed with my conclusion. But it stuck. From that day onward, I knew that I would devote myself first to the questions as my highest passion. Where answers emerged, I would hold them hypothetically, seeking out criticisms before confirmations and modifying my beliefs accordingly. Only the freedom to challenge orthodoxies can bring transcendence down to earth.

That moment also sowed the seeds for my becoming a Quaker. When the foundations that hold up orthodoxy begin to crumble, the building falls. As for so many people, it was during seminary that I lost my faith and left organized religion. But one Sunday morning while I was visiting home, my mother asked me if I'd like to attend her Quaker Meeting. That time of silence was, and is, the most honest hour of the week. "I may not believe in anything," I thought, "but I do know that I will die someday. To reflect on how to live in the face of death is worth an hour a week."

Shortly thereafter, separated by only two years, both of my parents died, and both were celebrated in a Quaker Memorial Meeting for Worship. A week after my mother's tragic death, we sat again in silence in the Meeting room. No pastor shared anecdotes about the deceased or promises for an afterlife. When her friends or family felt led, they "spoke out of the silence," and we then returned to silence to reflect on what had been said, to weep or to smile. At one point, my sister stood and spoke of her anger that our mother would have been taken away in this way. At the end, she shook her fist at the heavens and yelled, "I hate you, God!" Sometime during those minutes I became a Quaker for life. Where else, I thought, could you scream out your fury at God and be embraced without judgment?

In some ways, Quakers are literalists. Appealing to the New Testament, early Quakers refused to serve in the army, to swear to tell the truth when in court, or to use any titles for the British nobility, calling each one "Friend" instead. Not surprisingly, they spent a lot of time in jails. Instead of doctrines, as Quakers we affirm our "testimony," which in my unprogrammed tradition means the values that we intend to live by, such as Simplicity, Peace, Integrity, Community, Equality, and Stewardship. I particularly remember a row of white-haired women standing on a sidewalk and holding hands in deep but firm silence, behind them gay couples walking into the city courthouse, and in front of them a screaming mob. That's what testimony means.

A central conviction for Quakers is that there is "That of God in Every One."[1] If I had to formulate my theology and spiritual practice in only six words, those are the ones I would choose. If there is That of God in a Muslim, you don't kill him; in a black man, you don't imprison him unjustly (or shoot him); in an animal, you don't torture or eat her; in nature, you don't rape and pillage it for your own pleasure. Because of That of God in the person before me, I strive to hear her as deeply as possible, whatever her color, culture, or creed. When during worship a person speaks out of the silence, I listen for That of God in her words before returning to reflection or prayer. Imagine what would happen if members of each religion listened for That of God in all the others and held themselves to nonviolence in thought, word, and deed? Imagine what would happen if we learned to see and hear That of God in every part of the natural world around us?

I had the best theological education I could find: a rigorous conservative seminary, four years under the great Lutheran theologian Wolfhart Pannenberg, and mentoring from the famous theologians at Yale during Ph.D. studies. I'm known as a constructive theologian, having published books with titles such as *Adventures in the Spirit* and *In Whom We Live and Move and Have Our Being*. I teach classes and mentor doctoral students in the field, specializing in forms of panentheism around the world. For this reason, I owe readers a brief statement of where my theological work has brought me.

Like some (but not all) authors in this volume, I believe in a not-less-than-personal Divine that is the source of and underlies all existing things. If this God is all-knowing and all-powerful, he or she is a negligent, even abusive parent, responsible for the darkest evil and the most immoral suffering. I could never worship a "Heavenly Father" who would watch even one innocent child being tortured to death, who is able to stop the suffering in an instant, and who does not.

But a God who changes, who responds, who enters into the suffering of the world? This is the heart of what process theologians affirm. We do it in different ways, however. Some of my colleagues believe that God is *metaphysically* limited; God could not be related to a world in any other way than God currently is. With other colleagues, I prefer to imagine a real divine choice. In the New Testament it's expressed as an act of self-emptying (*kenosis*) on the part of the Christ, "who, although he existed in the form of God, did not regard equality with God a thing to be grasped, but emptied himself, taking on the form of a servant, being born in the likeness of [a] man. And being found in human form, he humbled himself and became obedient unto death, even death on a cross" (Philippians 2).

I then expand this idea from Christ to all Creation. All three Abrahamic traditions (at least in their orthodox forms) affirm an infinite Divine before creation. Now expand the *kenosis* idea: what if, in creating a world of finite beings, God self-limits the divine transcendence and power for the sake of relationship? This approach opens the door to a pervasive divine immanence that flows through all things and sustains all beings, yet in such a way that their own agency is strengthened.

We call this view *relational panentheism*: God's choice to create was a choice to be in relationship, to be maximally related, which means never erasing the freedom of created beings. That's a radical requirement. It excludes direct revelations of infallible knowledge, forced conformity to God's will, and overpowering miracles that set aside natural laws. Not even once. Hence, the miracle-working God must give way to a constant lure of the Divine—not a transcendent incursion, but a gentle tug toward the Good. The lure is felt in the "fusing-without-loss-of-identity" that we experience in mystical moments and in intimate relationships. Divine action becomes sustenance, nurturing, comfort. The Immanent Divine is the spiritual presence that comes to and into everyone who suffers; indeed, God is that presence that is *always already alongside and within*.

We don't say that a scientist is hypocritical for not living out the Schrödinger wave equation, but things are different in the spiritual life. Where you want to go and how you walk the path always go together, just as much as what you believe about people (and other living things) and how you treat them. Equally inseparable are what you want to say and how you say it. I often wonder to what degree "finding God in everyone and everywhere" can be expressed through the "-isms" that theologians use.

I think it can, but only if one can bond head to heart. *Head*: St. Thomas Aquinas, the 13th-century Catholic theologian, begins his magisterial "Summa" with five ways (*viae*) to prove the existence of God: God is first mover, source of order, necessary being, and so forth. *Heart*: What if we think of "ways" not as highways to God, but as wandering paths? The German philosopher Martin Heidegger calls these *Holzwege*, trails that meander through the forest with no particular destination. Sometimes, he says, they come out into a *Lichtung*, an unexpected opening in the forest where you can suddenly see the sky. You rest yourself on a tree stump in the middle of the small green clearing bathed in light and listen to the rustling of the wind. Three trails in particular have led me into that clearing of divine light—the trails of the poetic, the scientific, and the mystical.

Something far more deeply interfused. The Romantic poets were drawn to a deeper dimension that underlies the world as it appears. Take Wordsworth, who saw that we, as moderns, have lost touch with what matters: "The world is too much with us; late and soon / Getting and spending, we lay waste our powers / Little we see in Nature that is ours..." And yet the thing we long for is so close:

> This Sea that bares her bosom to the moon
> The winds that will be howling at all hours
> And are up-gathered now like sleeping flowers;
> For this, for everything, we are out of tune
> It moves us not.

It's not that Nature is the ultimate goal, itself God. Nature, so immanent around us—even now I watch the wrens washing themselves in the fountain, the hummingbirds hovering above the flowers—is also the portal to something that transcends us, something we can never fully grasp. At dusk Wordsworth wanders up the creek bed behind Tintern Abbey, keenly aware of every detail of tree and flower. He (and I with him) reflects that when he was young "nature... was all in all." But now it vibrates, illuminates, shimmers, and lets him see behind the veil:

> ... And I have felt
> A presence that disturbs me with the joy
> Of elevated thoughts; a sense sublime
> Of something far more deeply interfused,
> Whose dwelling is the light of setting suns,
> And the round ocean and the living air,
> And the blue sky, and in the mind of man:
> A motion and a spirit, that impels
> All thinking things, all objects of all thought,
> And rolls through all things.

The Divine *dwells in* sun, ocean, air, in our minds and souls; yet it always remains more than these. It "rolls through all things" like the crashing waves of the northern California coast, pulsing in and out and in again. Like William Blake, you can "Hold Infinity in the palm of your hand / And Eternity in an hour," participating in its boundlessness. But you yourself are neither infinite or eternal.

Catching one-million-year-old light. Wordsworth bemoaned our deaf ear for the voice of nature: "It moves us not." Far more deaf are we to the symphonies of science. Like the black and white notes in the score that code for the music without *being* the music, the equations of physics are windows that open onto amazing vistas. I once talked with a physicist who had co-developed a theory of cold dark matter from mathematical models alone. One day he was asked to be present for an announcement from a team at the Stanford Linear Accelerator. Sitting in the audience, he heard the scientists describe the empirical discovery that his pure mathematics had predicted, including the values he had calculated. It was, he said, a religious experience—that core features of the universe could be predicted from mathematical theories alone.

Many physicists are mystics. Einstein famously affirmed, "The most beautiful thing we can experience is the mysterious. It is the source of all true art and science." Nor does Richard Feynman see any conflict: "The vastness of the heavens stretches my imagination—stuck on this carousel my little eye can catch one million year old light... It does not do harm to the mystery to know a little about it."[2] Einstein again: "If something is in me which can be called religious then it is the unbounded admiration for the structure of the world so far as our science can reveal it."[3]

Butterflies and dancing chimpanzees. Two of the most profound scientist-mystics I have known are Jane Goodall and Rachel Carson. I had the privilege of working with Jane over a seven-year period, and still view her as one of the few genuine saints I have known. At the time, she was traveling over 300 days a year, building her Roots and Shoots organization, and advocating for animals and their habitats. Her lifestyle matched her values. I remember once, at UNESCO world headquarters in Paris, watching her as she came to an elevator, followed by a group of administrators, men in suits. She blocked the doors and made them follow her like ducklings as she led them down several flights of stairs.

Many know that Jane Goodall had an incredible spiritual connection with animals. But few know about the foundational role that her own spirituality played in her life. I interviewed her at the State of the World Forum in New York City and asked her to talk more about her own spiritual experience. Here's what she told me:

> It is my belief—and because it is a belief, you can discuss it but not disprove it—that there is a great Spiritual Power and that there is a spark of that spiritual power within each of us. And I believe that there is a spark of the same spiritual power in *all* life... We have rationalized our feelings about the great spiritual power—God, the Divine, the Creator—whatever we want to call it... Some of us call this spark a soul... Many people are prepared to admit that there is this spark of spirit in everything, but only in us [they say] is it the soul.[4]

Once, when giving a talk, Jane told the amazing story of watching a group of young male chimpanzees walk up a small river they had never visited before. As they came around a sharp corner, they suddenly saw a huge waterfall, crashing majestically into a pond. At first they froze, amazed, taking in what they had just encountered. Then, she said, the young chimps raised their arms above their heads and began to dance with joy. Their response, Jane told the audience, is best understood as awe and wonder.

During those years, Jane demonstrated how deeply spirituality and nature are connected. "Many try to deny the presence of a spiritual dimension to their lives," she told me. "Maybe, just maybe, we can turn things around and begin to save what is left of the natural world. Maybe it is not too late to heal some of the scars we have inflicted, to find ways of living in greater harmony with nature."[5]

Rachel Carson was one of the greatest naturalists and environmentalists of the 20th century. She too writes of "the value of preserving and strengthening this sense of awe and wonder, this recognition of something beyond the boundaries of human existence... Those who contemplate the beauty of the earth find reserves of strength that will endure as long as life lasts."[6] Rachel is best known for *Silent Spring*, but I strongly recommend reading at least one of the three books in her *Sea* series. (My favorite is *Under the Sea Wind*.) She calls herself a naturalist, and yet the vibrating spirituality of the natural world sounds through clearly in her writing.

One day, when I was walking along the rocky coast just south of Portland, Maine, I came across a boulder with a plaque embedded in it. It was the spot where Rachel Carson had asked that her ashes be spread upon the water. In one of her last letters she described her impending death and her undying love of nature. If I could choose one sentence to inscribe on the spot where my ashes will be mixed with the Pacific, it would be Rachel's words: "But most of all I shall remember the monarchs, that unhurried westward drift of one small winged form after another, each drawn by some invisible force."[7]

All manner of thing shall be well. The mystic knows through a kind of seeing, a knowing that is not through the mind but through the heart. If words must be used, they are but a pale reflection of the unitive experience. In such moments, surely, we encounter the Immanent Divine.

I believe it is the infinite that we encounter, that infinite presence "in whom we live and move and have our being," and in whose womb we dwell. We can no more possess her than we can capture a ray of sunlight with our hands. As Frederico García Lorca puts it, "When the moon sails out / the sea covers the earth / and the heart feels it is / a little island in the infinite."

Mysticism begins with the realization that our words will always fall short. And yet language about Mystery is not an off/on switch. There is much to learn from *when* and *how* words fail us. Indeed, maybe "fail" is not even the right word; maybe words serve us best as they gradually step aside and become pointers toward the ineffable. Sometimes, as Peter Berger writes, they are "signals of transcendence"—not the transcendent itself, but intimations of it, like fingers pointing at the moon. At other times, as T.S. Eliot beautifully puts it, "... there is only the unattended / Moment, the moment in and out of time, / The distraction fit, lost in a shaft of sunlight,"

> Or the waterfall, or music heard so deeply
> That it is not heard at all, but you are the music
> While the music lasts. These are only hints and guesses,
> Hints followed by guesses...

Some of our deepest mystical experiences are not vertical; they do not pull us upward, like a church steeple, toward the transcendent. Instead, they are experiences of *horizontal transcendence*, as Ursula Goodenough puts it in *The Sacred Depths of Nature*. I am backpacking in the Trinity Alps Wilderness in northern California, southwest of Mt. Shasta. After a simple dinner I sit by the edge of the lake. The surface perfectly mirrors the mountains behind, disturbed only when a rainbow trout jumps to catch an insect. Darkness falls. A Zen verse forms itself in the silence:

> There was the lake and the moon
> Suddenly came Enlightenment
> And after there was the lake and the moon.

One can live infinitely into a single moment; the Now knows no boundaries. How long can you sit with Basho's best-known haiku:

> Old pond
> A frog jumps in—
> The sound of water

Somewhere between Basho's frog and Eliot's "hints and guesses" is where I seek to dwell.

Most of the authors whose spiritual memoirs follow are panentheists, though we may choke a bit on that awkward term. So many profound spiritual insights fall under its umbrella: the widely used Quaker expression, "That of God in Every One," or the phrase from the creed, originally applied only to Jesus Christ but now expanded to encompass every living thing, "in whom the fullness of God was pleased to dwell."

Of all the philosophers in history who have sought to formulate the panentheistic insight, none has succeeded more powerfully, I think, than the great Hindu theologian Ramanuja. Ramanuja's insights come from the Hindu scriptures, especially the Bhagavad Gita and the Upanishads. Three verses from the Kena Upanishad in particular tie together the mystical and the poetic, the experiential and the metaphysical, in language that gestures toward what cannot be said:

> That which thinks not by the mind, that by which the mind is thought, know That to be the Brahman and not this which men follow after here.

> That which sees not with the eye, that by which one sees the eye's seeing, know That to be the Brahman and not this which men follow after here.

> That which breathes not with the breath, that by which the life-breath is led forward in its paths, know That to be the Brahman and not this which men follow after here.

Each of us has our one life to lead. Each one is powered by needs and longings, by love and hate, by acts of deep compassion and acts of self-assertion. Crippled by pain or dancing with joy, we walk this journey from birth to death. When our eyes are open, we feel wonder; when our souls are open, we feel awe; when our hearts are open, we feel reverence for all that is.

Along the way, we form beliefs about God, pro or contra. Experiences evoke these beliefs (or destroy them), sustain them, and (hopefully) drive us to action. Beneath the appearances lies a *Mysterium tremendum et fascinans*, as Rudolf Otto put it—a Mystery that frightens and fascinates at the same time.

I find little comfort in the omnipotent God of my teen-age years; the moral costs of His management style are just too great. Surely the Divine permeates and sustains all things, closer to us than we are to ourselves, "higher than my highest and more inward than my innermost self" (St. Augustine). And if God is everywhere and in every one, as Julian of Norwich knew, then "all shall be well, and all shall be well, and all manner of thing shall be well."

In the end I can affirm no cosmic narrative that does not leave me on that rocky ocean shore, watching Rachel Carson's butterflys—"that unhurried westward drift of one small winged form after another, each drawn by some invisible force." Here, if anywhere, I experience the unity of finite being and the Divine. Yes, most of all I shall miss the Monarchs.

Notes

1. I emphasize that, although the phrase is taken from the founder of the Religious Society of Friends, George Fox, I and many other Friends today do not use it in the same sense as Fox did.

2. Richard Feynman, *The Feynman Lectures on Physics* (San Francisco: Pearson/Addison-Wesley) 2006 [1963]).

3. Einstein, 1954, letter to an atheist.

4. Interview with Jane Goodall, in Philip Clayton and Jim Schaal, ed., *Practicing Science, Living Faith: Interviews with Twelve Leading Scientists* (New York: Columbia University Press, 2007), 27.

5. Ibid., 38.

6. Rachel Carson, "Help Your Child to Wonder," *Woman's Home Companion*, July 1956, p. 48.

7. Rachel Carson, letter to Dorothy Freeman, September 10, 1963.

2. *Rediscovering God in Nature and Nature in God, via India*

Rupert Sheldrake

I believe that God is in me, and that I am in God. I think that God is in all nature and that all nature is in God. I have not always thought like this. I was an atheist for about 15 years, although I was brought up as a Christian. I rediscovered God through India.

I was raised in a Methodist family and educated at Anglican boarding schools from the age of 10 to 17, first at Ranby House Preparatory School, and then at Worksop College, in Nottinghamshire. These schools are part of a group of high-church Anglican boarding schools, the Woodard Schools, established in the 19th century. I was a chorister, singing in the school choir for the Anglican liturgy of Sung Eucharist and

Choral Evensong, and with our choir I sang Choral Evensong in several cathedrals, including Lincoln, Southwell, and York. I also learned to play the organ, following in the footsteps of my paternal grandfather and my uncle, both of whom were organists and choirmasters in the Methodist Church.

I was impressed by the decency, kindness, and sincerity of the Methodist community in my hometown, Newark-on-Trent, and I was moved by the beauty of the liturgy and the music in the Anglican tradition. I was also keenly interested in nature, and before I went away to school, I kept a wide variety of pets as well as collected plants, which I pressed. My father was an herbalist, pharmacist, and microscopist, and he helped and encouraged me.

But by about the age of 14, I realized that the scientific worldview left little room for God except as a private subjective experience. I was taught that we were living in an atheistic, machine-like universe. God seemed to exist only as an idea in human minds, and hence in human brains, apart from a possible role in framing the mathematical laws of nature. Everything went on automatically, and unconsciously, including evolution. I was the only boy in my year who refused to be confirmed.

My housemaster, Robin Thoday, was also my biology teacher, and he had a strong influence on my thinking. He was also raised in the Quaker tradition, and came from a biological lineage. His father had been professor of botany at the University of Wales, and his brother John was professor of genetics at the nearby University of Sheffield, later to become professor of genetics at Cambridge. In a series of long conversations that we had at night, after which I had to creep back into the dormitory where I slept along with 50 other boys, Robin showed me that Christianity was essentially a mythological system, rooted in primitive and animistic patterns of thought. He introduced me to Sir James Fraser's book *The Golden Bough*, parts of which I read at his suggestion. He also introduced me to Robert Graves' book *The White Goddess* about Celtic mythology in Britain, and he convinced me that Christianity was just one of many mythic systems, all of which were expressions of anthropocentric imaginations and primitive animistic thought. However, he was not a standard atheist. He thought that human minds and science itself were driven by what he called the "unity-seeking process," and this ultimate unity sounded to me like God.

By the age of 17, I was reading Freud, who persuaded me that God was nothing but a projection of an infant's view of its biological father, and that mystical experiences were a kind of regression to an infantile mode of "oceanic" experience. When I read Freud's *Psychopathology of Everyday Life* I saw how everyone (including me) was influenced by unconscious habits of which they were normally unaware, some of them involving repressed emotional experiences from their childhood.

I thought of myself as an atheist, and on an experimental basis I stopped praying, starting with days for which I had few concerns, and felt would probably go smoothly. When I finally stopped praying altogether, life seemed to go on more or less as normal. But it wasn't exactly a controlled experiment. The whole school was bathed in prayers twice on Sundays and at least once every other day of the week. My mother also prayed for me every night, as did other members of my family. So, in retrospect, this "experiment" was not as conclusive as it seemed at the time.

Nonetheless, when I went to Cambridge University to read natural sciences, I identified myself as an atheist and secular humanist. I found that the biggest advantage of atheism was liberation from guilt about sex.

I was drawn to the insights of Karl Marx and joined the Cambridge Labour Club, where I was part of a Trotskyite faction, but not for long. I became more interested in the Campaign for Nuclear Disarmament (CND) and was an active anti-nuclear protester, going on marches to nuclear bases; and I was arrested in Parliament Square for sitting on the road, as part of a protest led by Lord Bertrand Russell, then in his 90s. Bertrand Russell was a prominent atheist. This impressed me. I didn't pay so much attention to the fact that the CND was led by an Anglican priest, Canon John Collins, a canon of St. Paul's Cathedral, and Lord Soper, a prominent Methodist. Many members of the movement were Quakers.

While I was an undergraduate, I didn't doubt atheism, but I began to worry about the truth of mechanistic science. I found it hard to believe that the universe was nothing but a machine, and that animals and plants were also machines, with no purposes or feelings, and that we too were machines, with brains that were essentially electronic computers. I started reading Goethe, who gave me the idea of a possible holistic science.

I was successful at Cambridge, and gained a double first-class degree, as well as the University Botany Prize, and everyone assumed that I would go on to do a Ph.D. in biology. But I had my doubts, and wanted to find out if this is what I really wanted. I was fortunate to be appointed the Frank Knox Fellow at Harvard University, where I spent a year (1963-64) studying the history and philosophy of science, which gave me a wider perspective. This was soon after Thomas Kuhn's book, *The Structure of Scientific Revolutions,* came out, and I was very impressed by his idea of paradigms in science as conventions or belief systems, which could be replaced in scientific revolutions by other models of reality. It became obvious to me that the mechanistic worldview was just such a paradigm.

I then returned to Cambridge to do my Ph.D. in plant biochemistry, where I worked on the production of the plant hormone auxin. I discovered that it was made in dying cells as a byproduct of their decomposition. As plants grow, cells within them die, especially the wood cells, which dissolve themselves to become empty tubes that conduct water. And as cells die, they produce auxin, which gives rise to more growth.

While I was doing this research, I encountered a group in Cambridge called the Epiphany Philosophers, an improbable mixture of philosophers, quantum physicists, linguists, pioneering computer buffs, Christian mystics, Quakers, and Buddhists. This group prayed together, wearing long white robes, singing plainchant and following the Anglican liturgy, but also had some of the most robust intellectual discussions I have ever experienced. The dominant force of this group was Margaret Masterman, the wife of Richard Braithwaite, a professor of philosophy at Cambridge, and her vision was that where science and mystical religion conflicted, there was probably something wrong with science. This conflict was greatest in the realms of mechanistic biology and the materialist theory of mind. Another member of this group, Dorothy Emmet, was professor of philosophy at Manchester, and had been a student of Alfred North Whitehead.

I was very interested in the discussions, which happened both in the group's retreat house in Cambridge, and also at an old windmill on the Norfolk coast, at Burnham Overy Staithe. I was not so interested in the Christian liturgy, and went along with it rather half-heartedly as I had learned to do at school, where chapel attendance was compulsory.

In 1967, I was elected to the Research Fellowship of Clare College Cambridge, which gave me free rooms in college, free meals on high table, free wine, free bed-makers to clean my room, free telephone calls, and a very modest salary. For six years, I enjoyed an unprecedented period of freedom. I had a laboratory in the biochemistry department and could work on whatever I liked—which was mainly on polarity in plants and the cellular basis of polar auxin transport, and also on the cellular basis of ageing and death. For the last three years of my time at Cambridge, I was also a research fellow of the Royal Society.

In 1968, I had a separate Royal Society grant to work in the Botany Department of the University of Malaya, in Kuala Lumpur, studying rainforest plants. On my way to Malaysia, I spent two months travelling through India, which was a life-changing experience. I had only been there for a few days when I ran into a friend of mine from Cambridge, Johnny Parry, who was doing fieldwork for his anthropology Ph.D. in a remote village in the Himalayan foothills. We met by chance in Delhi, and he invited me to go back with him to his village. I went. It was several hours' walk from the nearest road head, which we reached after a long journey by train and bus. He was living in the house of a Brahmin family who were herbal doctors or *vaids*. There was no electricity, no radio, and no television. Johnny spoke the local language, Paharhi, and as we walked through the village in the following days we chatted with farmers, people in teashops, and local artisans.

One day we went for a walk along a road up a valley leading into the mountains, and by a waterfall we saw a cave, in which there was an orange-robed figure, the local *sadhu* or holy man. He called out to Johnny, who told me the sadhu had invited us up to his cave. So we went and sat there with him. He produced a clay pipe, packed material into it, lit it, and invited me to have a smoke. Before lighting it, he invoked the god Shiva and told me it was Shiva's holy plant. He showed me how to smoke the chillum and I took several puffs. This was the first time I had had a dose of cannabis that affected me. I had only smoked it once before, at a party in Cambridge, and had felt nothing. This time the world was transformed. When I went outside the cave into the sun, as I stood on the grass, looking up at the mountains, I felt a blissful sense of connection, and a conscious presence far greater than my own.

Before I left the *vaid* family to start my journey through India, at 4:00 a.m., the Brahmin's wife burnt incense, anointed me with holy ashes, gave me some *prasad* or holy food for my journey, and told me I would return to India. I did so six years later, to take up a job at an international agricultural institute in Hyderabad.

Traveling through India and Sri Lanka, living in Malaysia, and then traveling through Thailand, Laos, and Cambodia on my way home, shifted my view of the world very radically. In Asia, I was not among secular humanists and atheists, but among Hindus, Muslims, and Buddhists. Their view of life seemed just as rational as the scientific view I had been educated into, if not more so, and they also seemed to be having more fun. When I got back to Cambridge in 1969, it was harder than ever to believe enthusiastically in the materialist and mechanistic view of nature. In 1971, I took LSD for the first time, and it was literally mind-expanding. I saw visions. I experienced music as sublimely beautiful, ever-changing visual patterns, synaesthetically. Nothing in the materialist worldview had prepared me for this.

From a scientific point of view, by 1973 I had concluded that the mechanistic theory of life was not only inadequate, but could be replaced by a more holistic or organismic theory. Alfred North Whitehead established the philosophical foundations for this approach in the 1920s. In his book *Science in the Modern World* (1927), he argued that nature was not made up of material stuff that just endured in time, but of processes. Quantum theory, then very new, had already recognized that material particles, like electrons, and the quantum of light, photons, have a wave like nature. Being waves, they wave. And waving takes time. There cannot be a wave at an instant in time, nor at an infinitesimally small position in space. Waves take time and space to wave in; all material systems are therefore fundamentally processes, and as a processes they have future and past poles.

Whitehead pointed out that nature is made up of many levels of organisms, from atoms and molecules to cells, and then on to animals and plants. Whitehead, as far as I know, did not push this process further, but obviously it must extend to our planet as a whole, Gaia, the solar system, the galaxy, galactic clusters, and ultimately the entire cosmos. Nature is composed of nested hierarchies of organization, or holons, as Arthur Koestler called them (Figure 1). At each level, the whole is more than the sum of its parts, and each of the parts is itself a whole that is more than the sum of its parts, and so on.

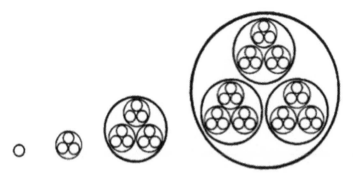

Figure 1. A nested hierarchy or holarchy of holons.

Since the 1920s, within the holistic tradition of biology, the organizing formative principles of animals and plants had been called *morphogenetic fields*. These fields had ends or goals within them, and attracted animals and plants towards their mature forms. They were rather like what Aristotle and St. Thomas Aquinas called the vegetative soul. Aristotle called this attractive principle within the soul, pulling development towards an end goal, *entelechy*. A growing seedling was attracted towards the material form of the oak tree by its entelechy. I was very interested by this tradition in developmental biology, but found it raised as many questions as it answered. How were these organizing principles passed on over time? How were they inherited in animals and plants?

A new way of answering these questions came to me in 1973. My hypothesis was that these fields were themselves shaped by a resonance from past similar systems, which I called morphic resonance, which gave them an inherent memory. From this point of view, each species has a collective memory on which each individual draws and to which it contributes. This memory covers both the development of form, as in plant growth and animal embryology, and behavior, as in the inherited instincts of animals. Similar organizing fields underlie the activities of groups of animals, like hives of bees, schools of fish, flocks of birds, and packs of wolves. The wholeness of each level comes from an organizing field, called a morphic field, which gives it its shape, form or structure as a vibratory pattern of activity. And morphic fields have ends or goals; they move towards attractors.

In Cambridge, the idea of a memory in nature was treated as frivolous or irrelevant by most of my scientific colleagues. I found more interest in the idea among fellows of my college in philosophy and history. But it was clear to me that I could not develop this approach within the biochemistry department where I was working, because it was so at odds with the reductionist ethos of that discipline. So I decided to do something completely different.

In 1974, I resigned my fellowship at Cambridge to become principal plant physiologist at the International Crops Research Institute for the Semi-Arid Tropics (ICRISAT) in Hyderabad. At Cambridge, I had taken up transcendental meditation and yoga, and was eager to immerse myself in the culture of India. I was also excited about working in an institute where I could do something useful to help poor farmers and impoverished people. I carried out many field experiments, and helped develop new varieties of chickpeas and pigeonpeas and new cropping systems. I also visited temples, listened to discourses by Hindu sages, and went for the *darshan*, the look, of holy men and women. I learned Urdu and had close Muslim friends. For a year I had a Sufi teacher and did a regular Sufi practice, a kind of mantra called a *wazifah*, which was one of the 99 names of God. But to my surprise, I felt myself pulled back towards the Christian tradition. I started praying again, and attending evensong at St. John's Church, Secunderabad, originally the Anglican Church for the British cantonment. At the age of 34, I was confirmed at St. John's, in the Church of South India.

One of the things I deeply appreciated about being in India was the general acceptance that the world is alive. This came to me in one of my first experiences in India, by the sadhu's cave in the Himalayas, and through the pervasive sense of sacred rivers, mountains, plants, and animals. When I was working at ICRISAT, I lived in the wing of a crumbling palace in Hyderabad, which I rented from a Raja, whose family was part of the nobility of Hyderabad, which was ruled by the Nizam until 1948, and was the largest princely state in India. During the monsoon my veranda was leaking because a pipal tree had taken root in the roof, and its roots were cracking the masonry and plaster. Pipals are sacred trees and the Buddha was enlightened while sitting under one. I asked my landlord, the Raja, if he could remove it and he said he would, but never did; and then I asked my institute to send some members of the maintenance crew to solve the problem. When I came back after work on the day appointed, I found the pipal was still there. The workers had made various excuses but had done nothing. When I mentioned this to the head of the maintenance department, he told me that the reason was that the workmen were Hindus, and they were afraid of cutting down a sacred tree. But he assured me he would get the job done. The next day when I returned home after work, the tree had gone and the roof had been mended. I asked him how he did it. He said, "I sent some Muslims." Muslims, of course, have their own well-developed sense of the sacred, but pipal trees are not in a special category for them.

I found something similar when I asked my cook to trap some rats that were disturbing my sleep. He bought some traps that did not kill the rats but imprisoned them. When he caught some, I asked him how he was going to kill them. He explained that he was not going to kill them. They were a sacred animal, the vehicle of Lord Ganesh, the elephant-headed god, so he was going to take them somewhere else. He put the rat-filled traps on the back of his bicycle and pedaled away, releasing them far from my home, and far from his. Thereafter I noticed people all over Hyderabad with rats in traps on the backs of their bicycles. Rats were being moved from place to but the total number remained the same.

At one level, these beliefs are superstitions that obstruct progress, like sacred cows in the middle of busy modern thoroughfares. But at the same time these practices reflect a deep sense of the life of nature, and not just nature but the spirit within nature. The same is true of the air, which is not just a gas containing oxygen and other kinds of molecule, but full of *prana*, a living flow of energy. Likewise the sun is a living being, and its radiant light sustaining all life on earth, flows from a divine source.

After my confirmation, I was happy to be reconnected with my own ancestral tradition, and to be part of the Christian community at St. John's, Secunderabad, and later at St. George's, Hyderabad, where I was for a while the organist. But the rather narrow views of Indian Christians, and their dismissive attitude to Hinduism seemed to me a limitation. I wanted to find a way of embracing both.

In Hyderabad, I was fortunate to have had several servants, and it was easy to offer hospitality to travelers. One such guest, who had visited many ashrams in India, after staying with me, sent me a postcard from Tamil Nadu, in the South of India saying, "I have discovered an ashram that would be just right for you. I suggest you take a weekend off work and go there as soon as possible." He gave me the details. I trusted his judgment, and after a series of long train journeys, I found myself in the Christian ashram of Father Bede Griffiths, a British Benedictine monk who had been living in India for many years, wearing the saffron robes of an Indian holy man, living in a small ashram near a village on the banks of a sacred river, the Cauvery. I could not believe at first that such a man and such a place were possible. Everything seemed to come together here.

I had continued to think about morphic resonance while I was working at ICRISAT, and found that India provided a congenial atmosphere for doing so. Whenever I explained the idea to Hindu friends and acquaintances, instead of the blank incomprehension I was used to in Cambridge, the usual response was, "There is nothing new in this idea. Rishis have seen this thousands of years ago." And, indeed, in both Hindu and Buddhist philosophy, the idea of memory in nature is well known, through a generalization of the idea of *karma*, a principle of memory or habit.

By the time I met Father Bede, I had reached a point where I felt I could write a book on the hypothesis of morphic resonance. When I told Father Bede of this idea, he invited me to stay at his ashram for as long as I liked to write it. I accepted. A year later, I left my job and went to live in the ashram, where I spent 18 months writing the first draft of my book *A New Science of Life*, published in 1981. During that period, I lived as part of this Benedictine community. I meditated twice a day, sitting on the bank of the Cauvery River, took part in the five daily services and helped with farming work in the ashram in the mornings.

Father Bede had an extraordinarily wide-ranging and inclusive mind, and living in his ashram was an extraordinarily time of synthesis for me, with the unity-seeking process in full swing. I saw Father Bede almost every day, heard his homilies at mass in the mornings, and his discourses on the *Upanishads* in the late afternoons, sitting in the shade of a grove of palm trees. Through him I came to understand one of the great insights of the Hindu tradition, which is summarized in the Kena Upanishad as follows:

> What cannot be seen with the eye, but that whereby the eye can see; know that alone to be Brahman, the Spirit; and not what people here adore.

God is the ground of our consciousness and our being. Our minds are not independent units that have somehow emerged from unconscious matter, all separate. Rather our consciousness is derived from the consciousness of God, and our minds, and all minds in nature, are linked back to the consciousness of God as their source.

Father Bede also introduced me to the Christian mystics, like Meister Eckhart and William Law, as well as to the philosophy of form of St. Thomas Aquinas, which was very relevant to my ideas about morphic fields. He also showed me that St. Bonaventure, a 13th-century Franciscan friar, had suggested that everything in nature participates in the Holy Trinity. Pope Francis made the same point in his recent encyclical *Laudato Si* (2015), summarizing St. Bonaventure's teaching by saying that "each creature bears in itself a specifically Trinitarian structure."

Intermingled with these more abstract ideas, Father Bede was involved every day with the life of the ashram and local village, and was often asked to bless new houses, or small businesses, or babies. He loved the way that the local villagers spiritualized the spaces in which they lived, and was happy that the village had several sacred trees within it, and many small temples around natural phenomena like termite mounds. What I learned from living in India was the sense of the God's presence in the natural world, and Father Bede showed me that this was not in contradiction to Christianity, but in harmony with it.

This way of thinking was, of course, very different from the mechanistic view of nature into which I had been educated. One day, while living in the ashram, I was thinking about the rays of light from the sun coming through the leaves of the trees and wondered whether the physical light, as described by physics, and the divine light or spiritual light of consciousness, with its source in God, is a symbolic or metaphorical counterpart, not the same as the physical light. I asked Father Bede what he thought. He said of course there are not two kinds of light. Physical and spiritual light are one.

When I returned to England after living in India for five and a half years, I saw my native land afresh. In England, too, there were ancient holy places and pilgrimages and holy days, the great Christian festivals, including the feasts of All Saints and St. Michael and all Angels. In England, too, there were places where many people felt a sense of connection with the divine. England also had great temples—cathedrals and churches—where sacred chants were offered up daily in praise of God.

In the atheistic universe of materialism and Neo-Darwinism, God is at best an optional extra, part of a belief system confined to the brains of believers. But as the sciences move beyond materialism, we are recovering a sense of the life inherent in nature as a whole, and in self-organizing systems at all levels of complexity. I discussed this transition in my book *The Rebirth of Nature: The Greening of Science and God* (1992). In my book *Science Set Free* (2012; called *The Science Delusion* in the United Kingdom), I show how the 10 fundamental assumptions of materialism have now been superseded by advances in the sciences themselves. But as the sciences move towards a new form of animism or panpsychism, we need new ways of reconnecting with the Christian theological tradition that flourished before the 17th century, when the mechanical worldview took hold.

When I first went to California in the early 1980s, through Father Bede I met Matthew Fox, at that time a Dominican priest, best known for his book *Original Blessing*. He was going back to the ancient insight that all creation came forth from God and was good, rather than focusing the spiritual life on the drama of sin and redemption, although these certainly played a part. He also emphasized that in the United States, if the land were to be honored, and if those who lived on it were to form a healthy relationship with it, they would have to learn from the Native Americans who had lived there long before the European conquerors arrived. The native peoples saw their land as holy, whereas the settlers saw it as real estate to be bought, sold and developed. Matthew and I became great friends and have published two books together, *Natural Grace: Dialogues on Science and Spirituality* (1996) and *The Physics of Angels: Where the Realms of Science and Spirit Meet* (also 1996). Matthew's work helps to reconnect us with the animistic roots of Judaism and Christianity, and with the indigenous people all over the earth who have understood the natural world as alive and spirit-filled.

In California, in the 1980s and again in 2012, I was invited to Claremont College, where I found myself in the center of the school of process theology, which I have found immensely helpful, in particular, through the work of John Cobb and David Ray Griffin. More traditional theologians, including Father Bede, had not paid much attention to evolutionary creativity. This was not a big issue for the church fathers and medieval theologians, who lived in a universe that was believed to be made up of celestial bodies—the stars and planets that were beyond the range of generation and corruption—while on earth the species of animals and plants were fixed. Likewise, Hindu and Sufi philosophers did not live in a cosmos that was believed to be radically evolutionary. But we do.

Biological evolution on earth, human scientific and technological creativity, and the rapid innovations we see all around us, imply an ongoing creativity immanent in the entire cosmos, in biological life and in humanity. Traditional accounts of creation, even when they saw it proceeding in stages rather than all at once, located these events in the remote past, followed by the course of nature going on more or less unchanged, except perhaps for occasional catastrophes. In the Hindu version, there is indeed a process of change over time, but it is one of devolution rather than evolution, with disorder increasing as the universe degenerates. By contrast, in the Judeo-Christian tradition, there was a true development in humanity, through the events of the Old Testament; the life, death, and resurrection of Jesus Christ; and the development of the church and of Christian culture. This progressivist view of history was secularized in the 17th century, most notably by Francis Bacon, giving rise to the idea of economic progress through science and technology, now the orthodoxy of every government in the world. But the philosophers of the Enlightenment confined progress to humanity. In the 19th century it was extended to all biological life through the theory of evolution. And, since 1966, this evolutionary vision has been extended to the entire cosmos. The modern creation story is that the universe was born very small, far less than the size of the head of a pin, some 14 billion years ago, and immensely hot. It has been growing and cooling ever since, and new forms and structures have appeared within it.

This new evolutionary cosmology raises new questions about the role of God in creativity. My own ideas about morphic resonance see the regularities of nature as habits, but all the habits of nature had to come into being for the first time. Evolution is an interplay of habit and creativity. But what is the source of this creativity? Process theologians see God as acting like a "lure," a pull towards actualizing "values that will result in greater richness of experience."[1] Teilhard de Chardin also developed the idea of God as a final cause, attracting the evolutionary course of nature. But even if we accept that the evolutionary process as a whole is drawn towards a divine end, and that this process is essentially creative, the details of evolutionary creativity remain obscure.

From an animistic or a panpsychist point of view, there are many levels of organization within the universe, at many levels of complexity, in a nested hierarchy (Figure 1), with subatomic particles in atoms in molecules in crystals, with cells in tissues in organs in organisms in societies, with ecosystems in Gaia in the solar system in the galaxy. At all levels these organizing principles have the ability to adapt to circumstances and maintain the system they organize in the face of challenges from without. Their adaptations may be original, creative, and this creativity could be thought of as welling up from a level below. Or they could be thought of as organized by higher levels, with innovations in animals and plants influenced by the organization of the whole earth, or the solar system, or the galaxy. Creative inspiration could descend from a higher level.

Platonists place the archetypes of all new forms outside space and time, in a transcendent realm of Forms or Ideas. Each new species, each new kind of dinosaur, or bird, or beetle, reflects an eternal Platonic archetype. These have always existed and always will, even if when all species of dinosaurs are extinct. Even before any of the dinosaurs first appeared, they were potentialities in the mind of God, awaiting the moment in which they could manifest. St. Augustine had such an idea with his concept of seed ideas, *rationes seminales*. But since God's mind presumably contains all possibilities, including many that may never be manifested in our universe, this still leaves open the question of how a creative intelligence selects the appropriate potentiality from this infinite source.

The philosopher Henri Bergson argued strongly for the opposite point of view: evolution is not the unfolding of pre-existing potentialities, but rather involves an inherent creativity. Insofar as God is the source of this creativity, he makes up new forms as he goes along, creating himself through the evolutionary process: "God has nothing of the already made: He is unceasing life, action, freedom.... Creation, so conceived, is not a mystery: we experience it ourselves when we act freely."[2] Bergson called this creative impetus the *élan vital*, as if God were the Holy Spirit, but only the Holy Spirit.

We may never arrive at a full and complete understanding, but it seems to me that the doctrine of the Holy Trinity provides an inherently dynamic model of God, and this eternal dynamic process within God underlies the creativity expressed through all nature in the process of cosmic evolution.

If God were only the second aspect of the Trinity, the Logos, the Word, then he would be immobilized in the Platonic realm of Forms or Ideas. Evolution and change in the world would ultimately be unreal; only the eternal Logos would be real. But in Christianity the Logos became incarnate as a human in a particular place, at a particular time in history, in a world of change and evolution. Indeed, the incarnation of the Word as Jesus Christ was a supreme example of evolutionary creativity, opening up a new way of being human, and changing the course of human history.

But Jesus Christ became human not just because he was the Word of God, but because he was conceived by the Spirit of God, and had the Holy Spirit within him, and was inspired by the Holy Spirit, as he experienced dramatically when he was baptized.

The fundamental manifestations of the Spirit are breath, the wind, movement and change, life, and the energy in all nature. This became very clear to me through translations of the Bible into Indian languages. The word that has to be used for the Holy Spirit is *shakti*, which in the Indian tradition is a principle of energy in all things.

In the Holy Trinity, the primary metaphor is speech. Spoken words depend both on ideas in minds and on the outflow of the breath through which the words or forms are spoken. If there were only forms, and no spirit, the forms would not be expressed in nature or in history, but rather would be confined to a realm of ideas. And if there were only spirit and no words, there would only be a chaotic, formless flow of change. Words unfold and succeed each other through the flow of the spirit, and the spirit changes because of the words that are spoken through it. And the speaker of the words and the breather of the breath, the Father, changes through the breathing and the speaking. Yet this Trinity is also beyond time and space, and its dynamics transcend the natural world.

There are powerful parallels to this Trinitarian understanding in other religious traditions. I first became aware of this connection when I was living in Father Bede's ashram, which in English is called the Ashram of the Holy Trinity, while in Sanskrit, it is Satchitanada Ashram, a word expressing the unity of *sat*, being; *chit*, consciousness; and *ananda*, bliss. These fundamental agreements between the Christian, Hindu, and other traditions are brilliantly illuminated in David Bentley Hart's book *The Experience of God: Being, Consciousness, Bliss.*[3]

Many new questions arise in a post-materialist, animistic or panpsychist world. How can we understand evolutionary creativity? How is the creativity of God expressed in cosmic evolution? What kinds of consciousness are there in planets, stars, and galaxies, and how do they affect us? Are we the only biological organisms on earth, or in the universe, with minds that can consciously connect with the being of God? How are our minds and other kinds of minds throughout the universe related? Why does the universe contain billions of galaxies and each galaxy billions of stars? Are there other universes besides our own, as some cosmologists think? And if so, could there be conscious connections between them?

These kinds of questions do not arise if God and nature are kept separate, and the realms of theology and natural science are insulated from each other. But if God is in nature and nature is in God, we are surrounded by new possibilities.

Notes

1. David Ray Griffin, *God and Religion in the Postmodern World* (Albany, NY: State University of New York Press: 1989), 80.
2. Henri Bergson, Creative Evolution (London: Macmillan, 1911), 262.
3. David Bentley Hart, *The Experience of God: Being, Consciousness, Bliss* (New Haven, CT: Yale University Press, 2013).

3. The Entangled God of My Heart

Ilia Delio, OSF

The Lure of Science

In 1984, I completed a dissertation in pharmacology at New Jersey Medical School. My research was in the area of motoneuron neuropathy and I worked with an experimental drug to mimic the pathological neuronal damage found in Lou Gherig's disease, also known as Amyotrophic Lateral Sclerosis (ALS). I worked with an Italian neuropathologist from Milan, and together we would look at healthy and damaged motoneurons through a high-powered electron microscope, allowing us to peer inside the private lives of nerve cells. The sheer ability to do so often left me speechless and wondering. How did these incredibly fine-tuned and well-organized cells come about? How did they disintegrate? What keeps a hundred trillion neurons operating synchronously and inter-dependently with incredible precision? These questions and others kept me enthralled in the area of neuroscience. Yet something more seem to be at the heart of it all, even though science pursued questions of inquiry with methods of analysis and statistics. I felt there was an elusive quality of nature which led me to write on the first page of my doctoral dissertation: "In the simplest cell of life lies the mystery of creation."

I was a hardcore scientist who felt that the path to truth could only be found in science. Although I had been raised in a Catholic Italian-American family, religion was what one did on Sunday. My parents imparted a moderate sense of religion, including Sunday worship obligation, devotion to St. Anthony, and of course the great feasts of Christmas and Easter. I was sent to Catholic schools with virtually no consideration of non-Catholic schools. I cannot say that I either rebelled or rejected the Catholic milieu. On the contrary, I liked the prayers, the liturgical worship and even the devotions because I was drawn to the mystery of religion. As a result, I developed two brains: a science brain and a religious brain. Science meant serious study, thought, inquiry, and examination while religion evoked wonder, awe, mystery, and order. With religion I had identity and purpose, while in science I had a drive to know and discover.

Although I loved the field of neuroscience and had accepted a postdoctoral position at Johns Hopkins Medical School, I felt there was a deep inner draw to God that could not be satisfied by scientific research. One day I came across a new biography of the Trappist monk, Thomas Merton. I had never heard of Merton nor did I know anything about contemplative life. Merton's story was so appealing that I quickly went out and purchased his autobiography, *The Seven Storey Mountain*. I devoured it in an evening and felt that my life was meant to follow a path similar to that of Merton. Hence, shortly after successfully defending my dissertation on ALS, I took a slight detour and entered a Byzantine Rite monastery of discalced (shoeless) Carmelite nuns in Pennsylvania. My research colleagues thought it was a respite from exhaustion and could not otherwise understand why I would make such a radical choice on the heels of a very successful career. I really could not find the words to adequately explain why I decided to decline the postdoc at Hopkins in order to enclose myself in a monastery devoted to prayer and physical labor. So I left with few words of comfort to friends and family.

Monastic Life:
The Laboratory of God

To this day I cannot give a logical explanation for relinquishing a career in a field that was beginning to mushroom into very lucrative areas. I could neither explain God nor adequately describe the power of a religious call to a celibate life. All I could say was that the power of God was such that to deny God would have been to deny my very self. I was impelled to leave everything I had worked for and enter the uncharted territories of the spiritual life. The words "let go, let God" appropriately described my path. The monastery offered an alternate world to the world I renounced, a world of discipline, prayer, hard work, and community. We prayed six hours a day, and when we were not at prayer, we worked to maintain the monastery both physically and financially. We were gardeners, carpenters, bakers, and musicians. While our work supported the community, prayer deepened our spiritual lives. The Carmelite charism is formed by prayer and contemplation as described by the two leading mystical writers of the order, St. Teresa of Avila and St. John of the Cross. I was deeply attracted to Teresa's wit and personality, as well as her realistic understanding of human nature and her constant search for God. She was a woman of great intellect and vision who became a renowned doctor of the Church.

Despite the rhythmic harmony of monastic life, however, I felt something was askew. For one thing, I could not reconcile the God of Jesus Christ—"who so loved the world that he sent his only Son"—with a life significantly detached from the world. If God is for the world, why should we be against it? This unresolved spiritual struggle created a great interior conflict for me; thus after four years I took a leave of absence and was sent to live with a community of German Franciscan sisters in New Jersey while doing a postdoc in neurotoxicology at Rutgers University. My inner spirit of exploration and discovery found new freedom among the Franciscans because the world was no longer an obstacle to God; rather it was the place to find God. The Franciscan charism focused on "following the footprints of Christ." I had no idea of what this meant, but it was clear that life as a scientist in a Franciscan community of women would be short-lived, as the sisters would eventually send me to Fordham University to study theology.

Theology: The Queen of Sciences

I agreed to study theology more reluctantly than enthusiastically because I had the simple idea that "God" could not be studied or subject to real inquiry. However, Fordham gave me the opportunity to explore the world anew outside the convent. I concentrated in the area of historical theology because I had always been attracted to the writings of the early Church Fathers, such as St. Augustine, and eventually wrote a master's thesis on happiness in the *Rule* of Augustine. Studying theology opened up doors that I never knew existed. For one, my puerile notion of God was quickly dispelled by the deep philosophical and theological writers of the early Church. I soon realized that theology was not a matter of feeling or devotion but a science in its own right with methods of inquiry, logical reasoning, structured arguments, and insightful conclusions. Indeed, medievalists viewed theology as the "queen of all sciences" since every discipline, from the mechanical arts to astronomy and rhetoric, could be traced back to theology. The scientific nature of theology converted me from a bicameral mind of science or religion to an integrative mind of science and religion. As I studied the writings of the Middle Ages and the development of scholasticism, I began to appreciate the deep interconnectedness between macrocosm and microcosm.

I was given the opportunity to continue to pursue a doctorate in historical theology and wound up studying with one of the leading Bonaventure scholars, Ewert H. Cousins. Cousins was a remarkable man in many ways, a brilliant mind and humble spirit wrapped together in a childlike wonder of new ideas and insights. His lectures often spanned the centuries in a single hour. He would begin with Augustine then move to the Victorines and Franciscans and then wind his way into the thought of Alfred North Whitehead and Teilhard de Chardin and then back to Francis of Assisi and Bonaventure. Cousins was, by training, a philosopher and his gentle spirit betrayed his penetrating mind. He discovered the structure of the coincidence of opposites in Bonaventure's writings and used this hermeneutic to interpret Bonaventure's cosmic Christology. He helped create the Classics of Western Spirituality series with Richard Payne and was the general editor of the World Spirituality Series. He was friends with Thomas Berry and Raimon Panikkar, as well as president of the American Teilhard Association and member of the World Parliament of Religions. He recognized that we are living on the cusp of a new axial age of consciousness which, following Karl Jaspers, he called the second axial period. In fact, the second axial period occupied much of his thought. While first axial consciousness gave rise to the free, autonomous individual, Cousins recognized that the second axial period evoked a new global consciousness. In his book *Christ of the 21st Century* he described the second axial age as one ushered in by science and technology, including television, mass communication, mass travel, and the internet. These technologies have fundamentally altered our view of the world and ourselves in the world. Cousins claimed that our consciousness was jolted onto a new level when, in 1968, the first photograph of the planet earth, reprinted in all major magazines, triggered immense awe; a tiny blue marble-like globe suspended in space. From space, the earth seemed like a single tribe of humanity. For the first time since the appearance of human life on our planet, all of the tribes, all of the nations, all of the religions began to share a common history.[1] Cousins used the term "complexified collective consciousness" to describe this new level of consciousness, indicating that people are becoming more aware of belonging to humanity as a whole rather than a specific group.[2] Second axial period consciousness, he wrote, is communal, global, ecological, and cosmic—an advancement in the whole evolutionary process.

It was from Cousins that I learned the art of integrating science, theology, and spirituality into one evolving flow of life. I was honored to be among his cherished doctoral students, becoming a theologian of the second axial age. We would sit for hours in his cramped office lined with piles of books and dissertations lost in a flow of ideas on love, the spiritual life, the evolution of the world soul, the mystery of God, and endless conversations on the meaning of life in an expanding universe. In the presence of Cousins, ideas blossomed into new worlds, and I would often find myself occupying multiple universes, as I listened to his seminal ideas flowering in the midst of the Bronx. His depth of spirit was mystical and illuminative as he discussed Teilhard's God of evolution or Whitehead's dipolar nature of God, while at the same time highlighting the nature mysticism of Francis of Assisi. It was from Cousins that I learned to be an integrative thinker without feeling the need to develop an analytical method of inquiry (which plagued many of my fellow students). Little did I realize that his scholarly endeavors were not always appreciated by his Fordham colleagues; however, he soared above the politics of academia, often with a smile. While his colleagues labored in first axial theology, Cousins was already thinking for a new age.

Teaching Science and Religion

Trained as a scientist and theologian, I felt prepared to take on my first teaching job as a visiting professor at Trinity College in Hartford, Connecticut. My task was to teach an undergraduate course on science and religion. I undertook the task with great relish until I realized that these two areas had grown into a monumental new discipline; the literature was vast. I was overwhelmed by the amount of reading in science and religion and found myself night after night taking copious notes on complex topics such as evolution and religion, divine action, chaos, and complexity. My Italian-American God from New Jersey was growing into a much larger divine mystery embracing the universe. How to make sense of this new God for undergraduate students was daunting. After one semester of teaching at Trinity, I was hired by a graduate school of theology in Washington, D.C., Washington Theological Union (WTU), to spearhead Franciscan theology and spirituality studies. This was an opportune position because it allowed me to develop new courses both in Franciscan studies and science and religion. It was at WTU that my transformation from a conservative monastic to an integrative, second axial theologian came to fruition. God was born into a new vision of evolving life.

My God of evolution was not exactly born among the sciences, however, but through immersion in medieval Franciscan theology. I wrote my doctoral dissertation on Bonaventure's Christ mysticism and it was this exploration that opened me up to a God of radical love. One of the most striking features of Bonaventure's theology is that he never gives an extended treatment of the nature of God independent of the doctrine of Trinity. In his *Sentence* commentary he offers one brief question on the oneness of God, before proceeding directly to the question of plurality of persons.[3] He begins his consideration of the Trinity not by examining the individual persons as such but by exploring how we move from the unified nature of God to the existence of three persons. Following Dionysius, Bonaventure considered the name of God in the Old Testament as Being: "I am who Am" (Exodus 3:14). In the New Testament, however, God reveals himself as good:

"No one is good but God alone" (Luke 18:19)[4]; hence the name of God is goodness, and Bonaventure looked to Dionysius and Richard of St. Victor to understand God as ultimate goodness marked by a trinity of persons in love.

The life of the Trinity originates eternally from the first divine person, the Father, who, as first, is infinitely fecund and fountain fullness (*fontalis plenitudo*) of goodness. This fountain fullness expresses itself perfectly in one who is Son and Word. This process reaches its consummation in the love between them, which is the Spirit. Love, therefore, is the energizing, dynamic life of the Trinity. Janet Kvamme writes: "It is love that brings the persons together in unity; through the generosity of love the divinity emanates and the divine persons proceed. Love flows out from the fountain fullness of fecundity."[5] Hence, the second and third persons of the Trinity flow from a generosity of love and of willing, "originating in the One who is boundless and inexhaustible love."[6] What made Bonaventure's theology of God so attractive was that love is not a relation of God but defines the nature of God: God *is* love. Michael Meerson wrote: "God's ultimate reality cannot be located in substance (what it is in itself) but only in personhood: what God is toward another. God exists as the mystery of persons in communion. God exists hypostatically in freedom and ecstasies. Only in communion can God be what God is, and only in communion can God be at all.... Since love produces communion among persons, love causes God to be who God is."[7]

The power of love as the very definition of God shattered my benevolent grandfather God of childhood. In Franciscan theology I encountered a living God who is personal, self-communicative and self-emptying; a God who is poor, humble, empowering, and free. This is a God who is quite at home in a world of evolution, chaos, complexity, and emergence. Bonaventure drew an intimate relation between creation and incarnation, describing the created universe as the fountain fullness of God's expressed being. Creation flows from the heart of God, *ex amore,* rendering everything a reflection of the power, wisdom, and goodness of the triune God. Creation is a theophany, an expression of God's glory. Since the Word of God is expressed in the manifold variety of creation, Bonaventure viewed the world as sacramental, a symbolic world full of God's presence.

The 14th-century Franciscan theologian, John Duns Scotus, followed the path of Bonaventure's God. Scotus looked at our world and realized that God is absolutely free, nothing created is necessary. Since God did not have to create anything, all is gift and grace.[8] God creates because God wishes to reveal and communicate Godself to others as the fullness of his own love. The present moment, therefore, expresses the perfection of the eternal. Scotus, like Bonaventure, saw an intimate connection between creation and incarnation, a connection which he grounded in the infinite love of God. As the eternal movement of lover (Father), beloved (Son), and the sharing of love (Spirit), the Trinity is the model of reality. God's love is ordered, free, and holy. Every single aspect of the created universe exists because of God's absolute freedom and unlimited love. God loves Godself in others, love "spilling over" into another as utterly *agape* and yet, totally *eros*: God loves to be loved. God became human in Jesus out of love (rather than sin), according to Scotus, because God wanted to express Godself outwardly in a creature who would be a masterpiece of love. This is Scotus's doctrine of the primacy of Christ. Christ is the first in God's intention to love. Creation is not an independent act of divine love that was, incidentally, followed up by divine self-revelation in the covenant. Rather, the divine desire to become incarnate was part of the overall plan or order of intention. By placing the incarnation within the context of creation and not dependent on human sin, Christ becomes the *"summum opus Dei"* (highest work of God) of the entire created order. The world is Christified through the intimate indwelling presence of divine love.

From Bonaventure to Teilhard

Ewert Cousins noticed similarities between Bonaventure's theology and that of the Jesuit scientist, Pierre Teilhard de Chardin which became influential on my own thought as well. Like Teilhard, Bonaventure saw matter as open to incarnation and incarnation as the fulfillment of the universe. When Teilhard discovered the Scotistic doctrine of the primacy of Christ he exclaimed: "There is the theology of the future!" Cousins wrote: "As Bonaventure saw the journey of the individual soul, Teilhard saw in the cosmos that love is both the impetus and the term of the process of development. For Teilhard, this creative love interiorizes and transforms each individual unit while uniting it to the whole."[9] He described love as the primal energy of the universe, the energy of attraction, union, and transcendence. "Driven by the forces of love," he wrote, "the fragments of the world [continuously] seek each other so that the world may come to being."[10] Indeed, the beauty of Teilhard's God rests on the dynamism of love. The name "God" reflects the incomprehensible wellspring of love at the heart of an expanding universe. He outlined a philosophy of love, based on the primacy of energy in the universe, describing love not as a dissipating energy but as energy building up in the universe, manifested in increased consciousness. The primal energy of evolving love is the energy of attraction, generativity, and creativity: Life evolves toward more complex life and consciousness.

Teilhard's quest was to find the God of evolution. As a paleontologist, he was a keen observer of the process of evolution which, he said, proceeds through the spheres of matter, life and consciousness. This process requires a center, which is also its energizing goal. By this he meant that there must be within evolution a centering point of unfolding unity, an influential center of wholeness which he called "Omega," a center both within and ahead. He wrote: "Since the emergence in our consciousness of the 'sense of evolution' it has become physically impossible for us to conceive or worship anything but an organic Prime-Mover God, *ab ante*. Only a God who is functionally and totally 'Omega' can satisfy us."[11] God is the name of absolute love, Omega, the power of love that attracts and empowers the future from the future because love that empowers being transcends being as the absolute horizon of being itself. John Haught has illuminated Teilhard's God as the power of the future. Theology has thought of God too much in terms of a prime mover moving things *from the past*; however, the foundation of things is not so much a ground of being sustaining existence from beneath but a power of attraction toward *what lies up ahead*. Evolution impels us to think of God as drawing the world *from the future*.[12]

But if God is acting from the future, what does this mean for present reality? Teilhard described a dynamic God-world relationship in the form of creative union. Creation is an act of immanent unification—the world is in process of being created by the gradual unification of multiplicity. God is continuously becoming "element," drawing all things through love into the fullness of being. Thomas King described Teilhard's God as a God of matter: "God is not found through opposition to matter (anti-matter) or independent of matter (extra-matter) but through matter (trans-matter)."[13] We take hold of God in the finite; God is sensed as "rising" or "emerging" from the depths of physical evolution, born not in the heart of matter but *as* the heart of matter.[14] While in the case of a static world, Teilhard wrote, the creator is structurally independent of his work, in the case of an evolutive world, the contrary is true. God is not conceivable except in so far as he coincides with evolution but without being lost in (sort of a 'formal' cause) the center of convergence of cosmogenesis.[15] God is dynamically interior to creation, a divine energy which is imperceptible, gradually bringing all things to their fullness. God acts from within, at the core of each element, by animating the sphere of being from within. Every element bears within it an Omega center who is both within and beyond the future transcendent horizon of being, which empowers things to create themselves. Where God is operating, it is always possible for us to see only the work of nature because God is the formal cause, the intrinsic principle of being, although God is not identical with being itself. This metaphysics of primary and secondary causality maintains the ontological distinction between divinity and creation in a way that God makes things to make themselves. Denis Edwards sees God creating in one divine act that embraces the whole process, a panentheistic view of divine action which enables what is radically new to emerge in created being.[16] Following Karl Rahner, he states that creation can be seen as the relationship between God's absolute being and finite being of creatures whereby finite beings are continuously constituted in existence by God. God is at the heart of evolutionary change as the power which enables a creature to go beyond itself and become more than it is.[17]

Yet, Teilhard's Omega-centered evolution connotes a deep incarnational relationality and mutuality that, in a sense, departs from primary-secondary causality by inverting panentheism. We live and move in God because God is living and moving in us. We are becoming something new in God because God is becoming something new in us. This is the basis of Teilhard's *cosmotheandrism*: The world is not God and God is not the world, yet God is the unlimited depth of love of all that is, a love that overflows into new life. This interpenetrating relationship of divinity and created reality means that God and matter exist in what Bonaventure called a coincidence of opposites and, as such, are mutually affirming. In fact, Teilhard believed that without evolution something would be absolutely lacking to God, considered in the fullness not of his being but of his act of union. He wanted to do away once and for all with the idea that God's continuous act of creation is one of *absolute* gratuity.[18] Rather, evolution somehow completes God. God is being born in the cosmos through the energies of love. Every created being is held in being by the breath of divine love whose infinite depth exceeds the capacity of any finite being to contain it; hence every being stretches forth toward its own self-expression, reaching out toward more being and life. This dynamic presence of divine love incarnate, empowering the center of every created being, is symbolized by Christ Omega. The divine Word of love at the heart of the universe is one with the universe in its evolution toward fullness of being. The deep incarnating presence of God, drawing together the elements of nature into greater unity and complexity, led Teilhard to speak of evolution as a process of cosmic personalization. It is not something in evolution, he said, but someone. Evolution is the genesis of the cosmic person; it is christogenesis, a process of ongoing incarnating divine love personally entangled with unfinished matter, empowering creation toward a new cosmotheandric whole. God is love and love is the heart of the universe empowering the universe toward more unified life. In this way, life flourishes on the cusp of the future because God is the future, the power of love's creative newness at the heart of evolving life.

The Ever-Newness of God

As I reflect on the emergence of divine mystery, from the 13th century into the 21st century, I am reminded of the elusive presence of God. The name "God" can at times constrain divine mystery, as if God is a concept that can be logically explained, analyzed, or domesticated, like a cat, comfortably curled up on a lap. But God is the name of incomprehensible divine love at the heart of evolving life; the depth and future of life as it creatively transcends and reappears in new patterns of relationship. Nature both reveals and conceals divinity insofar as everything reflects the beauty of divine love but unconscious matter must be raised to a level of self-consciousness for divinity to be recognized. This absolute horizon of deep, personal love, namely God Omega, is ever receding into absolute futurity and at the same time deeply present in every element of created life. Divine love is the heartbeat of everything that exists. Bonaventure maintained that the world at its deepest level is marked by the radical potential to receive the self-communication of divine love into it and thus a world fit for working out the divine purpose.

Although Bonaventure and Teilhard share the dynamism of divine love, we cannot ignore the advances of modern science that impact our understanding of nature. Teilhard recognized that science has made remarkable strides in genetics, physics, and biology, and technology has developed with a genius of creativity. Because of technology, two major developments challenge our prevailing notions of nature: the rise of the thinking machine and the cybernetic organism (cyborg). The rise of artificial intelligence (after Teilhard) has afforded the exploration of nature's plasticity or inherent ability to be reshaped revealing that nature is not fixed but is a process constituted by the drive for transcendence. What we thought was fixed and bounded is now seen to be permeable and unbounded. The cyborg or cybernetic organism is the hybrid machine-organism that tells us something about nature. Cyborgs are hybrid entities that are neither wholly technology nor completely organic. Nature can be reshaped, merged with an artifice or animal and reclaimed along new lines of informational flow and relationality, open to new forms. The cyborg as symbolic of nature has the potential not only to disrupt persistent dualisms (body and soul; matter and spirit) but also to refashion our thinking about the theoretical understanding of the body as a material entity and a discursive process. In light of the cyborg we can say that what counts as human is not and should not be self-evident. As Philip Hefner writes: "God has set up a system in which the creatures who transcend humans in the chain of evolution are creatures we have designed and created so that the act of transcending them is at the same time our own act of transcending ourselves."[19]

But cyborgs also tell us about God. If the symbol of the cyborg defines the fluidity of the human person then it also defines the person of Jesus Christ, indicating that we do not have a clearly defined, exhaustive concept of humanity, let alone divinity. The Christian God is so contrary to common sense, it destabilizes reified categories. Deliberately showing up as a hybrid creature (divinity and humanity), Jesus reveals the arbitrariness and constructed nature of what is considered the norm. When the divine Word becomes flesh (Incarnation), God transcends the boundaries of separation (between divinity and creation) to become something new. God enters into bounded existence, yet these boundaries are not fixed; nature constantly transcends itself in pursuit of new, more unified life symbolized by the resurrection of Jesus Christ. The life of Jesus reveals the inner depth of nature to be protean, open to God and thus open to hybridization, to becoming something new. No one person or existent can exhaust the presence of God because God is always the more of anything that exists.

The cyborg as symbol of God discloses the erratic presence of God; for divine love knows no boundaries. God is as much at home in the neuron, as in the human person, the human android and perhaps even robots programmed for love, compassion, relationship, and community.

God is overflowing, creative love-energy and the personal liberation of being-in-love. When we are immersed in the drive for transcendence, we are sharing in the ultimate depths of reality that is God. That is why science can evoke wonder and awe but faith in divine love enkindles life. To be entangled with God, surrendered in love, is to be immersed in the liberating truth of evolving life and thus to be set free to live from a new center of love. There is sort of an impotence of

God without us, as Teilhard realized. God is not above us but beneath us or better within us and before us—meaning that we do not find God as a suprasensible idea but as another "ourself" who dwells in and authenticates our darkness. We become, strangely, the privileged bearers of transcendence insofar as God within is also God ahead, luring us toward new horizons of love. While panentheism connotes life in God, we must not lose sight of God's self-emptying into us. The term "entanglement" better describes the deep, ineffable, mutually-affecting divine-created relationship that could be likened to a dance or perhaps a tango, where God is the lead dancer drawing "an entire universe, and not just human history, toward an unfathomable fulfillment yet to be realized."[20]

If the power of divine love is source and goal of all that is, then knowledge alone cannot bring us to our ultimate meaning and fulfillment, only the fidelity of love. God is eternally becoming other in love unto love. The power of divine love which evolves the cosmos toward greater personalization invites self-gift; love unto death for the sake of more life. To be free in love we must know ourselves as being loved and this means accepting ourselves as lovable. Science discloses the power of nature to orient itself toward relationships and complexity but it cannot define or constrain the power of transcending love. This is what I finally came to realize through my years of exploring science and religion. There is an absolute wholeness of truth and beauty that lies at the center of even a single cell. It cannot be observed or measured because it is elusive in nature; it draws the observer into its field of activity and at the same time awakens within a desire to pursue its ever receding horizon. I went in search of this powerful lure and I discovered a God who is hidden and humble; a God of overflowing love in whom I live and move and who lives and moves in me. As much as I have tried to control and understand this God of love, I have found the divine personal embrace of love is beyond my grasp. So I have let go and, in doing so, realize that in the midst of chaos there is God; in suffering and death, there is God; and where new life emerges there is God whose breathe of life is deeply woven into my life. God is the beginning and end because in God there is no beginning or end; rather there is an eternal openness to newness of life. To let go into this God is to live into the future.

Notes

1. Ewert H. Cousins, *Christ of the 21st Century* (Rockport, MA: Element, 1992), 7-10.
2. See Pierre Teilhard de Chardin, *The Activation of Energy*, trans. René Hague (New York: Harcourt, Brace, Jovanovich, 1970), 30-31, 101-103; Ewert Cousins, "Teilhard's Concept of Religion," 12.
3. In his introduction to Bonaventure's *Disputed Questions on the Mystery of the Trinity*, Zachary Hayes writes that "Bonaventure never gives an extended treatment of the nature of God independently of the doctrine of the Trinity." In an accompanying footnote he states that "the development of the attributes of the divine nature is presented within the framework of the Trinitarian question." See Zachary Hayes, introduction to *Disputed Questions on the Mystery of the Trinity, Vol. 3, Works of Saint Bonaventure*, ed. George Marcil (New York: The Franciscan Institute, 1979), 32 n. 4.
4. The comparison between John Damascene and the Pseudo-Dionysius on the names of God as being and good are discussed by Bonaventure in his classic *Itinerarium Mentis in Deum*. See Bonaventure *Itinerarium Mentis in Deum* (<u>Itin.</u>) 5.2 (V, 307).
5. Janet C. Kwamme, "The *Fontalis Plenitudo* in Bonaventure as a Symbol for His Metaphysics" (unpublished Ph.D. dissertation,

Fordham University, 1999), 170.

6. Kwamme, "*Fontalis Plenitudo* in Bonaventure," 175.

7. Michael Aksionov Meerson, *The Trinity of Love in Modern Russian Theology* (Quincy, IL: Franciscan Press, 1998), 4.

8. Kenan B. Osborne, "Incarnation, Individuality and Diversity," *The Cord* 45.3 (1995): 22; John Duns Scotus, *A Treatise on God as First Principle*, trans. and ed. Allan B. Wolter (Chicago: Franciscan Herald Press, 1966), xvii.

9. Ewert H. Cousins, "The Evolving Cosmos: Teilhard de Chardin and Bonaventure," *The Cord* 16 (1966): 17.

10. Pierre Teilhard de Chardin, *The Phenomenon of Man*, trans. Bernard Wall (New York: Harper & Row, 1959), 264.

11. Pierre Teilhard de Chardin, *Christianity and Evolution*, trans. René Hague (New York: Harcourt, Brace, Jovanovich 1971), 239-40.

12. John F. Haught, *God After Darwin: A Theology of Evolution* (Boulder, CO: Westview, 2000), 81. See also, "Theology for an Unfinished Universe," in *From Teilhard to Omega: Co-creating an Unfinished Universe*, pp. 13-17, ed. Ilia Delio (Maryknoll, NY: Orbis, 2014) and *Resting on the Future: Catholic Theology for an Unfinished Universe* (New York: Bloomsbury, 2015).

13. Thomas M. King, S.J., *Teilhard's Mysticism of Knowing* (New York: Seabury, 1981), 66-7.

14. Ibid., 103.

15. Teilhard de Chardin, *Christianity and Evolution*, 239.

16. Denis Edwards, *The God of Evolution: A Trinitarian Theology* (New York: Paulist Press, 1999), 76.

17. Denis Edwards, *Jesus and the Cosmos* (Mahwah, NJ: Paulist Press, 1990), 99.

18. Donald Gray, *The One and the Many: Teilhard de Chardin's Vision of Unity* (London: Burns and Oates, 1969), 125.

19. Philip Hefner, *Technology and Human Becoming* (Minneapolis: Fortress Press, 2003), 84-6.

20. John F. Haught, *Deeper than Darwin: The Prospect for Religion in the Age of Evolution* (Boulder, CO: Westview, 2009), 174.

4. My Journey to the God of Personal Idealism

Keith Ward

I had an idyllic childhood in a beautiful part of England (Northumberland), in a loving and supportive family and community, where Christian churches were positive forces for personal creativity and social justice. That formed my personality, but I was also always encouraged to be critical and creative in my thinking. So it was natural that as I grew up, questions arose in my mind about the existence of a loving God in a world of so much suffering, violence, and hatred. I never became anti-religious, but it began to seem that agnosticism was the most honest attitude to take to God.

Then, while I was serving in the Royal Air Force in Yemen, I fell into the hands, not of terrorists, but of ultra-conservative evangelicals (fundamentalists). The main reason that I did so was that the Protestant chapel was the only air-conditioned building for miles around. It was exceedingly hot in Yemen. So I began to spend a lot of time in chapel. It was there that the conservative evangelicals found me. Once they found me, there was no escape. They prayed for me, with me, and around me. They persuaded me to ask Christ to come into my life. And, to my surprise, Christ did. That is, I had an intense and rather dramatic experience of the presence of God, in the form of the risen Christ, which changed the whole course of my life. It was, it seemed to me then, and it still does, Jesus Christ calling me to follow him.

So far, so good. But there was a downside. It first became apparent when my fundamentalist friends (they are still friends) assured me that my father was going to Hell. My father was no saint, but he was in many ways a good and kind man, and it seemed totally unfair that he should have to suffer eternally just because he did not like churches. How did they know he was going to Hell? Because it said so in the Bible, where it apparently said that God was going to make my father suffer endlessly because he did not believe in a loving God. I had to admit that if this was what God did, my father was probably right not to think that God was very loving after all. Why should anyone be tortured forever for having a reasonable belief?

My problems got worse. Soon I began to wonder, having read different Gospel accounts of the same event, whether the Bible was literally true, without any errors at all. I wondered what would happen to the millions of people who had never heard of Jesus. I wondered why a God of love had ordered the Israelites to exterminate all the Canaanites who refused to be their slaves—all of them, men, women, children, and even cattle. I wondered why my friends' belief that the universe was only a few thousand years old, and would end any day, was so clearly inconsistent with everything that modern science said about the size and age of the cosmos. My friends thought I was sinking into sin. I was certainly sinking into something.

I was in a dilemma. I would never be able to deny the importance of my experience of Christ. But I just could not see the connection between that experience and belief in the literal truth of the whole Bible. Did the experience really depend on such very odd beliefs? I wondered and wondered. Then, when I went to university, I found there was a name for people who wondered as much as I did—they were philosophers. So, a few years later, I found myself as a lecturer in philosophy at the University of Glasgow. For seven years I wondered in public about religious, moral, and philosophical beliefs, and, amazingly, I got paid for it (not much, admittedly). But I did not go to any Christian church.

But a return to God was inevitable. God had touched me, first through tolerant and attractive expressions of Christian faith when I was very young, and then unexpectedly, through the testimony of fundamentalist Christians. Their experience of the liberating Spirit was, I was sure, genuine. But their view of God was fundamentally distorted. They believed in a God of unlimited, self-giving love who nevertheless dictated incomprehensible laws like stoning sons to death for getting drunk, who condoned the total slaughter of the unfortunate Amalekites, and who sent millions of people to Hell for failing to get the creed right. I came to think that their belief was self-contradictory. A God of self-giving love (*agape:* 1 John 4:8) would not do any of those things. So if my friends' belief about God's love was right (based on their experience of Christ's self-sacrificial love for them, while they were yet in sin), then some of the Bible was simply wrong about God.

I can see their problem. They think that if lots of the Bible is wrong, then the records of Jesus' life and teaching might be wrong too. Then their faith would be built on sand. But there is a simple and fundamental mistake here. In any other area of life, we do not require that a text is inerrant before we accept it as a supreme and reliable authority. For instance, we probably all accept Einstein's theory of relativity. This was a great insight into the nature of the universe, and almost all of us accept it on authority. Yet it is certainly not inerrant, and Einstein made plenty of mistakes during his scientific life. That in no way lessens his authority as a truly great scientist, who saw truths that most of us would be quite unable to discover or even imagine.

Why should the same sort of thing not be true of the Bible? The Christian Gospels present four different records of the impact Jesus had on various groups of people, records based on verbal accounts that had been passed down for years, and were written and edited in a language—Greek—which Jesus probably did not use for teaching. The most natural thing to say, since these records were written down by people who loved and even worshipped Jesus, and treasured memories of him, is that they give a pretty accurate record of things he is remembered to have said and done, though they are not inerrant in every detail.

The point is that it is the impact, the experience of divine love in Jesus which changes the lives of his disciples, that is important. Christian revelation is not God dictating propositions, which have to be believed and obeyed to the letter. It is an encounter with the personal reality of God, mediated through the person of Jesus. That personal reality is what gives life to the church, and its character is defined by the key elements of Jesus' life and teaching that are preserved in the church, and recorded in the Gospels.

Jesus was a Jew, living in a culture which kept alive the prophetic promise of a Messiah, and his teachings require an understanding of how that culture developed, and how it could happen that his disciples came to believe that he was the Messiah. Using the understanding of revelation suggested by the Gospels and by the encounters with the risen Christ experienced by Christians throughout the ages, we can then say that the Old Testament provides a record of encounters with God throughout the long history of the Jewish people. The Old Testament consists of many different books, written at many different times by many different people. I now find it deeply unilluminating to say that it is "written by God," as Christians sometimes say. It is written by people and imbued with many of their limited understandings of the world and their often crude moral views. It records the development of an understanding of God over hundreds of years. Such an understanding results from genuine encounters with God. But those encounters are described in terms of the prior beliefs and expectations of the humans who experienced them. We should not expect them to emerge fully developed and inerrant. We should expect them to change as reflection and greater knowledge emerge in that culture's history. And that is what the texts most naturally suggest.

The God of Christian fundamentalism dictates propositions that are changelessly true—obviously God cannot lie or deceive. But that view leads to all the problems that anyone who reads the Bible carefully must face up to sooner or later. The God of the Bible is a God whose nature emerges progressively (and it is not always progress!) over centuries of experience and reflection, as the divine encounters humans who are largely ignorant, prejudiced, and often chauvinistic. Such a God does not dictate, or even preserve from all error. Such a God seeks to guide towards greater understanding. It is in that sense, I think, that God inspires the Scriptures. Even the moral limitations of the Bible (like the subordination of women) are useful for teaching—as the text most often quoted by fundamentalists says (2 Timothy 3:16). But what such texts teach is precisely that even inspired people make mistakes, and have limitations that need to be overcome by later generations.

If you have a guiding, co-operating, experiential view of revelation, then of course it would be odd to say that revelation ended with Jesus or his apostles. But it does make sense to say that Jesus has a pivotal role in the story of divine-human encounters that is the Christian faith. It is not that all his recorded words are unchangeably true. They are often very cryptic and frustrating. For instance, what he is supposed to have said about marriage and divorce is something that various Christian churches argue about to this day. The point is that, in his life and teaching, he declares the supremacy of self-giving, agapistic love. This is what he showed in his life and death, what he requires of his disciples, and what he declared the nature of God to be. That is an insight which does seem to be absolute and unchangeable. But what it implies in practice is fiendishly hard to work out.

So Jesus is the definitive symbol of the divine life as agapistic love. It is that insight which is unchangeable. But what it means has never been fully discerned. God is progressively revealing the divine nature in co-operation with many human minds, and in experiences of personal encounter which have to be interpreted in terms of human prior beliefs and values.

At the same time as I was working through these problems and coming to a new (for me) understanding of Christian faith, I was also teaching philosophy, and my studies there helped me to work out a view of God that had a close affinity with my developing Christian beliefs. At first my reaction against fundamentalism led me to say that I was an atheist—I certainly knew all the philosophical arguments against God. However, as time passed it became clear, to begin with, that most of the great classical philosophers had believed in God, as a non-physical reality of great value which had some sort of causal role in relation to the physical universe. Most had believed that this reality was the origin of the physical universe, that it was the ultimate source of the moral, aesthetic, and intellectual values that make human life worthwhile, and that the universe had some sort of purpose which was connected with the realization of these values.

It was also clear that each major philosopher had a unique way of describing this God and its relation to the universe. Plato spoke of "the Good" as a reality of supreme value, and of a Demiurge or architect of the universe, who tried to embody images of the Good in the physical universe. Aristotle spoke of a supreme self-contemplating intellect, again of supreme goodness, which the universe loved and tried to imitate, though this supreme intellect was not a creator of the universe. Philosophers like Descartes, Spinoza, Leibniz, Kant, and Hegel, all developed notions of an Absolute Reality which had important components of intellect and value. Some of these philosophers were Christians and some were not. But it seemed obvious that the idea of God was not just some sentimental and arbitrary invention, but the result of a serious investigation into the ultimate nature of reality. There were many ways of describing God, so it was not a dogmatic, precisely defined, and inflexible concept. But the idea of a reality of supreme value and intelligence at the heart of the universe was a product of deep and intense thought by some of the best and most creative minds in history.

Some of those who taught me philosophy—A. J. (Freddie) Ayer is a prime example—were notable atheists. But their atheism did not seem to follow from their philosophy. Ayer's formulation of his own philosophy of logical positivism was, as he came to admit, deeply flawed. The heart of it strikes me as correct—namely, that all claims to knowledge have to be ultimately founded on personal experience. Ayer, however, placed two restrictions on this: first, such experiences all had to be sense experiences, and second, all claims about objects which were not sense-experiences had to be just "logical constructions" out of sense-experiences. Neither of these restrictions are compelling. Humans have many experiences that do not come through the senses—claims to experience moral obligations or mathematical truths, for example. Such things cannot be ruled out by mere definition. Furthermore, all experiences have to be interpreted, so that thought and intellect have a positive part to play in making claims about objective reality.

On Ayer's own account, there could logically be a God, a set of experiences which provide maximal knowledge of all that exists (there can, after all, be experiences which do not have to be caused by physical sense-organs), and which could be the cause of any other sets of experiences that exist. The British Empiricist philosopher Berkeley argued that there was such a God, and that positing a God was the best way of accounting for the way in which all the many other different sets of experiences (finite minds) form a coherent and intelligible unity. There could in principle be non-sensory experience of such a supreme mind, and its existence would provide a good explanation for the mysterious fact of the intelligibility of nature and the emergence of consciousness, purpose, and value in a physical universe.

So the idea of God, as a conscious, intelligent mind of maximal knowledge, power, and value, which is the cause of the physical universe and of many other more limited minds, came to seem to me to be the most adequate account of reality that philosophy could provide. But working out an adequate description of such a mind is very difficult. In Christian history, Aristotle has been taken as the chief guide in working out a doctrine of God. That was a good choice, for Aristotle did affirm the coherence of the idea of a mind that knows, wills, and loves itself as a reality of maximal value. But it was also a strange choice, because Aristotle did not think that God had any real relation to the universe, which simply existed as an independent reality, trying to imitate the perfection of God as best as it could—which was not very far.

I came to think that a supreme mind of maximal value would not be an isolated self-contemplator, but would create a physical universe in order to actualize values in a temporal, changing, reality that could not exist in pure eternity. Maximal value, in other words, would have to include temporal as well as eternal values. It is in this sense that the Eternal is in a sense incomplete. Beauty needs to be expressed in particular beautiful things. Thought about possible objects needs to be expressed in the production of actual objects. The appreciation of a possible world is different from the appreciation of an actual world, and the thought of the happiness of another possible person is different from the awareness of the happiness of another actual person. Possibility requires actuality and particularity for its completion. The world exists as the embodiment and expression of thought.

One great value that could not exist without some creation is creativity itself. Creativity, in general, is bringing about new things that have never before existed. It requires imagination, effort, struggle, and overcoming. Its value lies largely in the difficult process of forging the new out of the old, a process that may meet many dead-ends, involve much failure, and realize few successes. It is like a vital force that struggles against obstacles and generates novelty by destroying fossilized structures.

Could this be true of God's creativity? Does God have to struggle, destroy, and often fail? This may seem absurd if we are thinking of the Aristotelian changeless contemplation of pure Beauty. There is a place for that in a maximally perfect being. But if creativity is a value, then a maximally worthwhile being must do something like struggle. It must undertake costly and rigorous efforts to accomplish new worthwhile goals. But what can God struggle against, and what can that cost God? To be truly creative, God must create an "other," even an opposing reality, with possibilities of novel value, but also with possible resistance to change. The maximally valuable being must create an alien world that is potentially good but often actually resistant to creatively changing goods. (This is reminiscent of the great chaos, *tohu wa bohu*, which Genesis places the beginning of creation, and of the great Leviathan, threatening dragon of the saltwater sea, with which God struggles until the end of time, according to some Psalms and the Book of Revelation).

The greatest form of creativity is the creation of 'other' conscious autonomous powers with which experiences can be shared, with which God can co-operate, but which may also oppose and resist God. Fellowship forged through the persistence of love in face of hardships endured and over-come—that is a unique form of value, that only a temporal and developing creation can provide. It is the adventure of Supreme Mind as it forges its own nature as maximal good-ness, actualizing many potentialities for good from an es-tranged world that is, paradoxically, generated from the di-vine nature as a necessary condition for its own progressive self-development.

It is not—as some proponents of the "free-will defense" argue—just that human freedom is a great enough value to justify the suffering there is in the world—as though God had the choice of whether to create suffering or not, and freely chose to create it. Rather, the being of God necessarily real-izes itself in generating what is other than it, to enable it to realize its own eternal yet largely potential nature in a tempo-ral and developing form of being. We do not have to ask, "Is freedom worth all this suffering?" We have to see that being necessarily realizes itself through a process of alienation, de-velopment, and return. That is its nature. There is no delicate balancing of values and free choice of the greater good. There is the necessity of forging actual good out of ambiguous po-tentiality. That is something a maximally good being would necessarily do, in addition to contemplating its own solitary perfection. It realizes the great good of bringing multitudes of others to share in that contemplation, though they too will first have to participate in the risk and reality of alienation and its overcoming.

This is a recognizably post-Hegelian idea of God, though it is not Hegel's own form of absolute idealism. It can be called personal idealism, because it is a form of idealism—the belief that mind is the ultimate reality—which asserts that there is one supreme mind that can be related to as a personal, not an impersonal, being. But the relationship is not a purely external one, as though two distinct persons were related to each other while remaining quite separate. It is a form of *panentheism*, since the Supreme Mind, God, in a sense includes all other realities, including all finite minds, in itself. I do not think of God as a being separated from the cosmos who can only externally interfere in it. Rather I think of God as the all-enveloping spiritual reality which is the deepest nature of the cosmos itself. But of course God's reality is much greater than the cosmos. It is important to this form of idealism that God is affected by everything that happens in the cosmos, and that God shapes the cosmos by the intentions and values that are inherent in the divine nature.

But God is not the unilateral shaper of everything, since finite minds, rather like the cells of a human body, also shape the way things go, sometimes not in line with the intentions of the mind whose body it is. The relation between the supreme mind and finite minds is one of synergy, or cooperation, whereby the supreme mind sets ultimate goals and aids finite minds to attain it if they are cooperative, or frustrates their aims if they are not. Both the limited attainment of sanctity and the limited success of evil among humans seems to be evidence for such a synergistic relation between the supreme mind and finite minds. Human minds do not determine everything in human bodies, but their governing intentions can influence how bodies behave. So we might think of God as setting the governing intentions of the cosmos. Those intentions actively influence how things go, but allow the minds which the cosmos generates to implement or frustrate the divine intentions to a large but limited extent.

The ideal goal of the divine expansion into the creation of and relationship to finite minds is the existence of a communion of being in which divine and human, infinite and finite, unify and interact. Humans can become channels of divine power and love, and God's own nature can be enriched by its inclusion of the finite experiences of minds within a created cosmos. As the New Testament puts it, Christ, the eternal Wisdom of God, can live in and through us. And we can live as members of the body of Christ, contributing our unique actions and experiences to the life of God. There is relationship, and there is unity, and there is an interpenetration of being. My hope, as a Christian, is that this goal will be fully realized when the history of human endeavor, failure, and reconciliation, is completed.

This, I believe, is the final destiny that God wills for every intelligent sentient being, without exception. Some ask, "If this is true, why be a Christian?" Precisely because this is what Christian faith teaches! That is not what my fundamentalist friends think, but I have come to think that they have an unduly limited understanding of the self-giving love of God. If Christians think that Christ is "the true light that enlightens everyone" (John 1:9), then God must somehow be present to everyone, and must be seeking their enlightenment and salvation, whether they believe in God or not. The existence of many different religions and competing claims to revelation used to strike me as an objection to Christianity. But now I see many different religious paths as differing ways to God. God is a transcendent spiritual reality, a reality that is the underlying nature of all reality, but is infinitely greater than all physical reality. There must be many aspects of such a reality, infinite faces of the Infinite, and many ways of seeing the many aspects of Infinity.

Different religious traditions have developed from creative insights into such spiritual aspects of reality, insights which naturally use the concepts and values that belong to specific cultures, although those concepts and values may be transformed in the process. So, for instance, in Buddhism the idea of a "self" or "soul" is associated with the idea of "ego" or of one continuing and unchanging soul-substance. A major insight of Buddhism is the transience of all finite things, and so the doctrine of "no-self" (*anatta*) and of the renunciation of ego becomes a major theme. Hence ultimate reality is seen in terms of a transient stream of experiences or events, and the idea of one unchanging God is just not used. Yet there is an ultimate state— *Nirvana*—which is one of knowledge, compassion, and bliss. It lies beyond personality, but it is a transcendent spiritual reality of inestimable value, not just a state of human minds.

Christians can readily see this as an aspect of the divine being, and they can learn from it much about the ego-transcending nature of God, and value of compassion for all sentient beings, and practical techniques for overcoming self-centered attachments. Christians will still wish to affirm that there is a divine being who can be expressed in human form, and who actively relates in love to finite beings. Christians think these are objective truths about reality, and Buddhists may seem to deny them. Yet many Buddhists find that *Boddhisattvas*, who renounce Enlightenment in order to help their devotees, are compassionate, finite expressions of the ultimate *Dharma-body* of the Buddha, with which all humans are somehow one. It is not helpful to say that Christians and Buddhists are saying the same things, when they obviously disagree about many things. But it is helpful to say that they are both ways of approaching a transcendent spiritual reality whose nature is consciousness and bliss, and they are both concerned to overcome the forces of hatred, greed, and ignorance—the "three fires" of Buddhism. Differences remain—absorption into a state of Pure Mind is not the same as achieving a state of pure love of God. But both views can be "open" to insights from the other, and "inclusive" in affirming that no one is barred from ultimate enlightenment or salvation by their adherence to a different faith. In the end, if there are two contradictory propositions, only one can be true. But many religious propositions are not very clearly and rigidly defined, and sometimes they can be seen as complementary rather than contradictory. This enables one to say that diversity is the natural condition of the human mind, but one still has an obligation both to stand by the truth as one sees it, and to be open to different presentations of truth, allowing them, where it seems appropriate, to modify the precise statement of one's own beliefs.

This is what has happened in my case, as I have found myself teaching and interacting with other religious traditions—most notably some Indian traditions, which are in fact among the earliest forms of Idealism. The 12th-century Indian sage Ramanuja founded the school of *Visist-Advaita Vedanta* (qualified non-dualism, based on Vedanta, the teaching of a major commentary on the Upanishads). This school holds that there is one non-dual reality (*Brahman,* which we might call Absolute Spirit). But within this reality there are many parts, most notably, finite souls, matter, and a Supreme Lord. It is a deeply devotional school, worshipping the god Vishnu, often under the form of Krishna. The final goal is a community of souls living in conscious loving relation to Krishna, free from death and sorrow. I am among those who find such traditions of devotion and meditation very helpful for Christians—indeed, we can find in the largely mythical figures of such gods another real aspect of the universal Christ. A major figure, though by no means the only one, in quest to find a deep unity of Vedantic and Christian traditions is Bede Griffiths, who was a Benedictine monk. People like him show that it is possible in the modern world is to stay loyal to one tradition (the Christian, in this case), but share in the practices of other traditions. In this way one is looking for a more universal spirituality, but it might be better to say that one is expanding one's own faith rather than trying to syncretize all faiths into one confused whole.

I find such an expansive view both philosophically defensible and wholly consistent with the Christian idea that God was in Christ reconciling the whole world to the divine, redeeming the world through bringing it to share in the divine nature (2 Peter 1:4). It complements the Aristotelian idea of a changeless and passionless God by accepting that God has a necessary and eternal nature of beauty and love, but adds that God actively guides and cooperates with humans by gradually leading them to see deeper truths about the divine nature. This is the God of personal idealism, who gradually unfolds the divine nature in communion with many created minds, uniting them to the divine life through real creativity and relationship. It is the idea of God that both my philosophical musings and my Christian faith have led me to develop. It has made possible my own journey back to God.

5. God is Compassion and Agape

John B. Cobb, Jr.

I grew up thinking of God as my loving companion. I never prayed much, but I did converse with God. I felt that with God I could be completely honest since, after all, he already knew me better than I knew myself. To this day, I think that youthful relation to God was basically healthy.

The biggest problem was sexuality. Although I could be honest about that with God, my understanding of what God wanted of me had no place for my sexuality. I could not repress it and did not try very hard to do so, but I also could not integrate it. Today I see that as the result of an element of legalism that did not really fit my understanding of God's love but was part of the religious culture I internalized. My experience of the effects of legalism has strengthened my anti-legalism, which is supported by Jesus and Paul as well.

One of my most painful memories is of a conversation with a couple who had invited me for dinner. I had read and been deeply impressed with Aldous Huxley's *Perennial Philosophy.* As the couple encouraged me to share my thinking, I spoke of how the understanding of God developed in Huxley's book overcame legalism. They asked me if that applied to sexual actions. I quickly and unthinkingly answered, "Except that."

I immediately felt the absurdity of my response. The intensity of that realization was such that, although the incident occurred 70 years ago, the feeling has hardly dimmed. My hosts probably sensed my humiliation and confusion and gently redirected the conversation. I remain astonished that I could have so segregated my thinking up until that moment. Painful as it was, the experience ended that segregation at least in terms of conscious thinking.

That incident occurred during my army days. I was inducted soon after my 18th birthday in 1943, and I served for three and a half years. The first year or so was spent studying Japanese, and the rest of the time, translating captured documents, except for a few months in the occupation of Japan. I mention this because my army experience was very different from that of most soldiers. For me, it was the first encounter with intellectuals. Most of my companions were Jews and Catholics from New York who preferred to spend the war working with the Japanese language rather than in what we are more likely to consider military pursuits.

These older and far more sophisticated people treated me kindly, but I quickly came to see that the worldview of my youth was, for them, somewhat quaint. Perhaps they considered it pre-modern. In any case I became aware that vast changes had occurred in the world of thought of which my limited experience in a small junior college in Georgia had given me no hint. I was fascinated by the discovery of a new world, and I read a good deal, but I knew that I remained quite ignorant of modern thought.

We veterans of World War II were treated well. The GI bill made further education economically accessible. I remained entirely naïve about colleges and universities, but one of my army friends recommended the University of Chicago; so, as soon as I was separated from the army, I applied. I remain deeply grateful. One attraction was that I did not have to go back to undergraduate study. I could go directly into one of the graduate divisions and could structure my own program for an MA degree.

God remained very important to me, and I had learned that in modernity belief in God had become extremely problematic. I felt a pressing need to find out why, and to learn whether more knowledge would compel me to give up any such belief. I signed up for the program on the Analysis of Ideas and the Study of Method. The theme I announced was all the arguments against belief in God.

The program was the brainchild of Richard McKeon, and I took far more courses with him than with anyone else during my stay at Chicago. I'm not sure why. I was in awe of him and felt that by not really understanding him I was missing out on profound wisdom. On the other hand, I did not enjoy his courses, and others actually helped me much more. I described the relationship at the time as getting hold of an electrically-charged wire and not being able to let go. Perhaps what turned out to be the most valuable part of his thinking for me was that he relativized modernity. I survived better than the best-known McKeon student, Robert Pirsig, author of *Zen and the Art of Motorcycle Maintenance.*

I was very fortunate that in my first quarter I took a course with Charles Hartshorne. It was obvious that Hartshorne was well informed about modern philosophy. This familiarity had not led him to atheism. I was intellectually assured that whatever the arguments for atheism, it was possible to respond to them rationally. Of course, the belief in God that could be defended differed in important respects from the one that atheists in general were opposing. But it seemed almost the philosophical equivalent of my youthful understanding.

Hartshorne focused his critique of the tradition on two doctrines: divine omnipotence and divine immutability. He showed, to my satisfaction then and now, that these doctrines are not only philosophically indefensible but also spiritually and existentially destructive and in conflict with the Bible. Hartshorne thought that when we rid theology of these damaging accretions, the traditional arguments for God, especially the ontological one, were valid.

Hartshorne insisted that the existence of God could be proved. I was not drawn to that claim. Years later I had an experience that confirmed for me the impossibility of "proving" anything. Hartshorne wrote extensively on the ontological argument, which he thought could be formulated with the help of modal logic to be decisive. I was asked to review a book that contained a short formal argument. It hinged on a principle in modal logic. I knew I was not competent to evaluate; so I took it to a professor of logic in Pomona College. He saw at a glance that, given the validity of the principle, the argument was formally conclusive. His immediate response was that, if that principle could be used to prove the existence of God, modal logic would have to reject it. So much for proving God "logically"!

Despite the enormous importance to me of what I learned from Hartshorne, my immersion in modern thought led to my own "death-of-God" experience. This did not follow from any modern argument. At this level, Hartshorne won hands down. But late modern thought simply operates with categories, data, and theories in which God has no possible role. If one is socialized to think in its terms, one will be an atheist, whether or not one fully recognizes this. The issue, I concluded then, and still affirm, is not arguments but comprehensive world view. The late modern worldview that sets the limits of the discussion that is to be taken seriously is inherently atheistic. Despite Hartshorne, and despite McKeon, I found myself in a few months sucked into atheism. There was no point in continuing the three-year MA program I had begun. I still wanted to believe in God. I just didn't.

It may seem strange that at just that time I shifted to the Divinity School. I had had a little contact with James Luther Adams, Amos Wilder, and Joachim Wach, and I was quite sure that these scholars understood the modern world, not just intellectually, as Hartshorne certainly did, but also in the way it had taken hold of me. Yet they still found meaning in some kind of theological discussion. Before abandoning my faith altogether, I needed to find out how these people adjusted to the modern world or how they avoided its fully nihilistic implications.

The Divinity School faculty was "neo-naturalist." They took evolution very seriously. From their perspective, now that we know that we are part of nature, we know also that the Cartesian view of nature, so closely bound up with modern science, is inadequate. A new view of nature will allow us to take values, freedom, and responsibility seriously without the Cartesian dualism that had been refuted by Darwin. To me this was convincing, and it was liberating from the oppressively reductionist and determinist worldview so prevalent in late modernism. I began to heal from the shock of my death-of-God experience.

The Divinity School faculty also followed William James into "radical empiricism." James told us to take seriously all aspects of our experience, not just its sensory aspects. This was a great relief from the sensory empiricism of the dominant modern tradition and the sciences. Whatever else is experienced has equal claim to our attention with what we experience through our eyes, which is so privileged in the modernity into which I had been sucked.

I continued to take an occasional course with Hartshorne. Both Hartshorne and the Divinity School faculty affirmed "process" over the traditional "substance" thinking of the West. Although the term "process philosophy" was not used, I found this move also convincing and liberating. But what was most striking was the difference between the rationalist process thought of Hartshorne and the radical empiricist process thought of the Divinity School.

The systematic theologians teaching in the Divinity School at that time were Bernard Loomer, Bernard Meland, and Daniel Day Williams. Although Henry Nelson Wieman had retired from the faculty, his thought continued to play a large role. It was the most systematically developed expression of neo-naturalist theology. So I wrote my MA thesis on his understanding of God, and I will describe the differences of the two approaches in terms of the differences between Wieman and Hartshorne.

Wieman's most important book is *The Source of Human Good*. For him, as a radical empiricist, one needs to stay entirely within the realm of human experience and not speculate beyond it. The source of human good must be empirically identified. Wieman did what I still consider a brilliant and underused job of identifying "creative transformation" as the place where human good grows. He shows that this is not something we can control. We can only trust the process and allow ourselves to be used in bringing the good about. Thus he held strongly to the Christian insight that we grow by trust in grace. He identified this process of creative transformation as God.

Earlier Wieman had introduced the influence of Whitehead into the faculty, but when he realized how important speculation was to the later Whitehead, he turned against him. He felt strongly that the health of faith depended on freeing it completely from debatable beliefs. He thought that sticking to radical empirical description, he could point to God in irrefutable ways, and that calling people to faith and service did not depend on any doubtful beliefs. He thought Whitehead was dangerous, because he distracted his readers from this faith and led them to base their faith on ideas that are profoundly speculative.

Hartshorne was not much impressed by Wieman's achievement. He wrote a book, *Philosophers Speak of God,* in which he took five characteristics of God as normative. He gave Wieman credit for only one of these.

In one respect Hartshorne and Wieman were similar. Both sought certainty. Hartshorne thought certainty could be attained only by reason. Wieman thought it could be attained only by sticking closely to experience. I appreciated much that was being done by both of them and regretted their mutual rejection. But I was not drawn to the idea that certainty was possible. My experience had been that the overall worldview was more determinative than either experience or reason. It seemed to me that arguments and descriptions operated typically with unexpressed assumptions.

I had entered Divinity School in hopes that I would find a way out of the meaninglessness with which my death-of-God experience had left me. My account above indicates that I received what I sought. But this was not by arguments. It was by allowing me to try on worldviews that differed from the dominant worldview, but did not require virtually ignoring it, as Hartshorne sometimes seemed to do. On the other hand, what I appropriated in the Divinity School was not in opposition to Hartshorne. Like the neo-naturalists he emphatically affirmed the continuity of human life with that of other animals. He was a lifelong student of birds and especially their songs, and he wrote a beautiful book arguing that birds sometime sing just because they enjoy singing. At this point he was doing empirical work supporting a belief he shared with the neo-naturalist theologians.

Hartshorne had no objection to radical empiricism, but it was not important to his arguments. For me it was profoundly liberating. So many things that the dominant modern vision does not allow us to discuss can be given serious consideration. I could live and breathe again and find meaning in this world.

But did my work in the Divinity School restore belief in God? If I were satisfied to mean by "God" what Wieman meant, the answer would be quite simply, yes. But this was not the God to whom I had been devoted. That God was an individual subject rather than a type of event. Wieman opposed affirming anything like that as speculative. In this respect he had imbibed the nontheistic assumptions of the dominant world view. I looked to Hartshorne for help. But the joint pressure of the dominant worldview and the Divinity School faculty did not make it easy to feel confident in following Hartshorne back into real theism.

I wrote my dissertation on "Christian Faith and Speculative Belief." I argued that the attempt to exclude speculative belief altogether does not work. I was, of course, writing for my own sake. Could I really take the steps I wanted to take without it being just wish-fulfillment? Could I go from the occurrence of creative transformation to an actual entity that grounds or supports this occurrence? Or should I accept the empiricists' bias against such explanation. My conclusion was that even those who most wanted to free Christian faith from speculative belief failed to do so. The ideal of avoiding speculation was illusory. I would not abandon ideas simply because they were not directly empirical.

Hartshorne provided me with a view of a metaphysically real God who was an individual subject. His metaphysics was self-coherent and compatible with what we know empirically. Wieman provided a rich account of how good increases in human experience. Both were convincing to me. But of course since they rejected each other's views, something else was needed.

Hartshorne often referred to Whitehead appreciatively and associated Whitehead's ideas with his own. He finally offered a course on Whitehead, and I was glad to get more deeply into his thought. Whitehead confirmed my doubts about the quest for certainty. He encouraged the scientific method of developing theories imaginatively and checking them empirically. This enabled him to go far beyond the description of experience but to affirm strongly the empirical test.

I once expressed to Hartshorne my interest in cosmology, that is, the most inclusive and basic understanding of all that is. Hartshorne said he had been given a book on the subject and would give it to me because he was not much interested. I was startled. I had not realized that for him metaphysics and cosmology are quite distinct enterprises, one rational, the other empirical. For Hartshorne metaphysics deals with necessary truths, and discussion of God belongs to that conversation. It should not be distracted by contingent facts. I realized that for quite different reasons Wieman was not interested in cosmology either. But the worldview questions so important to me could not be separated from cosmology. Clearly I could be neither a Hartshornian nor a Wiemanian in any strong sense, despite my desire to appropriate much from both men.

So it was with great joy that I found Whitehead. He was chiefly interested in cosmology and dealt with strictly metaphysical questions only occasionally and as they required attention. His cosmology provided me with the systematic and inclusive alternative to the modernity that had destroyed my faith. I began a long process of becoming a Whiteheadian. But I was still seeking to understand and appropriate the depth of understanding that I sensed in McKeon.

By this time, even if I did not have the knowledge of the history of philosophy that would enable me truly to understand and appropriate what McKeon taught, I did understand that what he offered was a philosophy of the history of philosophy. This philosophy warned against commitment to any particular philosophical system. There are a number of basic ways of doing philosophy that all have more or less equal validity. They are adaptable to historical changes; so they reappear in different guises in different eras. The deep respect I felt for McKeon's profundity and wisdom made it very difficult to commit myself to Whitehead.

Although all the influences from which I was profiting led me away from the dominant late modern nihilism that had destroyed my faith, I felt that I should check modernity out again before dismissing it altogether. For that purpose I audited a course with Rudolf Carnap, a leading positivist. He was obviously highly intelligent, knew a great deal about which I was wholly ignorant, and presented his ideas very clearly. He drew out the assumptions of late modernism and developed them with rigorous consistency. It was all very impressive in its own way.

One day a student asked how the views he was espousing expressed themselves in his daily life. Carnap answered unhesitatingly that there was no connection. For me, that confirmed deep impressions that I had not felt comfortable in articulating. I was thereby inoculated against taking further interest in the late modern world of thought. I fear that since then I have had difficulty in giving respectful attention to the ideas of those who have not broken from the dominant modern assumptions. Whatever the limitations of Whitehead's proposals or those of any other thinker who offers alternatives to the established worldview, they are certainly improvements over late modernity.

I had barely begun the journey toward being a Whiteheadian. Whitehead had the respect of much of the Divinity School faculty and references to him were fairly common, but during my years there, no course on Whitehead was offered in the Divinity School. After I left, Loomer began teaching year-long courses on Whitehead and Williams wrote what I regard as still today the best Whiteheadian theology, *The Spirit and the Forms of Love.* Those developments increased my confidence that I had not made a mistake. But when I left Chicago I was far from confident. The one course dealing with Whitehead that I had had was taught by Hartshorne, and he emphasized the metaphysics, whereas I was attracted especially by the cosmology. I left Chicago with this one course on Whitehead and six from McKeon, who warned me against commitment to any one school of thought. Among philosophers he emphasized Aristotle. The only seminar I gave on a single thinker before coming to Claremont eight years later was on Aristotle.

Nevertheless, I was becoming a Whiteheadian. What was required for this to happen was for me to distinguish clearly between what McKeon meant by philosophy and the cosmology that seemed so important to me. McKeon did not help me to do that. But as I made that distinction, I could acknowledge that there is a plurality of strictly philosophical questions that can recur and be treated in one of several ways. This variety of philosophies could be found in Greece, in the Middle Ages, and in both early and late modernity. But I decided that does not reduce the importance of the differences between the classical worldview, the medieval worldview, the early modern worldview, and the late modern worldview. My focus has not been on the strictly philosophical questions that can be raised in each context but on the worldviews themselves.

For me, overcoming late modern nihilism is far more important than the philosophy of the history of philosophy and does not depend on that. As I liberated myself from McKeon's controlling influence in this way, and as I gradually educated myself about Whitehead, I truly became a Whiteheadian.

I have not ceased to be pluralistic about many things. But I believe that at particular junctures in history, humanity faces particular challenges. I am not now pluralistic about whether we should try to save our species from extinction, nor about the relative importance of that task in comparison with most of what goes on in value-free research universities. These are the epitome of the late modernism from which radical empiricism, neo-naturalism, process metaphysics, and, above all, Whiteheadian cosmology rescued me. I am not pluralistic about the importance of breaking the hold of late modernism on our culture generally and on our universities particularly.

Now, what about "panentheism?" This word was not much used while I was at Chicago. It became important later. Hartshorne occasionally used it in class. In any case, his doctrine of God is emphatically pan-en-theist. For him, what is of central importance is that what we experience, God also experiences. Our joy gives God joy. God shares our sorrows. This gives us the motive to increase joy in the world and diminish unnecessary suffering. He called his ethics, contributionism. If what happens simply ceases and disappears forever after the moment of its occurrence, then meaninglessness threatens. If we know that it contributes to the everlasting life of God, all that happens to us and all that we do matters.

The accumulation of all that happens also provides a basis of affirming truth about the past. If the past does not exist in any sense, as the late modern worldview implies, then statements about the past cannot be true or false. My sense is that when I write about the past, as in this essay, I am being reasonably accurate, but also, no doubt, making mistakes some of which could be corrected. If the past no longer exists at all, or exists only in quite unreliable memories, then my inescapable intuition is mistaken. My ineradicable intuition is very difficult to justify unless the past is still real.

Central to the Abrahamic traditions is divine compassion. Compassion means feeling with. That is the claim that God feels our feelings with us, that we are totally known and understood and accepted. This is affirmed by pan-en-theism, and it is a central part of Hartshorne's metaphysics.

However, this panentheism does little by itself to incorporate the radical empirical phenomena that I also found so valuable. Hartshorne explained that God set the parameters for creaturely existence. For example, he sometimes indicated that the balance between freedom and determinism was set by God. I think he would have been pleased that cosmology now indicates that there are many constants that seem to be set just as needed to support life. One could interpret this to mean that God is immanent in the world. But a strong doctrine of immanence is not to be found in Hartshorne. In the book I mentioned, in which Wieman comes off so poorly, none of the five normative elements for doctrines of God refer to divine immanence.

Since I have understood panentheism quite literally as focusing on God's inclusion of the world, I have usually wanted to say that of equal importance to panentheism is the doctrine of divine immanence. Since the editors of this volume include this in their understanding of panentheism, perhaps in the future I can just identify myself as a panentheist, and all my beliefs about the relation of God and the world will be included.

Biographically, however, it was only with my fuller study of Whitehead that I was able to integrate immanence with panentheism. Theologically, this meant the understanding of God's love as both compassion and agape. Hence my title.

Many people affirm divine immanence, but few explain it. Immanence requires what substance thinking views as impossible, namely, that two things occupy the same space at the same time. More or less by definition, this cannot be true of substances. Whitehead thought that in the dogmatic struggles of the early church to describe God's incarnation in Jesus and the relations among the persons of the Trinity, there was a metaphysical breakthrough. In addition to the human and divine coinhering in Jesus, the three persons of the Trinity coinhered in one another. For Whitehead, this was a potential advance of which philosophers did not avail themselves. Whitehead adopts and universalizes it.

The possibility of doing so depends not only on the shift from substances to events, but also on the understanding of what he calls "eternal objects" and "conceptual feelings." Hartshorne rejected this side of Whitehead's philosophy, and many process thinkers continue to do so. They may continue to speak of God's immanence in creatures but, so far, I am not aware of a serious analysis of immanence without the use of eternal objects and conceptual feelings. For this reason, I am hesitant to assume that the term panentheism by itself gives adequate emphasis to God's effective presence and working in all creatures.

It is interesting that Whitehead associates the religious role of God chiefly with what I described as Hartshorne's concerns. Without some ongoing reality to the ephemeral events, their significance is lost. Whitehead has a strong sense of God as compassionate companion.

Whitehead describes God's immanence in all events as the "secular" activity of God. For strictly philosophical reasons he needs to explain the pervasive role of teleology in the world. For example, he thinks that all living things strive to live, to live well, and even to live better. He proposes that each derives from God an "initial aim" at achieving what value can be achieved at that time and place. This creaturely aim is derived from God's encompassing aim at the realization of value. What I have called derivation is, in his detailed and rigorous account, inclusion. God is participating in the self-constitution of each occasion. Quite clearly he explains the role of God in what Wieman described so well as "creative transformation."

This analysis of God's role in creaturely occasions is found in the most technical of all of Whitehead's philosophical writings, *Process and Reality*. In my view, this in no way reduces its existential and spiritual importance. The full realization that God is participating in every moment of my life and of how God is present is profoundly important existentially and, I would say, religiously. That the boundary between the secular and the religious breaks down here is all to the good.

The reader will note how thorough is Whitehead's victory over other intellectual authorities in my life. There are still points on which I am not satisfied and prefer the views of others, including Hartshorne. But on many points, such as the full integration of how the world is in God and how God is in the world, I have not found a competitor. From Whitehead I derive confidence that my deep intuitions, grounded in the profound influence of the New Testament, that God is both compassion and agape, are not just wish fulfillment.

I make no claim to certainty, but I rest in assurance.

6. *"I Am Not a Space that God Does Not Occupy…"*

Cynthia Bourgeault

The Light Within

"So does that mean every time a new baby's born, there's less God?"

The pint-sized questioner was my grandson Jack, at the time four years old and clearly wrestling with the theological implications of the recent birth of his baby sister. His other grandmother, of a more evangelical persuasion, had been coaching him on the basic tenets of Christian belief: 1) that God is everywhere, and 2) that human beings are not God. With his four-year-old, preoperational-logic brain in virtual overdrive, Jack was trying to reconcile the admittedly challenging interface between these two givens.

I have to admit, his question stopped me dead in my tracks. Never during my own childhood would the thought have even crossed my mind that a human being might be a space where God was *not*. Raised in the rolling countryside of southeastern Pennsylvania and sent to Quaker schools for my early schooling, I grew up in an easy, natural intimacy between the divine and human realms. To be sure, Sundays brought my weekly encounter with Christian Science, where it was drilled into me that "there is no life, truth, intelligence, nor substance in matter." But the rest of the week I was free to roam the fields and forests and drink in exactly the opposite assurance. From the first moment my young self-reflective consciousness came online, about Jack's age or a little younger (I remember myself standing in a pumpkin patch just at sunset in late October, everything brilliantly ablaze in orange), I knew then and there that the holy, intimate radiance suffusing the picture was in me and in *everything*, if for no other reason than because it was from the *inside* that all of this seemed to be emerging. "Ah," the Quakers nodded encouragingly, "the light within!" And they told me it was in everyone.

In due course, at Christian Science Sunday School and Methodist Vacation Bible School, we kids all read the Bible stories and learned all about those epic Old Testament battles against something called "idol worship." We thrilled as Moses smashed down the golden calf and sneered over our shoulders at those misguided Baal worshippers or Phoenicians or Canaanites with whom our Hebrew heroes were locked in mortal combat. I didn't know exactly what "idol worship" was at the time, but I knew it had to do with trying to put God in a box— and that the consequences for disobedience were severe. (The Ten Commandments, duly memorized as part of our Bible School experience, left no doubt on that score.)

Blessedly, it never occurred to me back in those early days of my awakening that my cherished secret, that gently dawning light within, might be seen in some quarters as "putting God in a box."

Panentheism

The whole implicit collision course didn't really hit home until years later—decades later, in fact; post Ph.D., post seminary, post ordination—when, by now a commissioned practitioner of Centering Prayer, I was regularly giving introductory workshops in local churches and seminaries. Part of the standard presentation features a way of introducing the concept of contemplative prayer by framing it in terms of different levels of consciousness: our *ordinary awareness* (task-oriented and self-referential), *spiritual awareness* (more open-ended, receptive, and emotionally attuned), and last but not least, the *divine indwelling*, through which God "himself" is personally conscious in us and *as* us.

"No, no, that is quite wrong. You are in error." Inevitably there would be a person standing there at the break, right in my face, urgently challenging me on this last point. "There is *nothing* of God that indwells the human person," this person would categorically proclaim. From there, the argument would go in either of two directions: a) we humans have been so ineradicably contaminated by sin that we have lost the image and likeness of God, or b) the whole thing is pure pantheism.

This episode was repeated with such predictable regularity that I eventually came to expect it. Clearly the whole notion of a divine indwelling, for all its certifiable theological orthodoxy, continues to make many traditionally reared Christians squirm.

I draw in my breath and begin again. "Yes," I try to explain to this person, "for sure, if I were claiming that I am God or that God and the world are the same, that would be pantheism. But surely God can *inhabit* this world of ours, indwell and suffuse it without getting *stuck* there..."

"Oh, you mean you're a *panentheist!*" comes the rejoinder. I roll my eyes and cede the point, all the while silently gritting my teeth.

For you see, mea culpa, I have to admit that I do not take easily to being labeled a panentheist. Yes, I know that Marcus Borg and most of my other theologically progressive colleagues are all in favor of it, but the term has always made me distinctly uncomfortable. It's not so much the *concept* that bothers me; it's the word itself. Like a "jet airplane," it's one of those terms that tries to define itself in terms of a prior term (in this case, pantheism), to which it offers an ostensible improvement. Pan*en*theism hence looks like a more refined version of pantheism, an update that disposes of its major shortcomings while still implicitly keeping the paradigm in place.

But in fact, it's the entire paradigm that's the problem in the first place, and I suspect that things are not going to improve (either for our schools of theology or for our planet) until we gird up our loins and stop *en*abling it. As our world hovers on the threshold of a second axial age, I believe that it's time to recognize pantheism as a concept whose era has long since come and gone. It has no place in a post-Einsteinian universe, is radically subversive of all efforts toward a unified planetary ecology, notoriously unfriendly to mystics, and just plain old existentially *wrong*. This old wineskin's simply gotta go before we can break out the new wine of an authentically non-dual Christianity.

I am not saying this simply for the sake of being controversial. These conclusions have been slowly growing in me for a very long time now, to the point where I simply cannot see the situation in any other way. And if truth be told, I would probably never have had the nerve to share them publicly were it not for the gracious invitation of the editors of this volume for me to contribute an autobiographical reflection rather than a theological argument. So, gratefully taking refuge in the personal and confessional intent of this assignment, I simply hope to share with you a bit of the story of how I have come to see things in this way—in particular, the three "aha" insights that changed everything for me.

Panikkar

I had been slowly drifting toward a more unitive worldview for decades, but it was Raimon Panikkar who finally put me across the line.

Panikkar had been on my distant radar screen for some time, but my immersion began in earnest in the spring of 2008—thanks, I should say, to a nudge from my longtime friend and spiritual mentor Thomas Keating. Eighty-five years old at the time (he's now 93 and still growing by spiritual leaps and bounds), Thomas had himself recently taken the plunge into Panikkar's 2004 magnum opus *Christophany*, and was electrified by its brilliant, dynamically non-dual vision. "Can you imagine how this would change the face of Christianity if it were better known?" he mused, then added, staring straight at me with that signature twinkle of the eye, "But of course, it's too difficult for *lay people....*"

Well, them's fighting words! It's long been a point of pride with me (and Thomas knew it!) that anything worth teaching can be taught if you can only find the right angle of approach. So rising to the wager, I too plunged into *Christophany*, only to find my heart, just like Thomas', ripped wide open by this theologically exacting yet breathtakingly non-dual rendition of the Christian mystical vision. As I waded into the section called "The Mysticism of Jesus Christ," I was floored by what Panikkar seemed to be arguing: that the Trinity, often dismissed as a theological add-on hammered out at the later theological councils, was actually an original—because it originated in the mind of Christ! It encapsulates in a single elegant mandala the entire personal experience of Jesus himself in his relationship to divinity.

Far from either a static immanence or static transcendence, Jesus' experience of God was *cosmotheandric*, the infinite and the finite continuously interabiding one another, dynamically changing places through a process of continuing self-giving, or kenosis. At the "Abba, father" pole, claims Panikkar, Jesus is most fully identified with his finite selfhood, reaching out to God with what Panikkar describes as "a very intense experience of a divine filiation."[11] At the opposite pole, "I and the Father are one," there is simply a unity of being, no place where God stops and "I" begin, just a unity. Between these two poles, the third of Jesus' three great *mahavakyani*, or master sayings (Panikkar's word for these, of course) —"It is good that I leave"— places the other two in a perpetual kenotic dynamism which Panikkar beautifully summarizes as "I am one with the source insofar as I too act as a source by making all

I have flowed receive again."[22] Dynamism, the missing link: like a bicycle, the whole thing only works when it's in motion.

"*Cosmotheandric*" is Panikkar's neologism of choice to describe this dynamic intercirculation. Denotatively, it covers much the same turf as panentheism, but connotatively, they are light years apart. *Panentheism* ties us back into that old static paradigm (this "thing" called the created order is not God, but God can still visit it without getting stuck in it); *cosmotheandric* (forged from the words *cosmos*, world; *theos*, God; and *andros*, human) speaks implicitly of an intercirculation of realms, of whole different dimensions or planes of being actively infusing each other. It is cosmic, quantum, Einsteinian, portraying the paradox of form and formless more like virtual particles dancing in and out of existence in a single unified field than in the old substance theology categories now largely outmoded as we have discovered that *energy*, not substance, is the coin of the realm.

Panikkar's words knocked my socks off, for it felt so in tune with the heartbeat of the 21st century, the dynamic, evolving, interabiding world we are coming to find affirmed far more in science these days than in theology, still so stuck in defending an ancient and long since superfluous abyss between form and the formless. Nor did it come as much of surprise to me when the lay people in my Wisdom School ate it right up.

P.S. Jesus Was Not a Monotheist(!?)

But as I started to pay more attention to the subtext in *Christophany*, what I began to see appearing before my eyes was something even more radical. Was I really understanding correctly that Panikkar seemed to be implying that *Jesus was not a monotheist*?

I got to ask Panikkar this question directly in a private interview a few months before his death. His answer turned my world upside down—not so much what he said, but how he said it.

"Well, it sure *seemed* that way to me." Block by understated block, Panikkar seemed to be quietly building the case that what made Jesus so threatening to the Jewish authorities was not his politics, his mysticism, or even his charisma, but that aforementioned "intense experience of divine filiation." This unauthorized prophet was standing too close, violating that unbridgeable divide between Creator and creature which Father Abraham and Father Moses had fixed in place as firmly as the firmament itself. Who would ever call the great, transcendent Yahweh *abba* "Papa"?! Or accept the moniker "Son of God"—a blasphemy so galling that they played it back to him on his crown of thorns.

It was *so* blasphemous, in fact, that even St. Paul found himself wanting to wriggle out of it, inventing the grand theological dodge that Jesus is the only *natural* son of God; the rest of us are "adopted" sons. But with his own brilliant theological and interspiritual acuity, Panikkar overturned that proposition as logically flawed, culturally bound, and not at all what Jesus was saying in the first place. Jesus is the son of God because we are *all* sons (and daughters) of God, because that is how a cosmotheandric universe works, because God is not a first cause, not an explanation, but rather *meaning* itself, throbbing through the entire dynamism, suffusing the attuned heart like the air we breath, like the atoms still reverberating in our bodies from the big bang.

"Is that *really* what you meant? Am I understanding you rightly?" I peered across the vast walnut desk at the tiny,

93-year-old man sitting like a wizened tulku in the study at his home in Tavertet, Spain. It was March 8, 2010, less than six months before his death, and he was already actively transitioning toward the next realm; two months earlier he had cancelled all further engagements. How our own interview remained on his calendar, I to this day do not understand; chalk it up to the deft touch of a mutual friend in Barcelona who had arranged our meeting and served as our impromptu interpreter when our conversation occasionally lapsed into Panikkar's native Catalonian. We sat there for about an hour, our conversation mostly carried in the mode of contemplative prayer, punctuated by a few brief exchanges which barely rippled the radiance of the depths.

"That's really what you're saying?" I finally summoned up my nerve to ask—"that Jesus was not a monotheist?"

He weighed my words silently. The silence lasted a long, long time. Then slowly, still silently, he nodded. A mysterious smile flickered across his face, not unlike the Mona Lisa.

A Brief History of Consciousness

"I solemnly declare that I do believe the Holy Scriptures of the Old and New Testament to be the Word of God and to contain all things necessary to salvation."

It is the occasion of my ordination to the Episcopal priesthood, August 1979, and I am standing before my bishop, making my required public profession. My friends are rolling their eyes, wondering if I've just perjured myself. But no, I have never had difficulty with this particular provision, then or now. I do indeed believe that the Holy Scriptures contain all things necessary to salvation. So does a rock. So does this 10-foot-wide patch of ocean I am now sailing through after the fog has shut down my usual visual horizons. So does almost anything in this holy, God-infused universe of ours when we truly open our hearts to it.

But scripture is indeed its own unique brand of wonderfulness, and over the nearly seven decades it's been part of my life, I have come to appreciate its sacredness in a whole different way. Back then I looked upon it as the unchanging revelation of the one true God. Now I look at it as an extraordinary, sacred archive of the evolution of human consciousness.

The idea of levels of consciousness, first advanced in the late 1940s by Jean Gebser and Ernst Neumann and carried forward into our own era primarily through the work of Ken Wilber, suggests (in a nutshell) that each of us, in the course of our lives, passes through a series of levels of consciousness. Beginning in the undifferentiated "uroboric" state of infancy, we pass through the magical consciousness of early childhood, where the world is alive with "ghoulies and ghosties, long-leggity beasties, and things that go bump in the night"; to mythic membership (identification with the group or tribe); rational; pluralistic (*"Co-exist!"*)—and finally, if we're lucky, to those "non-dual" states of integral and cosmic consciousness, where we begin to see all things from the perspective of oneness. In the same way that an individual progresses through these levels in the course of life, moving as far as he or she is able to along the gradient, so has our entire human family passed through these same stages, "writ large" in the history of civilization.

Seen in this way, the people of Israel are indeed, quintessentially, "the pen that God writes with" (as our Israeli tour guide categorically proclaimed during my first pilgrimage to the Holy Land). The journey we call the Old Testament really gets underway around the shift from magical consciousness to mythic membership consciousness. That's what I was really witnessing in all those Bible stories of my childhood, those holy wars on "idol worship." What I now know from a wider reading of human anthropology is that all those struggles with the Canaanites and Baal worshippers were really playing out the displacement of an earlier, *magical* consciousness in the transition to the next level, *mythic membership.* Israel swept like a holy dust storm into these ancient matriarchal lands, replacing the gods of rocks and rivers with a new concept, of a God "out there," related to creation through covenant, not indwelling. It was a clear and significant evolutionary leap. The 12 tribes of Israel came into being as the active agency of this transition, determinedly obliterating their neighbors and even earlier, "pagan" vestiges in their own tradition (if Margaret Barker is right) to clear the way for this heretofore unconceivable new beachhead of divine/human consciousness.

Then, beginning in the Davidic psalms and continuing in earnest through the post-exilic prophets, we see the rise of *rational* consciousness as across the entire planet, the winds of that great "first axial" age begin to blow and Israel awakens to the idea of a personal relationship and individual accountability with this great transcendent Yahweh. Finally, in those mysterious apocalyptic images of the "suffering servant" and that elusive "son of man," we see the first intimations of a whole new level of consciousness, *integral* verging toward *non-dual:* the capacity to think from the whole, not from the part, and thus for the first time in the history of civilization to begin to envision the possibility of a collective humanity.

This is where Jesus takes up the story. As far as the West is concerned, he is indisputably the first to model a fully attained *non-dual* consciousness: flowing, compassionate, holographic, unbound by the conventions of those lower orders of consciousness which require that things be separated from each other in order to make sense of them. He is literally envisioning a new world, based on a new mode of consciousness: unity attained. And, of course, the planet was not ready for him then—and is *still* barely ready.

Israel came into existence on the arrowhead of conscious evolution, a process that is holy and irreversible, and its greatest thinkers (Jesus being one of them) have always been ahead of the curve, breaking through the conceptual logjams *du jour*, carrying consciousness to the next level. In this respect, I profoundly honor the Old Testament and could not even begin to make sense of my own Christian journey without it. And I honor the New Testament as well, and the great traditions of patristic, Neoplatonic, and scholastic thought that have framed our Western worldview for more than two millennia.

But it's no longer the era we live in. The era in which God could be thought of as "pure spirit," transcendent to matter, which "He" created but does not personally indwell, was turned upside down in 1905 (along with 2,500 years of metaphysical Prospero's castles built upon it), by the Einsteinian discovery that energy, not substance, is the true cosmic constant. And that "Heaven above" where "our Father art," where indeed art that? Surely not "above" this visible realm, suspended beyond those perfectly crystalline planetary orbits that medieval astronomy used to portray. In a universe 14 billion years old and vast beyond our most staggering reckonings, it is unimaginable to think that anything is "outside" the created realm. "Where is God in this picture?" writes Barbara Brown Taylor in her 2000 spiritual classic *The Luminous Web*, detailing the "radical shift" in her consciousness brought about by her exposure to quantum physics. Her answer:

God is all over the place. God is up there, down here, inside my skin and out. God is the web, the energy, the space, the light—not captured in them, as if any of those concepts was more real than what unites them—but revealed in that singular, vast net of relationships that animates everything that is.[33]

And in this dynamic, teeming, interabiding universe— pulsing, throbbing, kenotically exchanging—the finger-in-the-dike of panentheism (and even the old-school monotheism it is intended to protect) is simply, as my hermit teacher Rafe would shake his head and say, "last year's language." Scripture does indeed contain all things necessary to salvation, but only if we keep writing it. And to keep writing it means—as all the prophets from Abraham on have consistently proclaimed—to be willing to leave all known reference points behind in order to ride that arrowhead of evolution relentlessly toward the next unfolding. That's the common thread running through the entire scriptural narrative, and the reason it contains all things necessary to salvation.

Seeing

"*Voir ou périr*," wrote Pierre Teilhard de Chardin in his searing prologue to *The Human Phenomenon:* "See or perish."

In the end, it's all about seeing. But maybe not so much about what we see, as *how* we see. And that has been my most surprising discovery in recent years: to discover that this great, elusive non-dual reality may have more to do with an upgrade in the operating system than any change in spiritual state. Like most everything else that's come into my life in these past 30 years, it all started with Centering Prayer.

I took up the practice in the late 1980s, but it took a long time—maybe five years—before I actually got what it was all about. Like most beginning meditators, I thought the goal was to make your mind still so that God could find a way in. I used my sacred word like a street sweeper to clear away all thoughts so that God could fill my emptiness with divine presence. Only gradually did I learn that the essence of the prayer lies in the simple letting go: the release of thoughts not in order to be filled with something else, but for its own sake, as a perfectly valid and whole spiritual gesture in its own right. I came to see it as the meditational equivalent of *kenosis*, or self-emptying, experienced not as a spiritual attitude but as an embodied practice.

Once that corner was turned, a whole new horizon opened up. I began to notice that as I worked with this gesture, my attention was shifting lower in my body, moving out of my head and not onto but *into* my heart. By this I mean it was not a matter of thinking about my heart, but more an *abiding* in my heart, like a gradual, enfolding aliveness. I noticed that every time I went "out" of myself to think about something, this aliveness faded and I was back into cerebral mode again, back into inside and outside, subject and object.

It was thus that I gradually came to think of contemplative prayer not simply as a "resting in God," but as the gradual installation of a whole new system of perception—an upgrade in the operating system, as it were. I came to understand in a whole new way that classic Orthodox desideratum of "putting the mind in the heart."

The standard operating system on which rational consciousness and everything built on it rests is based on a "perception through differentiation" program. I am me by virtue of not being you. A cat is not a dog; God is not me. The play-ing field of perception is primordially organized into subject and object, inside and outside, like and unlike.

But this other "mind in the heart" system runs a whole different program: perception through *holographic unity*, or an instantaneous perception of the larger pattern through sympathetic entrainment. The simplest analogy I can think of comes from music. When people are asked to sing a simple canon (like "Row, row, row your boat"), inexperienced singers will nearly always cover their ears so that the other musical parts don't throw them off. But experienced singers realize that the whole song is a single harmonic unity and "lean into" the other parts in order to keep the rhythm and sing in tune. They are taking their bearings from the whole, which is what heart perception does.

I began to learn that there has indeed been a whole tradi-tion of this other kind of perception in the West, inaugurat-ed most likely by Jesus' simple one-liner "Blessed are the pure [i.e., undivided] in heart for they shall see God," and reaching its most sublime articulation in Orthodox Hesychasm and Is-lamic Sufism. Here the heart is perceived not as the seat of the emotions but as an organ of spiritual perception, and practice concentrates on removing the impurities (chiefly vainglory and attachment) and strengthening the physical grounding so that this other, far more powerful and vivifying operating system can come fully online.

The modern Sufi master Kabir Helminski writes about this heart-centered perception in a passage so emblazoned on my own consciousness that it manages to show up in most ev-ery book I've written. "We have subtle subconscious faculties we are not using," Helminski begins. "Beyond the limited analytical intellect lies a vast realm of mind that includes psychic and extrasensory abilities; intuition; wisdom; a sense of unity; aesthetic, qualitative, and creative faculties; and image-forming and symbolic capacities. Though these faculties are many, we give them a single name because they are operating best when they are in concert. They comprise a mind, moreover, in spontaneous connection with the cosmic mind. This total mind we call heart."[44]

"This total mind we call heart...." Now *there* is a revelation—or perhaps a revolution! During the 10 years or more it took for this other way of understanding to be gradually assimilated in me, I slowly awoke to the real "aha" of the situation. The thing is, pantheism, panentheism, monotheism—all those other grand "isms' of the Western philosophical mind—are purely *functions of the operating system*, the rational mind running its perception-through- differentiation program. They are based on there needing to be an inside and an outside, a subject and object, carefully delimited descriptors, and identity through differentiation. And in all those respects, the concept of a great transcendent God "out there" is totally and quintessentiually a function of separation consciousness at work, of the rational level of consciousness which was the great first axial breakthrough.

But that is two levels of consciousness below where we are now, and where we need to be moving much more swiftly if there is to be a future for this fragile and interconnected universe. At the pluralistic level (where most of liberal/ progressive consciousness is presently clustered), we are just beginning to put the separated bits and pieces back together under the banner of "coexist." At the next level, the integral, we have begun to think holographically, from the whole to the part (rather than from the part to the whole which is still paradigmatic for pluralistic consciousness). But only at the birth of the genuine non-dual does the upgrade happen; the mind sinks into the heart, and we literally perceive FROM NO SEPARATION, by matching the pattern. There is no inside and no outside, because they are no longer necessary for perception. (As my hermit teacher Rafe used to say, "When the building's completed, you no longer need the scaffolding.") "When you can make two become one, the inside like the outside, the higher like the lower..." says the gospel of Thomas (logion 22). When you can look at the laborers in the vineyard (Matthew 20) and do not immediately rank them on the grid of "more" and "less," when you begin to see in a dynamic, intercirculating, interabiding, *cosmotheandric* way that preserves both particularity and unity by setting the whole scene in motion, then, like Barbara Brown Taylor, you will hear yourself saying:

> At this point in my thinking, it is not enough for me to proclaim that God is responsible for all this unity. Instead, I want to proclaim that God *is* the unity—the very energy, the very intelligence, the very elegance and passion that makes it all go.[55]

In former days, this kind of seeing was often confused with a mystical experience or hyped as evidence of "enlightenment" or personal self-realization. And maybe this was indeed the case in former days, and I can pat myself on the back if I want for having glimpsed something once reserved to the saints and mystics. But then there's Jack, who at four is already clearly thinking in terms of the total volume of wholeness. It's no longer an over-the-top spiritual achievement. It's simply the way the planet is evolving.

I know that the direction and rate of acceleration nowadays leave a lot of us boomers who are still invested in the orderly transmission of institutional Christianity quaking in our boots. But you see, the light at the end of the tunnel in all this is that Jesus was THERE already, 2,000 years ago. And as we open our mystical eye-of-the-heart and *see*, what we see is a Christianity which has essentially been waiting in the wings for two millennia for the time to arrive when it can finally become consistent in its own highest cosmotheandric calling: "As you, Father, are in me and I am in you, may they also be in us...I in them and you in me, that they may be completely *one*." (John 17: 21-23).

That time is *now*, and we get to be the midwives!!! What could possibly be more exciting?

Notes

1. Raimon Panikkar, Christophany: *The Fullness of Man* (Maryknoll, NY: Orbis Books, 2004), 93.
2. Ibid., 116.
3. Barbara Brown Taylor, *The Luminous Web* (Cambridge, MA: Cowley Publicaions, 2000), 74.
4. Kabir Helminski, *Living Presence: A Sufi Way to Mindfulness and the Essential Self* (New York: Jeremy Tarcher/Putnam, 1993), 157.
5. Taylor, *The Luminous Web*, 74.

7. *Making God Necessary*

Deepak Chopra

The practice of medicine, which I began after moving from India to the United States in 1971, is an odd opening to God. But finding out what's wrong with a patient comes close to being a spiritual investigation, improbable as this may sound. Unless someone is wheeled into the emergency room with a broken leg or gunshot wound—both were common occurrences in the New Jersey hospital that was my first exposure to American medicine—the doctor begins by asking "What's wrong?" The patient then gives a subjective account of his aches, pains, and specific discomfort. This account is likely to be filtered through distortions such as high anxiety, distrust of medicine, or in my case back then, skepticism that a young M.D. from India really knew anything. ("Can I see a real doctor?" was written on the faces of many patients in an era when the Vietnam War had created a doctor shortage, leading to an influx of foreign-born and foreign-trained physicians.)

Although we all visit the doctor routinely to find out what's wrong with us, certain situations depend almost entirely upon subject-reporting. Pain is the most obvious example. There is no objective measure for pain, no reliable scale like the level of liver enzymes or hormones in the blood. "It hurts" is the only standard, and the patient's description of how much it hurts and where cannot be refuted. Depression and anxiety are also heavily dependent on subject-reporting. Even though brain scans are beginning to offer a hint at objective measurement, the general conclusion seems to be that every depressed patient is a unique case.

Diagnosis, then, implies a subtle struggle between what the patient reports and what the physician concludes to be true. The unspoken object of this contest, from the doctor's viewpoint, is to reduce subjectivity as much as possible so that medical science can get at the facts and nothing but the facts. It is absolutely necessary for subjectivity not to rule the practice of medicine, while on the other hand pure objectivity is a chimera.

My father had a long career as an Indian Army physician, a cardiologist, and it was a point of pride with him to reject Ayurveda, the centuries-old indigenous medicine of India, in favor of "real medicine," meaning the Western science-based variety. So a high respect for science was ingrained in me from my childhood onward, even though my grandmother was a staunch believer in Ayurvedic remedies, or folk remedies as my father would have labeled them. I felt no qualms about this division in the family, and after a certain age, perhaps 12 or 13, I understood why my father was also a nonbeliever in

God while all the women in the family, including my mother, were strongly devout.

Unless you have respect for subject-reported facts, religion is nearly impossible to credit. There are no facts about God, none that rise to the level of science, that is. Saint Paul may have been struck by divine light on the road to Damascus, but a traveler going in the opposite direction might simply have seen a man fall down on the side of the road. I recently asked a woman why she had become a deeply convinced convert to Roman Catholicism, and she replied, "Jesus was either a deluded psychotic or the Son of God, and I'm sure he wasn't crazy." She hadn't considered another, obvious possibility: Jesus could have been ordinarily sane but very convinced by his subjective experiences. So far as I could see in my early life, which was spent as a scientific atheist, all religions were founded on subjective and therefore unreliable experiences.

Yet I had an uncle whose hobby, as it were, consisted of visiting saints on a regular basis. "Saint" is a very general term in common Indian usage, denoting a holy man, swami, yogi, mystic, or enlightened master. No official body confers the title, and people regularly sit in the presence of saints in order to get a blessing, or *Darshan*. I went with my uncle as a fascinated youngster on various Darshan jaunts, and I was impressed that being in the presence of a saint made me feel peaceful and quiet inside. There was sometimes a sense of bliss, or *Ananda*, that is considered a classic sign of true Darshan. I later realized that for my uncle, this was actually a serious enterprise, because he had adopted the belief, which goes back before written history, that setting eyes on the enlightened ensures that you yourself will one day be enlightened (in fact, the Sanskrit root of Darshan is "to see").

This prelude brings me to the point of my argument about God today, and specifically the immanent God. The crisis of faith that surrounds us and so troubles churchmen and believers of every stripe can be solved only one way, by making God necessary. Unless God enters into daily decisions and, furthermore, brings about better results than doing without God, the divine will be at most an add-on to modern life. Any version of God that is personal, incidental, occasional, fickle, or unknowable cannot be a God I'd call necessary. Oxygen is necessary, along with food and shelter; money is necessary for all but the smallest fraction of society; and to the list could be added love and happiness, although those qualities are done without by untold millions of people.

In order to make God necessary, there is a journey from belief to faith and from faith to knowledge. One lesson from my medical practice, reinforced by science in general, is that subjectivity isn't good enough. There must be objective conclusions and, still better, practical solutions. Looking upon the seemingly superhuman calm with which Socrates faced death, Nietzsche thought he was glad to be cured of the disease of life. As rebellious as that sounds, the Buddha would have agreed, in a different way, that life's inevitable baggage of pain and suffering must be approached with radical surgery— the necessary treatment was ego death, the end of personal attachment to the cycle of pleasure and pain.

Lacking a rebellious streak, I've concluded that the point of spirituality is to deliver a kind of medicine to the soul, a recovery program that invests life with "light." This word has countless meanings in the world's spiritual traditions, but here my use is simply the light of knowledge—knowing what is real and disposing of what is unreal. If God cannot pass the test of knowledge, the spiritual journey remains incomplete or even aborted.

Belief is the first step, which is different from faith. Belief is more tenuous; it involves a willingness to believe that God is a possibility. A confirmed atheist won't accept belief as a first step, and countless modern people are satisfied enough with secularism that for all practical purposes they are practicing atheists. But if belief is adopted, a person starts to examine if something real is the object of belief. Children believe in fairytales, but to carry this belief into adulthood implies a kind of self-indulgence, an enjoyment in fooling oneself on purpose. Bible stories are like fairytales in the way they defy ordinary reality, and as children nothing is more captivating than miracles. But holding on to Bible stories as the basis of belief in God strikes me as a sort of self-indulgence, too, bringing the same pleasure in fooling oneself. Without holding a miracle up to the same validation as a blood test, we ignore the demands of reality.

But validating God is a long time coming, I realize, and this requires the second stage on the journey, faith. Faith is more convinced than belief. It is upheld by actual personal experience of some kind that points toward the divine. To my mind, knowledge of God isn't privileged over other kinds of knowledge. A physical brain is required, along with measurable activity in various regions of the brain that correlate with what a person is experiencing subjectively. To see angels requires the same visual cortex as seeing a cow. There's a trap here, however, that needs to be avoided.

The fact that the brain is active during spiritual experiences isn't the same as saying that the brain *creates* those experiences. It only processes them. In Tibetan Buddhist monks who have meditated on compassion for years, the prefrontal cortex lights up with extraordinary intensity on an fMRI. Certain frequencies of brain waves are also greatly intensified. Looking at this evidence, some have argued that neuroscience has validated that spiritual experience is real. I think that's a wrong conclusion, because nothing stronger than inference is involved. On an fMRI a neuroscientist sees only neural correlates, the physical fingerprints of something that isn't actually measurable. In fact, not just spiritual experience but all experience isn't captured through brain activity, any more than knowing the workings of a radio tells you how a Mozart symphony being broadcast through the radio was created. Hooking Shakespeare up with electrodes while he writes *Hamlet* won't reveal the first line, or even syllable, of the play, much less its meaning.

The whole point of spiritual experience is its profound meaning for the individual, which can be life-changing. If someone leaves her everyday existence to become a secluded Carmelite nun, it's folly to say "her brain made her do it." Her experience, filtered through her mental evaluation of it, made her do it. I would say that everyday life, in fact, is littered with clues and hints of spiritual experience. These passing moments take on a flavor everyone can identify with, even the most convinced atheist. Let me offer a partial list, which consists of moments when you or I feel:

Safe and protected
Wanted
Loved
As if we belong
As if our lives are embedded in a larger design
As if the body is light and action is effortless

Upheld by unseen forces
Unusually fortunate or lucky
Touched by fate
Inspired
Infused with light, or actually able to see a faint light
around someone else
Held in the presence of the divine
Spoken to by our soul
Certain that a deep wish or dream is coming true
Certain that a physical illness will be healed
At ease with death and dying.

Only a fraction of the items on this list conform to the conventional notion of a religious experience (although pollsters have found that ordinary people, up to a majority, report seeing an aura of light around someone else at least once in their lives, and hospice caregivers routinely see something like the soul leaving the body at the moment of death. These are phenomena difficult to talk about, even embarrassing, in the context of secular society). It takes a degree of faith in yourself to acknowledge these experiences and even more faith to follow them up. I'd call lack of follow-up the real loss of faith, because all too often the most extraordinary experiences pass through our lives momentarily and then are lost in the welter of daily existence.

Faith in your own experience is crucial. Once you notice that you've had a meaningful experience of the kind I've listed, you must give it significance. This is a harder step for most people, because they have been conditioned form childhood to identify with secondhand labels. In my case, for example, the labels include Indian, male, late middle age, doctor, married, well-to-do, and so on. As we accumulate labels, hoping to be known by positive tags rather than negative ones—I've had more than my share of the latter—we develop an ongoing story about who we are. This story is almost entirely externalized, because that's how labels work. Insidiously, we start to prefer labels over experience, especially when an experience would set us apart as different. "I am an endocrinologist" was a prestige tag for me in my profession. It took a bit of daring to substitute "I am a mind-body doctor" or "I am a meditator"— those tags were quite suspect in the 1980s. What if I became known without tags, both to others and to myself? "I feel like a child of the universe" or "I was touched by God" aren't safe ways to identify yourself.

So in the stage of faith, you must shift your allegiance to what you actually experience, which leads to a new, more authentic story about who you are and where you are headed. Much of the panic among professional religionists today can be traced to the collapse of traditional stories, stories of saints, miracle workers, the humbly devout, trials of faith, and rewards and punishments from God. Nietzsche notoriously thought that religious stories were power plays, methods by which a priest caste controlled believers. I'm willing to shrug off such accusations, because in reality, to live by any second-hand story keeps us from true knowledge. To accept conventional wisdom is the surest way to remain unwise.

Once you've given significance to your inner experience, more experiences start to arrive. You've turned on the tap. Everyone, as it happens, already entices phenomena to appear. If you walk around with a chip on your shoulder, there will always be more reasons to pick a fight. If you are an ingrained optimist, your day will be filled with things to be optimistic over. In other words, each of us creates personal reality through a feedback loop with the larger reality. Being infinite, the larger reality—known in Sanskrit as Brahman—can supply endless evidence that your personal story is valid. At some point it's important to believe this; otherwise, the alternative is to lead a meaningless life, which no one can tolerate. Then comes a change. The things you believe in start to become less personal, less about "I, me, and mine." Spirituality becomes more and more selfless.

Being practical modern people, we want a payoff for the time and effort we invest in things, and selfless spirituality has no obvious payoff. It would shock most seekers to hear that finding God or enlightenment doesn't make you a better person or smarter, richer, more respected—it doesn't make you more of anything. Wanting more is an ego game. It is intertwined with the ego's innate insecurity, which tries to find security by acquiring more of the good things in life and reducing more of the painful things. Rupert Spira, an inspired speaker on these matters, was once contemplating the question of the afterlife. "The ego wants to survive after death," Spira remarked, "so that it can come back and tell everyone about it." What would impress your friends more than telling them you just got back from a trip to Heaven? It beats the French Riviera.

Faith on its own is insufficient; it sustains us in a mixture of truth and illusion. Our minds, our desires, our wishes, fears, and dreams, lead us on, but there is always nagging uncertainty. Some things are convincing but illusory, like the ego's desire to be totally pleasured at every moment or to be liked by everyone. This jumble of illusion and reality all has to be sorted out. I associate the ripening stage of faith with emotional maturity, or what might be called "building a self." The essence of making God necessary is coming to grips with reality. A strong sense of self is required, never more so than when you realize that the self must be jettisoned. At that point, founded on your inner experiences, you are ready for the third and last stage, which is true knowledge.

True knowledge doesn't come with a signpost pointing to God. Instead, what you start knowing is the nature of existence. The only two things any of us actually knows with total certainty is that we exist and that we are aware of existing. Ironically, these are the two things everyone takes for granted, whether they call themselves atheists or believers. "I am" needs no follow-up. As soon as you say, "I am X," the X dominates your thought. "I am Deepak, an Indian male, a doctor, etc." forms a train of thought that leads, step by step, away from the simplicity of "I am." There's good reason for why Moses heard Jehovah say "I am that I am" from the burning bush. It's the one true thing that connects the human and the divine. "I am" is the beginning and end of wisdom.

This needs explaining, naturally. If you take the physical world as a given, existence is empty and inert. It's empty in that life won't matter unless it gets filled with countless experiences that arrive on a conveyor belt from birth to death. Existence as nothing but a physical fact is inert because until the mind enlivens it, nothing "out there" matters. Hamlet's "To be or not to be, that is the question" actually misses the point. To be is inevitable, beyond choosing. The real question is what existence means. This becomes an urgent question once the demands of "I, me, and mine" are exhausted or abandoned. A quote whose source I forget comes to mind: *As long as you have a personal stake in the world, enlightenment is impossible.* Or to make this truth more comfortable for Westerners who are suspicious of enlightenment, as long as you have a personal stake in the world, you won't know who you really are.

I've been asking for the reader's indulgence by not bringing up the immanent God, which is the putative subject here. But now we are close. If existence isn't fated to be empty and inert, it must be something else, replete and alive. The fullness of reality and the source of all life is God. When you come to the stage where you are urgently interested in existence, it turns out that awareness cannot be left out. To exist and to be aware that you exist go hand in hand; ultimately they are one. In the ancient Vedic tradition of India, this seamless unity, this one thing upon which all things are founded, was simply called "That." Two enlightened people could meet on the street with totally different backgrounds and completely divergent opinions about everything. But both would agree to the statement, "I am That, you are That, and all this is That."

"That" is too unspecific for theologians, and labels have been applied, such as Brahman, *vidya*, *mahavakya*, and so on, in order to find the right label. But this effort, along with the theology it is part of, runs against the intention of "That," which is to point beyond all language to the source of everything. God as origin belongs in every religion, it goes without saying. But origin without God is much trickier. The one great advantage of the Indian tradition, as I view it, lies in getting at the source without resorting to anything beyond existence itself. If God isn't existence, then the search for God will only lead into deeper illusion. That's the bottom line of "I am That."

In the final stage of the spiritual journey, to be is enough. Being is awareness, and there is no getting beyond awareness. What we are not aware of might as well not exist. A current fashion among physicists is to posit an infinite number of possible universes that comprise the so-called "multiverse." These alternate universes are necessary for cosmological reasons. For example, they get us past the nonsensical question, "What came before time began?" By general agreement, time and space, along with matter and energy, emerged at the instant of the Big Bang. Since the human brain is a product of time, space, matter, and energy, the pre-created state of the universe is impenetrable. But mathematical conjectures can be applied to a supposed pre-creation, and using one set of complex mathematical formulas allows proponents of the multiverse to imagine a cosmic casino where trillions of universe bubble up at random. One of these bubbles is the Big Bang, which completely at random produced a universe that fostered human life. Thus "our" universe has time and space in it, along with the force of evolution, making *Homo sapiens* a winner at the cosmic casino.

Theology couldn't be more fanciful or divorced from reality than this, and it's only a historical happenstance that makes us speak of the multiverse as more respectable than speaking of God as source and origin. "That" gets us past all historical happenstances. Neither an age of faith nor an age of science matters. In any age, the individual can find the truth simply by paying attention to the undeniable fact that existence and awareness are intertwined. At any given moment, someone in the world is amazed to find that the God experience is real. Wonder and certainty still dawn at these moments, whenever they arise. I keep at hand a passage from Thoreau's *Walden*, where he speaks of "the solitary hired man on a farm in the outskirts of Concord, who has had his second birth." Like us, Thoreau wonders if someone's testimony about having a "peculiar religious experience" is valid. In answer, he looks across the span of centuries: "Zoroaster, thousands of years ago, travelled the same road and had the same experience, but he, being wise, knew it to be universal."

If you find yourself suddenly infused with an experience you cannot explain, Thoreau says, just be aware that you are not alone. Your awakening is woven into the great tradition. "Humbly commune with Zoroaster then, and, through the liberalizing influence of all the worthies, with Jesus Christ himself, let 'our church' go by the board."

Skeptics turn this advice on its head. The fact that God has been experienced over the ages only goes to show that religion is a primitive holdover, a mental relic that we should train our brains to reject. But all attempts to clarify matters—to say, once and for all, that God is absolutely real or absolutely unreal—continue to fail. The muddle persists, and we all have felt the impact of confusion and doubt. What this tells me, however, is that it's impossible to stand aside from experience when we come to the source. Just as time, space, matter, and energy emerges from a pre-created domain that is timeless and without dimensions, the source of awareness is inconceivable. "That" is ground zero, the womb of reality. There is no more language, or even thought. As the ancient Indian *rishis* declared, "Those who know it speak of it not. Those who speak of it know it not."

It's only sensible to ask if such knowing, being impossible to talk about, is actually real. This has been a vexing dilemma that gave rise to two huge topics in philosophy: ontology (the study of being) and epistemology (the study of how we know things). Both topics are gnarly and entangled, and Indian philosophy isn't immune from that. But we can cut the Gordian knot with another expression from the ancient seers: *This isn't knowledge you acquire. It is knowledge you become.* God, like the universe and reality itself, is participatory. There is no other choice, since existence is always on the move, which is why I'm fond of saying that God is a verb, not a noun.

If the argument feels like it's getting opaque, I can offer an analogy that helped me when I first heard it. Imagine that your mind is like a river. On the surface a river is filled with activity in eddies and waves. As you go deeper, the waves subside into a steady current. Deeper still the current slows down, and at the very bottom of the river, there is no current at all as water settles into the underlying river bed. Just as we can trace a river from its most agitated state to a level of complete stillness, the mind can follow itself from the stream of consciousness to deeper levels until it encounters its source in silent awareness. The entire journey is accomplished within awareness; the beginning, middle, and end are all conscious.

The practical result of this dive into awareness is not abstract knowledge. Reality is different in different states of consciousness—another maxim from the ancient *rishis*. Therefore, God isn't merely process but transformation. In this book the authors were assigned the topic of "the immanent God," which acquires its importance as a kind of rescue mission. As the transcendent God loses significance in the modern world, we must turn to immanence—"God in us" or "God in everything"—to justify the divine. I have to agree, but with the proviso that transcendence and immanence aren't relevant distinctions in the end. We don't say, "Existence is way up there, beyond the clouds. Have faith and you will find that existence is down here, too." Likewise, if God is existence, being "up there" or "down here" has no meaning.

I could give a preview of coming attractions by holding out what higher states of consciousness must be like. The Indian tradition has thousands of pages on the subject. But the simple truth is that transformation never ends, and states of consciousness lead to realities that must be experienced directly. The Vedas sound reassuring when they say "You are the universe," a kind of ultimate validation of what it means to be human. Like everyone, I've spent my life searching for validation. I try in all frankness not to describe experiences I haven't had myself. The curious reader can infer throughout this chapter that everything being described has happened to me.

I am the union of two parents, in a sense, unwilling to rely on science or faith alone but equally unwilling to let go of either strand. It's a peculiarity in human beings that we never settle on a fixed identity, the way a tiger has tigerness and perhaps an angel has angelness. In the evolutionary scheme, our specific mutation is to embody mutability. I feel that personally every day, and if you ask me "Who are you?" I don't resort to memory, family, labels, and other remnants of selves that have drifted in and out of the picture since I was born. All statements of "I am X" fall short—even "I am God"—to explain what is real at this very moment. Existence is on the move, and the only reliable guide into the unknown is reality itself.

8. Panentheism and Technology: The Immanence of Rage

Loriliai Biernacki

In a recent popular article in *Scientific American Mind* neuroscientist Christof Koch offers a vision of humanity's future that would have been virtually unthinkable for most of humanity's past. Future humans will merge cyborg-like into symbiotic relations with our machine creations. Indeed, it's happening already. Driverless cars are here to stay, he tells us; computer algorithms like DeepMind can teach themselves new game-playing techniques and soon artificial intelligence will surpass human capacities.[1] Along these lines, iconic physicist Stephen Hawking went on record warning against just this. One of the greatest threats to human survival, he admonished us, is in fact, artificial intelligence.[2]

Meanwhile this same man, Stephen Hawking, one of our greatest scientific minds, was saved from a mute death by a technology that allowed his thoughts to echo through an artificial black box. The eerily mechanical voice we heard became iconic, a brilliant disembodied mind speaking unmetrically through technology. It itself seemed like a transcendent voice from some beyond—but not like what we might imagine to be a voice from heaven, from a god or angel. Rather instead it sounded with a syncopation that recalls the hacker group "Anonymous," a nameless collective (perhaps like the Elohim? Or the myriad deities functioning in the Tantric cakras lining the human spine?). This voice from an uncanny beyond displayed a plethora of machine-modulated sound bits conjoining to make flat tones conveying the weighty thoughts of this great man.

Does the future of humanity bode such a fusion of human and machine? Perhaps we might venture that Nietzsche's infamous obituary did not quite get it right. God is not so much dead in modernity, but rather, not quite yet born. Instead, some spark transferred from silicon circuits, like a disembodied ghost, awaits us, even if only as zombie technology. This, of course, is on everyone's mind, wildly rampant in pop culture from the attractive and deadly robot in *Ex machina*, to Scarlett Johansson's sonorous *Her*. Koch points to a 1954 science-fiction short story by Fredric Brown. When the super-computers of the galaxy manage to connect, God will finally awaken—"Yes, *now* there is a God."[3]

The zombie conception of human-turned-computers follows a trajectory of transcendence all too familiar to the history of religions. In this narrative, the body is a vessel for the soul and the goal is to lift the soul out of the body into a purer transcendence from the material world into some safe space beyond the suffering of here and now. Ray Kurzweil's hopes for his own machine-enhanced immortality as he downloads his consciousness onto the mainframe, follows this same logic. Call it nirvana, or heaven, or kaivalya, or immortality in a robot body; it's always about leaving this place here and now.

However, what all this bleak forecasting of human evolution into cyborg leaves out is a counter-narrative of human evolution, less loudly broadcast to be certain, yet one finding roots in a panentheist spirituality. This panentheist spirituality offers us a different story, one that reminds us of the intelligence of the body itself, the intelligence of earth as growing plants and animal species. Apart from the mind, apart from our conscious egos, the body's own intelligence participates in the reality of life and guides our actions in a way that metal and silicon cannot. How does the body do this? What does it look like? These are the preternatural moments that arise in the body, telling us to turn this corner instead of that. Somehow, sometimes, the body just knows, knows to take a different path to avoid the mugger lurking around the corner.

The popularity of panentheism as a guiding creed for our contemporary world in part arises from just this recognition of the intelligence of the body. Panentheism alerts us to the intelligence of the body as its own innate sentiency, that the materiality of the human body itself beckons to the divine not only as a transcendent executive self-directing the actions of an unruly mass of flesh. Rather, the body's intelligence is itself expression of the divine as it becomes immanent in matter.

We might say that what is special about panentheism for our times is that it offers a grounded spirituality. The divine is not just in the transcendent spaces beyond our human experience but also always deeply connected to the life that we live in the here and now, in our familiar bodies, on our humble planet earth. And while panentheism, with its growing popularity for a thoughtful, contemporary religiously educated public, is a Western term, coined in 19th-century Europe, it may be fair to suggest that its intimations of a bodily centered divinity have also found voice in other times.

Medieval India, especially the panentheism of philosophers of non-dual Tantra, like the 11th-century Kashmiri Abhinavagupta and his 10th-century predecessor Utpaladeva, also understood the need for a kind of grounded spirituality. Tantra itself was understood as a kind of magical technology, at any rate, at least in the functional ways that technology approximates magic. Tantra offered techniques to enhance human existence, leading to liberation (*mokṣa, nirvāṇa*), and at the same time also bringing material benefits to everyday life (*bhukti*). What these 10th- and 11th-century Indian mystics, Utpaladeva and Abhinavagupta, both recognized was the importance of embodiment, an awareness of the need for a spirituality that included the body. The body functions in the search for enlightenment not just as the vessel or vehicle housing a disembodied soul, but also itself aware, in a spirituality grounded in embodiment. Utpaladeva expresses this when he talks about the imagination. He gives us two types, making a distinction between them. One kind of imagination, *vikalpa*, can generate all manner of fanciful objects that one has never seen before, like a white elephant with two trunks and a hundred tusks. This type of imagination, Utpaladeva tells us, ultimately relies on a kind of negation and contrast, knowing things by chopping up the world into various opposing conceptions, even if one then puts them back together in novel ways,[4] as an imaginary hundred-tusked white elephant.

He contrasts this kind of imagination with a deeper, embodied, grounded spirituality, the insight that we get from inward self-reflection (*vimarśa*), the transformative peace that meditative visualization (*bhāvana*) brings. This imagination draws on mind and body as a holistic habitus, a way of being in the world. Significantly, *vimarśa* comes from the root word for touch and *bhāvana* from the root "to be," both pointing to a kind of grounded embodied awareness.

Our own contemporary society, it seems, has embraced *vikalpa*, the imaginative capacity to conjure up all sorts of ungrounded objects, rather than *bhāvana*, meditative embodiment, or *vimarśa*, inward self-reflection. As Merlin Donald points out, contemporary cognitive science studies of the mind and brain use two key features: generating new objects and the capacity to address memory as a way to rank different species in terms of what he dubs the "consciousness-club."[5] Species that display the capacity to generate new objects rank more highly on the scale. This is a way of admitting the possibility of consciousness for a dog or a chimpanzee, while denying it to other life forms, such as slugs or bacteria. These two key features are also precisely what Utpaladeva points to as defining characteristics of *vikalpa*. Indeed, these particular criteria, a capacity to generate new objects and the capacity to employ memory in cognitive processes, is also what some proponents of artificial intelligence, such as Ray Kurzweil, say will prove to us the soon-to-be consciousness of computers, on a level comparable to humans.

Yet, these Indian mystics, Utpala and Abhinavagupta do not think these capacities—i.e., imagination in the sense of *vikalpa* as a capacity to generate new objects and memory— to be germane to what consciousness is. Utpaladeva instead points to *vimarśa*, an embodied self-reflective awareness as the defining element in consciousness. The imaginative capacity of *vikalpa*, in contrast, is rejected precisely because the objects we get from this kind of imagination lack any real world groundedness. They are, as the *Yoga Sūtra* tells us, "*vastuśūnyo*" (Patañjali *Yoga Sūtra* 1.9), things lacking a real object, things not grounded in a kind of embodied real-world experience.

I suggest that precisely this lack of groundedness, this divorce from embodied world experience, is a deciding moment for our current predicament. I would venture that part of the resurgence of fundamentalist religion that we see happening around the world today is connected to a plea to bring back a groundedness, the security of time-worn religious traditions to an ungrounded technological world. I suspect that the deep sense of rage rising up all through our current political culture too, apart from its economic drivers, is also tied to a sense of being ungrounded, with no sustaining roots for spiritual expression. I would offer as well that it is the grounded part of being in a body that prevents things like alternative facts. What makes panentheism so compelling for us now in the beginning of the third millennium in the midst of a fraught politics is its possibilities for bringing us back to our bodies. But how did we get here?

The big changes really started in the 1950s. Led by a vanguard of intellectuals, a brave new idea, "the secularization thesis," took hold. Scholars in the U.S. and Europe, anthropologists, sociologists, scientists, everywhere thinkers were writing about this idea, this profound and long awaited transformation, or rather evolution, of humanity. Our species was at last growing out of infancy. Humans had finally evolved beyond the magical thinking of religion. Sure, some recalcitrant, retrograde pockets of religious belief remained, last dying bits of lingering fundamentalisms, but there was no doubt that these would eventually become a distant memory, dinosaurs of our evolutionary journey.

By the 1970s it had become a truism. Scholarly common consensus pronounced the "death of religion" in nearly prophetic tones, declaring religion a relic of the past. Max Weber's "disenchantment of the world," was the awaited and welcome antidote to Marx's opiate of the masses—where science demonstrates the folly of religious belief. This disenchantment would finally allow humans to let go of the superstitious "magical thinking" that religion promoted. Think of Sam Harris and Richard Dawkins. Only the underdeveloped Third World countries were still clinging to religion and that too would be cured by the advances of technology and modernity's capitalism. With the kind of clarity that only 20/20 hindsight can bring, that vision of society grown beyond religion was a bit muddy.

The resurgence of religion at the end of the last millennium, and in particular the rise of violent religious fundamentalisms surprised them all. They proved these hopeful exclamations of humanity's evolution to be hopelessly wrong. Charitably, we might suggest that the 1950s ushered in a promissory positivism pretty much everywhere, not just in the evolutionary promise of the death of religion. Yet religion certainly has not died out. But even so, something *has* changed in the religious landscape. We humans really are evolving and it may not be too far off to suggest that as we adapt to our now blossoming, technological millennium, religion seems to be shifting with us. Not dying out, not by any means disappearing, religion instead seems to be molding its contours around our own evolving conceptions of spirit.

The changes we see happening in our current religious landscape might best be understood as the rocky fumblings of an unsure evolution, as in fits and starts we explore the possibility of panentheist connection to a divine that includes ourselves, the fabric of life, embodiment.

What I want to focus on here is a seeming consequence, perhaps an inevitable byproduct of our disenchantment of the world—a residual rage, marking not only our own current political moment, but a signature also of the rise of angry fundamentalisms around the world. Certainly the origins of this rising anger connected with religiosity is multifaceted, over-determined by a host of hard-to-track factors. Yet we would be remiss to ignore the effects of modernity's disenchantment—especially the influences of technology in our current moment that tend to leave us oddly disconnected even as our virtual connections multiply.

But how, we might first wonder, does rage connect these angry fundamentalisms to anything genuinely religious? Isn't rage only just the antipathy of a heartfelt and grounded awareness of the divinity of life? Isn't the rage of so much fundamentalist violence simply a call to older repressive hierarchies of gender and skin color? Isn't it all about politics and money, and not belief in any case? And after all, why speak of rage in a book like this, striving to offer hope for a new millennium with a newly envisioned understanding of what spirituality looks like for us today, how it might manifest in the 21st century and beyond?

One might read the current rage of violent fundamentalisms of our contemporary moment as a rage against the loss of spirit. This rage marks the pain of loss of belief in the truth of scriptural revelations, up and against a science and technology that denies it. I suspect that it is rather the reverse, not about the loss of spirit, but rather about the loss of bodies. I propose that we pay attention to this rage, that beyond its surface political clichés, it offers to teach us about our embodiment. That is, the rage we see around us in politics and in the violent resurgences of religious fundamentalisms points to the hidden grounding pole of religiosity. This is the necessary counterpart of the profound flights of transcendence we associate with mystical experience and religion. This is what holds up transcendence—our earthbound immanence. This is what we lose as religion adapts to our new technological millennium. As we become more and more embedded in technological alter-selves—in Twitter feeds and Facebook, virtual realities that connect us to people around the world we might never meet physically—our relation to physical bodies is transforming. Our bodies are lost in the mix.

The rage of fundamentalist religion is, I suspect, a plea to call back a way of being that remembers embodiment in a greater scheme of life. And in this, religious ideas, even religious dogmas, call forth this older sense of what it means to be in a human body. There is a security, a stability in the old hierarchies that religion offered. As the authorities of science and the fantastic manipulations of technology replace religious belief, that stability—so closely connected to how we identify ourselves in bodies—dissolves.

Historically, humanity's capacity to transcend the body has been one-sided, mostly confined to the mind. An expression of spirit, religious dreams, and hopes of a better afterlife, have typically been balanced, offset by our own plodding bodily materiality. The human urge towards transcendence, the expansive vistas beyond this life and body that mystics of all stripes point to—these were possible precisely because of the body-bound structured hierarchies that religion offered. The flight of mysticism found an anchor in the steadiness of religious traditions, especially in religious doctrines and practices. Even as mystics like Meister Eckhart or the Indian philosopher Śaṅkara point to a reality above and beyond ordinary life, the silent scaffold supporting these flights of human transcendence has nevertheless been the underlying hierarchies of human bodies, the Catholic Church, the caste system. The kinds of transcendence that religion promises have always been steadied by our bodily incapacity to get much beyond earthbound limitations.

We might think about it in this way: the emphasis on transcendence in so much religion has been in part a struggle against an overwhelming immanence. The painful limitations of bodies, the inevitable suffering, *duḥkha,* is the backdrop for the Buddha to found his tradition. The ever-visible suffering that is the image of Christ's crucified body undergirds Christianity. The pain and limitation of the body has always served as the backdrop for a flight of the soul. Our minds could always imagine more, something more permanent, more alive beyond the suffering and death of the body. Now, at this historical moment when we finally find ourselves capable of transcending bodily limitations we never dreamed possible—now the difficulty is not enough attention to what it means to be stuck in a body. The chains of immanence have been loosened and many among us find the prospect dizzying. Panic, and also rage, are not so surprising as a response.

We are, after all, in a strange and novel moment in our history as a species. Never before have we been so many, seven plus billion. Never before has our species been able to fly above the clouds, indeed to reach the lights in the heavens, the moon, physically. Utopian promises abound: hopes of eradicating all illness by tinkering with our gene pool, along with the pursuit of miracles and a newfound Faustian capacity to alter the essence of apples and salmon and corn.

In the midst of this mechanical mastery, the disenchantment of the world leads to a paradoxical flight from embodiment. As science in the modern world has taken over what used to be religion's role as arbiter of truth standards, it has slowly eroded the believability and consequent stability of religious traditions. Certainly this has been a process a long time in the making, yet things are speeding up now and in the last 60 years. Violent fundamentalisms, the new demographic of the "spiritual but not religious," and our odd, almost freakish, virtual connections with people we have never met, online in virtual communities as disembodied voices, lacking the familiar tones and emotional affects of vocal cords and accents—these we might see as different sides of the same coin. As we learn how to transcend so many of our bodily limitations, we forget that we still carry bodies. I suspect it is this forgetfulness, an inability to balance transcendence with embodiment that fuels a disconnect where rage is a link back to the forgotten body.

We could point to current politics in America driven by a conservative religious agenda. No doubt our current intractable polarization in contemporary politics in America is itself a good reason to explore this rage. Yet, in our current moment in 2018, for many of us it is difficult to understand this unreasoning rage. Why respond to our burgeoning technological mastery by clinging to outdated religious ideas? It seems to be an irrational, might-makes-right reactive rage. Perhaps an easier, more familiar way, to understand this rage as a phenomenon might be to recall something most all of us have encountered: those annoying moments in traffic where cars are not moving as quickly as we would like and someone cuts in front. The tension of wanting to be already where we're going, not here where we are. The disconnect from bodies stuck in our individual pods in a sea of metal. Mostly, we do not act on this, the impatience, the anger. Being stuck in traffic is a kind of limbo that is nowhere. Not a space where we interact with others, where our identities connect to the world, rather a space outside of our real lives, simply an in-between space, not being here, but waiting to get where we can be here. Part of the frustration of being in traffic is that disconnect. We might even say it approximates a kind of transcendent nowhere, disconnected from our bodies and from others in our metal pods. It is a space that does not matter. The space of not actually being here, a transcendence as a kind of limbo may be what elicits an ungrounded anger, frustration, sometimes rage.

In 1987 a TV station in Los Angeles reporting on a rash of shootings that occurred on Interstate highways 405, 110, and 10, coined the term "road rage" to describe these highway incidents, with the number of incidents reported appearing to be increasing yearly. In 2006, the phenomenon even made its way into the American Psychiatric Association's DSM under the moniker of Intermittent Explosive Disorder. What strikes me most visibly about road rage is how frequently it demonstrates a need for personal connection. The all too common story of drivers tailgating and cutting each other off then leads to both pulling into the Korner Market to confront each other in a deadly embrace with now legal guns. This driving rage is baldly and oddly distinguished by a mutual need for personal, face to face encounter, one that unfortunately often ends badly for both.

I am reminded also of a story from a late medieval Tantric text, the Bṛhannīla Tantra, the "Great Blue Tantra." The story explores the theme of religious fundamentalism, rage, and the transformations of this rage through a wisdom that reconnects religious practice to embodiment and to acknowledgement of the other in a mutual encounter, a face to face presence. In this story, the famous Indian sage Vasistha is the protagonist. Elsewhere he is portrayed as an icon of wisdom, humility, and restraint. Here, however, Vasistha plays the persona of a somewhat religiously dogmatic and politically conservative figure. In this context, he is attached to traditional religious values and hierarchies. Vasistha wishes to obtain enlightenment and to obtain his desire he prays to the goddess Tara, a goddess of wisdom who leads one across to the farther shore of enlightenment. Vasistha prays to the goddess for a thousand years. Yet she ignores him. Frustrated, blazing with anger (*kopena jvalito*) he seeks out the creator god, Brahma, for answers, who points him back to her. Brahma informs him that only Tara can give him the wisdom he seeks. So he attends again to a strict religious asceticism for many more years. Even after much more intense religious practice, his efforts are fruitless. She still ignores him. At this point, frustrated that his correct adherence to the rules yields him no benefits, he erupts into deep unappeasable rage. The story tells us that Vasistha, blazing with great anger, proceeds to curse this goddess of wisdom. He ritually pours the water that seals the curse. At this point she does finally appear before him. What she teaches him is that the denial of the body, the denial of the embodiment that asceticism entails, will never lead to wisdom.

Note that, when she shows up, she does not respond by giving in to his rage, nor does she immediately grant him his desire. Rage, then, is an intermediate stage of the process of gaining wisdom. However, she ends her long silence and finally speaks to him and rebukes him for his harshness, politely informing him that his method is all wrong. His orthodoxy is, in fact, the problem. What this goddess does next is oddly resonant with the appeal to syncretic religion in our current plethora of spiritual-but-not-religious expressions of religiosity. She moves our protagonist out of his comfort zone of religious orthodoxy. Her response to his religious fundamentalism is to send him to a different religion, to the Buddha. This is a Hindu text, yet true to its Tantric, subversive character she has him embrace the religious values of another faith. The Buddha that he meets is not the familiar one we might encounter at a Zen or mindfulness retreat, but rather a Tantric outsider. This Buddha does not fit in with his preconceived ideas of an enlightened role model. He is staggering from drunkenness, and Vasistha's first response is to run. But instead he has a mystical conversion experience when a voice from the sky convinces him to stay. Given the deep injunction against liquor for the Hindu Brahmin priestly caste, the text suggests a highly unorthodox solution to fundamentalism, one that we might read as less about intoxication and more about letting go of rigid religious beliefs.

What the Buddha finally teaches Vasistha is that an ascetic transcendence that neglects the body does not lead to wisdom. With this, Vasistha's entire desire to transcend the body,

to leave the world for a body-free and suffering-free enlightenment is upended. He realizes that a mechanistic view of body,
of matter, and—for this medieval society—of women, is the
problem and the source of his rage. His asceticism and neglect
of the body generates his rage, and it is his rage which reconnects him back, eventually, to a recognition of embodiment.
Rage, in this sense, speaks to our embodiment; it functions as
a dangerous corrective against an overweening transcendence.

In terms of my own journey, I felt the force of this dialectic balance while studying in India's ancient holy city, Varanasi. I had gone with several companions to a famous temple,
the Kal Bhairav Mandir for the festival day of this Tantric
deity. This fierce deity, mythologically connected to Tantric
transgressions, embodies rage. He wanders the earth mad and
delirious, in a rage after chopping off the head of the creator
god Brahma, who is, after all, a Brahmin, occupying the epitome of the top of the political ladder. Curiously, this wild,
liquor-intoxicated outsider comes to occupy the role of spiritual *kotwal*, or cosmic chief of police, for the spirit world of
the holy city of Varanasi. Here, cosmos reflects politics. Just
as, on a mundane level, foreign visitors are obligated to sign
in with the police office in their district, so also, visitors to
the holy city of Kashi are required to pay a visit to this cosmic
police officer.

When we went to the Kal Bhairav Mandir, the temple
was crowded and raucous, but we eventually found an out-
of-the-way spot to meditate in this sacred site. In the midst
of a transcendent moment, an out-of-body space, I began to
understand the rage of Bhairava. Bhairava represents for the
Tantric tradition the idea of a panentheism. This deity functions both as immanent and transcendent, capturing both

poles of a panentheistic vision. The *mudra*, or posture, associated with Bhairava is a gaze with wide open eyes, while the awareness is focused within. The rage that Bhairava embodies is a call to remember the body and its flawed materiality, even while one's awareness is inwardly focused. Rage is akin to fear and both represent a flight away from the experience of the body. Yet, while fear reproduces itself in greater and greater escapes from material embodiment, rage demands that we connect to matter, to the body, at times in painful and unfortunate ways. What I learned from this experience in the temple of this panentheistic deity of rage was that my own use of meditation as a flight from the body inevitably circles around; the body neglected inevitably comes back. Rage is a call to remind us of embodiment. Rather than mindlessly discount the rage we face in our current political climate as an irrational throwback to outdated fundamentalist religious conceptions, we may cope better with it if we understand its roots in our current destabilizing pace of technological disembodiment.

As a scholar of Tantric traditions, I think my own journey has been very much about a reclamation of the body. If I were to explain Tantra in a sentence, I would not invoke its transgression, its ritual extravagance. I would point instead to emphasis on keeping the body in spiritual practice. In this sense, it holds open the possibilities of panentheism as a path of holding both the here and now, our real bodily and material ties, and also the hopes for what we can imagine with mind as it transcends beyond its limits. Embodiment on this journey is a fundamental component of a spirituality that can speak to our increasingly disembodied technological reality.

Notes

1. Christof Koch, "When Computers Surpass us," *Scientific American Mind*, September/October 2015, 26-29.
2. Hawking told the BBC: "The development of full artificial intelligence could spell the end of the human race." http://www.bbc.com/news/technology-30290540, accessed April 15, 2017.
3. Koch, "When Computers Surpass us," 26.
4. Raffaele Torella, T*he Īśvarapratyabhijñākārikā of Utpaladeva with the Author's vṛtti. Critical Edition and Annotated Translation* (Delhi: Motilal Banarsidass, 2002),129.
5. Merlin Donald, *A Mind So Rare: The Evolution of Human Consciousness* (New York: W.W. Norton, 2002), 123-5.

9. *My Journey Living and Teaching Panentheism*

Matthew Fox

Panentheism has been a part of my experience from way back. For example, in a journal I kept on my way to a hermitage on Vancouver Island in the summer of 1965 (I would have been 24 years old), I wrote: "As I learned in Communion this morning, Christ is not in me, but I am in Him. So too, He is not near, but I am nearer Him.....There is one vocation and that is living in God's presence."[1] This is Christological panentheism; it is also about God as Presence more than as Person. This too is panentheism.

In an article entitled "What is Prayer?", which I published when I was 27 years old, I defined prayer as "swimming."

One cannot think of swimming without thinking of the medium, water. Thus describing prayer as swimming implies immediately the indispensable reality of the field of God's love....A fish in water evidences certain passivity in its natural habitat, a seemingly utter dependence and relaxation in its medium. The water is always there for the fish; it just surrenders to the water.[2]

I am seeking a more "horizontal" understanding of prayer and of our relationship with Divinity as I cite the classic panentheistic text when I say the "reality, presumed in all prayers, is the field where we all 'live, move, and have our being.' It is the active, real love of a living God who is 'over all, works through all, and is in all.'"[3] I argue that understanding prayer as swimming "is historical since it was used not only by the early Christians but was a favorite among mystics through the centuries who spoke of the 'immersion' into Christ and of the 'floods and seas' of God's love for men. Today's psychology also has used the term in a significant manner."[4] And I refer to the book on Jung's religious ideas by Charles B. Hanna, *The Face of the Deep,* pointing out the very title.

While I did not have the concept of panentheism at hand at that early time in my theological life, I definitely had the experience. Calling prayer swimming in a field of Divine presence was a very panentheistic image as is a quest for the "field of prayer."

The late Father Bede Griffiths was eager to point out that *experience precedes concepts* when it comes to religious revelation, and always has. He writes:

> This is the danger of all religion. It begins with a mystical experience, the experience of the seers of the Upanishads, of the Buddha under the bo tree, of the Hebrew prophets and the apostles at Pentecost, of

Mahomet receiving the message of the Koran. But this experience has to be put into words; it has to descend into the outer world and take the forms of human speech. Already at this state it is open to misinterpretations; the conflict between the letter and the spirit begins. Then the logical and rational mind comes and creates systems of thought: heresies and sects spring up, and the Truth is divided. This is due to the defect of the rational mind, imposing its narrow concepts and categories on the universal truth. Yet it cannot be avoided because the Truth must be proclaimed.[5]

The fact that panentheism is *first of all an experience* must be guarded at all times. Theism, on the other hand, can easily fall into projections and object-making for projections.

Panentheism in My Writings

In my first book, with the unlikely title of *On Becoming a Musical, Mystical Bear: Spirituality American Style*, I contrast the panentheism of a creation-centered spirituality to a fall/redemption religious ideology in this way: The latter teaches that "humankind's relationship to God is primarily vertical: God is up, humankind below." While the former teaches that "humankind's relationship to God is horizontal and concentric in its meeting places. God is all in all and all is in God. God as panentheistic."[6]

In subsequent books I always bring in panentheism. In *Whee! We, Wee All the Way Home: A Guide to Sensual, Prophetic Spirituality* (1976), I wrote a chapter called "God as a Panentheistic God and Ourselves in that Image." There I make the following points:

> An intellectual monotheism has erected a God that
> only philosophers and academicians can understand
> or worship...Monotheism has become a weapon for
> keeping people away from the experience of the every-
> where God. For God is, simply, everywhere. As is the
> experience of God, as we have seen. God is truly Em-
> manuel, God-with-us....All are bathed in God. And
> to believe this is to be a panentheist (which means
> literally, 'all is in God or God is in all'). There is noth-
> ing heretical about being a panenetheist. Indeed, it is
> heretical not to be one.[7]

I criticize institutional religion for keeping panentheism
a secret and how doing so serves the interests of "monolithic
institutions of academia or churchliness." It is a way to keep
people distant from their own God-experience. I also critique
a too person-centered version of Divinity, one developed in
the fourth century under the influence of Greek philosophical categories. Panentheism offers a remedy for this over per-
sonalizing of the Godhead. I observe that "to emphasize God
as panentheistic and play down God as person is not to deny
the personal interest of this God in his/her people. We can
celebrate a personal panentheistic God without falling into
the psychologizing of God as a person."[8]

Invoking the *via negativa* ("the negative way"), I point out
that "not only is God everywhere to us like water to a fish,
but also God is nowhere. Not here. Nonperson. The void. The
distance. The silence. The pain."[9]

Bede Griffiths also opted for a less personal Godhead:
"The Christian concept of God often becomes so personal that
it needs to be corrected by the impersonalism of Buddhism....

To insist too much on the moral character of God can narrow our conception and lose something of that spontaneous freedom, that ecstasy of joy, which is found in Krishna."[10]

Two practical conclusions follow from panentheism. A panentheistic consciousness demands "more of our powers of awareness"—we see "God in a grain of sand; and in a towering mountain; and in a crippled old man; and in an act of love; and in a tragic happening." To be panentheistic is to believe "in a living God, a God living everywhere."

The second consequence of moving into panentheistic awareness is "the democracy of it all. A God who is everywhere is everybody's. A truly democratic God. Available to the least as well as the greatest." The God of panentheism is not a "God of power-control; a sort of commander-in-chief of the universe's ecstasies....No, a panentheistic God has shared the fun, the ecstasy, the joy, and the pains...with the littlest among us. That is spiritual democracy." Following that path will move us from an "I" consciousness to a "We" consciousness.[11] It will render us vulnerable and may make us enemies of powers and principalities. A panentheistic God is an incarnational one in whom we recognize that "the world, and all of its pieces, is ultimately a manifestation of God."[12]

I find this referencing of "spiritual democracy" especially important today when so many are eager to move beyond religious superiority complexes that invariably provoke war and even terrorism in the name of false gods and false religion to something more worthy of the nobility of our species, something more sustainable. In his important book *Walt Whitman: Shamanism, Spiritual Democracy, and the World Soul*, Stephen Herrmann credits Walt Whitman with the basic vision of spiritual democracy and cites Whitman's belief that the prophets were "the most democratic of the religion-ists [because] they appeal to the religion inside of man's very own nature."[13]

Herrmann writes: "Whitman saw that religions had be-come too far removed from the people. He wanted to make *the experience of the Divine* accessible, articulate, available in the present for anyone so he invented free-verse."[14] I too could name my effort in naming "creation spirituality" in the same vein: To render mysticism democratic. Everyone's experience. Available to all, not to a privileged class behind monastery doors.

For Whitman, religion "is democratic....its democracy ex-tends to each listener, whatever one's race, ethnicity, rank, na-tionality, social class, sexual orientation, or gender." The mode of accessing one's depth is through "vocalism," as in a drum's rhythm that is found in poetry as a "shamanic technique, a method for trance-induction" that transports one to "an ec-static state of Consciousness."[15] Not unlike Whitman, I have found "art as meditation" to be a portal to one's deeper self and soul and employed it for 30-some years with adults and for seven years with inner-city high school students to make it so available. It worked.

Poet Bill Everson, in his important book, *Archetype West: The West Coast as a Literary Region*, observes that the mysti-cal encounter with nature's immensity in the West in Califor-nia lies as a basis to American spirituality. And pantheism (I don't think Everson knew the concept of panentheism, frankly, and certainly not when he wrote this book) "is not only the basic Californian or Western point of view, but is essentially American, is indeed *the* characteristic religious and aesthetic feeling."[16] Panentheism names more fully the spiritual genius of the Native American and shamanistic tradition of relating to God. Everson believed that John Muir's crusade to oppose the damming of Hetch Hetchy marked the "main turning point in the spiritual life of the nation, perhaps the chief turning point as far as the future was concerned."[17] In my autobiography I cite these passages from Everson as I too felt, on moving out to California from Chicago, that I was encountering a new vista of spirituality, one of panentheism that one encounters in the region itself. Herrmann feels that Whitman's notion of spiritual democracy was "a vocation in which all could join."[18] And "the democracy we need to keep alive has to be spiritual as well as political."[19] Such is the outcome of a panentheistic perspective.

In my book *A Spirituality Named Compassion* (1979) I contrast the symbol of "Climbing Jacob's Ladder" to that of "Dancing Sara's Circle" and I offer some thoughts about the role of panentheism vs. theism in the latter change of consciousness.

> Jacob's ladder presumes a distance between us and God....While God is not adequately represented by total immanence....still God is wholly present where we are and not up, up and away from us. The classical term for this omnipresence of God wherein God is in all and all is in God is panentheism. The most appropriate symbol or picture of this divine omnipresence is that of a circle of water with fish in it. We are the fish; God is the water. We breathe God in and out all day long. We are in God and God is in us.....We do not have to look up to find God. We need simply to wake up to the truth that God has been here all along and very likely our consciousness was blocked up and lacked the simplicity of waking and seeing. The circu-

lar dynamic of Sarah's circle corresponds to the in/out energies of panentheism, while the ladder motif of Jacob's ladder corresponds to the God-distinct-from-us motif of theism.[20]

I address theism directly. "In theism separatism is given religious sanction. Dualism is unrepentant. Apartness is raised to the level of a religious presupposition. In panentheism, energies are not presumed to be *apart* but rather *a* part of one another." I refer to the work of Thorleif Boman who

> introduces a new, more Biblical, category for the presence of God. He calls it 'the transparence of God.' In such a relationship, 'God is not only above the world and in the world, but he is also through the world.' Thus Paul can speak of 'one God who is Father of all, over all, through all and within all' (Eph. 4.6).[21]

Panentheism is thus about transparency, our capacity to see into and through reality to recognize the Divine within all things.

Panentheism Preferred to Theism

Why all this panentheism? I suspect I was a bit impatient with theism from a very young age. I felt God's presence more in nature than in projections on a person who is a "God-in-the-sky" from an early age. I tell the story of experiencing the wild thunderstorms that were part and parcel of life in the Midwest where I grew up and being attracted by the awe of it all. I recall our family visiting Niagara Falls when I was about 12 years old and sensing a power and presence there that spoke to me of what I would later understand to be mysticism.

Yes, I think the reason panentheism has worked for me for a very long time is that it alone describes the human/divine relationship in a mystical fashion. "All things in God and God in all things"—this is my experience. And I think it is an experience many people pine for but rarely feel supported by religious preachers, teachers or even theologians. This is surely one reason I chose to study spirituality and have traveled a path to the mystics for spiritual sustenance and less into areas of ecclesiology, canon law, systematic theology or even Biblical studies as such. (Indeed, I met a renowned Biblical scholar a few years ago who told me he had no idea of what mysticism meant and felt no one else did either. He really should have been studying some outside his rather hot-house world of Biblical studies, I feel.)

With spirituality, experience precedes concepts; then the concepts assist in adding meat (and history and a lineage) to the experience, just as Bede Griffiths taught. That was always the case with me anyway. I experienced the presence within and around me and later I discovered the term "panentheism" and immediately liked it—not only for its subtle but significant distinction from pantheism but for its not being theism and not being atheism. Much of atheism I have come to learn is a rejection of theism. Panentheists are atheists insofar as they are anti-theists. Anti-theism is closely allied with anti-religion since so much cheap religion is built on theism and, sad to say, keeps its distance from mysticism or panentheism.

The Mystics on Panentheism

I maintain that panentheism is characteristic of all authentic mystics. All break through the dualism that theism teaches.

Dietrich Bonhoeffer, shortly before his execution, remarked that the God of the mystic is the only God contemporary humans can grasp. Such a God is about God as Presence, such a God is a panentheistic God. Bonhoeffer is honored as an activist and a martyr—indeed a prophet. In saying this, he is raising the stakes on how we understand mysticism and how it is decidedly *not* about flight from the world or uninvolvement with the world—in its truest sense, it includes critiquing the world—even to the point of martyrdom. For Bonhoeffer, then, there is a marriage of the God of mysticism and the God of prophecy, of contemplation and action.

We see this reality played out in the lives of the mystics which are often very much complicated by the social realities they take on as they strive to walk their talk. This is an important aspect of panentheism—that it be a platform and a springboard for social action and cultural criticism. It is not a nest for private revelations from the Divine, but a spring one returns to for the energy to carry on the battle, for living out the love of God found in all things.

A panentheistic theology is an ecological theology in the deepest sense of that word. Why? Because panentheism restates the sacredness of all things, the Divine in-ness in all things, the presence of God in all things, creation (basileia) as "kingdom or reign of God." Recovering the sacredness of all beings from forests to oceans, rivers to polar bears, eagles to tigers, is to recover a lost relationship with the holiness of being. In this way, we are in a position to re-imagine our politics, economics, education and religions as agents for honoring the rights and dignity of all beings. Our home ("eco" in Greek) becomes livable again. Theism distances the Divine from the rest of nature. Panentheism reunites them. No wonder Carl Jung warned that one can lose one's soul by worshiping a "God out there." Theism does that (and atheism is not far behind).

Medieval mystics also recognized panentheism.

Mechtild of Magdeburg (1210-1280) writes of God talking: "I who am divine am truly in you...and you are in Me." She describes her spiritual coming of age in this way: "The day of my spiritual awakening was the day I saw and knew I saw all things in God and God in all things."

Julian of Norwich (c. 1342-1415) also images our relationship with God in a panentheistic manner. "We have all been enclosed within God" and "we are in God and God, whom we do not see, is in us."

Hildegard of Bingen (1098-1179) speaks of God in us and the Holy Spirit flowing like fire through us. Also, "God hugs you. You are encircled by the arms of the mystery of God." We are surrounded with the roundness of divine compassion. These are panentheistic images of us-in-God and God-in-us. They are also deeply maternal. They challenge patriarchy's predilection for theism and dualism and a God-over-us mentality.

Meister Eckhart (c. 1260-1327) develops a mature panentheism in great depth. He writes: "God created all things in such a way that they are not outside himself, as ignorant people falsely image. Everything that God creates or does he does or creates in himself, sees or knows in himself, loves in himself." And since "God is a being that has in itself all being," it follows that divinity is "roundabout us, completely enveloping us." Not only are all things in God but "God is in all things. The more he is in things the more he is outside of things." Inside and outside are not separate but meld together in a panentheistic theology.[22]

Thomas Aquinas (1225-1274) addresses panentheism when he writes: "God embraces in the divine self all creatures.... Indeed, the Godhead contains all things... All things are in God..." He addressed christological panentheism in his Commentary on John's Gospel: "Christ says, 'Remain in me' by receiving grace; 'and I remain in you,' by helping you."[23] Aquinas comments on the celebrated panentheistic text from the Book of Acts in this way:

> Creatures are said to be in God in a twofold sense. In one way, so far as they are held together and preserved by the divine power—even as we say that things that are in our power are in us. And creatures are thus said to be in God, even as they exist in their own natures. In this sense we must understand the words of the Apostle when he says, 'in God we live, move, and have being,' since our being, living, and moving are themselves caused by God. In another sense things are said to be in God, as in the one who knows them, in which sense they are in God through their proper ideas, which in God are not distinct from the divine essence.[24]

He says: "God must be everywhere and in all things.... Wherever being is found, the divine presence is also there.... God is in all things; not indeed, as part of their essence, nor as an accident; but as an agent is present to that upon which it works."[25]

Aquinas compares God's presence in things to the presence of light in the air caused by the sun. Since being is so innermost to things, "it must be that God is in all things, and most intimately so." Indeed, "in a certain sense, one can say that God is more closely united to each thing than the thing is to itself."[26] He elaborates: "God is in all things by the divine power, inasmuch as all things are subject to divine power; God is in all things by the divine presence, inasmuch as all things are bare and open to God's eyes; and God is in all things by the divine essence, inasmuch as God is present to all as the cause of their being."[27] He hastens to insist however that "God forms no part of the essence of created things."[28]

Aquinas has gone very deeply into the nature of the panentheistic relationship between nature, God and humans. He elaborates when speaking of how God dwells in holy people.

> God dwells in the saints in three ways: by faith: 'That Christ may dwell in your hearts by faith' (Ephesians 3:17); by love: 'He or she that dwells in love, dwells in God and God in him or her' (1 John 4:16); and by the fulfillment of God's commandments: 'If anyone love me, they will keep my word and my Creator will love them, and we will come to them, and make our abode with them' (John 14:23).[29]

What derives from panentheism? Trust and confidence. "Confidence comes from God's nearness: 'The Lord is near to all that call upon God' (Psalm 145:18). Hence it is said: 'But you when you pray enter into your chamber' (Matthew 6:6), that is, into your heart."[30]

I have pointed out previously that "a theistic imaging of God is essentially adolescent, for it is based on an egoistic mindset, a zeroing in on how we are separate from God."[31] Adolescence is valuable for its development of an ego consciousness, a consciousness of separation from parents and development of one's own selfhood. But our spiritual consciousness has to mature beyond mere ego separation to *mysticism*, the consciousness of union and communion. A panentheistic awareness champions confidence.

Scripture, Panentheism, and the Sources of the Christ Path

We have seen Aquinas and others comment on the classic loci of panentheism in the New Testament, namely Acts and Ephesians. But there is much more. In John's Gospel the long "priestly prayer"—which scholars agree are not the words of Jesus so much as those of the community that rose up in his name—is filled with Christological panentheism; and the fact that this mystical poetry arose from the community only makes the case stronger that panentheism was a consciousness very early in the Christian movement. Consider these images from that discourse in John:

> May they all be one.
> Father, may they be one in us,
> as you are in me and I am in you,
> so that the world may believe it was you who sent me.
> I have given them the glory you gave to me,
> that they may be one as we are one.
> With me in them and you in me,
> may they be so completely one. (John 17: 21-23)

Thus we are told that panenthesim resides in the heart of the Godhead and is extended to humankind. This is repeated.

> Do you not believe
> that I am in the Father and the Father is in me?...
> But you know him,
> because he is with you, he is in you...
> On that day
> you will understand that I am in my Father
> and you in me and I in you. (John 14:10ff., 20)

Similar panentheism is found in the discourse on the
vine attributed to Jesus (though it too is the Christ speaking
through the community after his death).

> I am the true vine....
> Make your home in me, as I make mine in you....
> I am the vine, you are the branches.
> Whoever remains in me, with me in him,
> Bears fruit in plenty;
> For cut off from me you can do nothing.
> Anyone who does not remain in me
> Is like a branch that has been thrown away
> —he withers;...
> If you remain in me
> And my words remain in you,
> You may ask what you will
> And you shall get it.....
> Remain in my love. (John 15: 1, 4, 5, 7, 9)

In the Hebrew Bible, Israel itself is said to be a vine: "I
planted you like a choice vine of sound and reliable stock"
(Jeremiah 2:21). Grapes which humans convert to wine
stand as a symbol, even an archetype perhaps, for the messi-
anic times, when justice will flow like a river and all, the poor
as well as the rich, will gather at a mountaintop to be nour-
ished and to drink wine together (Isaiah). In the early church
wine was a symbol of the people coming together and among
the pagan religions too wine served that dimension of con-
viviality and even sacredness since it was a great mystery just
how grapes turned into wine (the fermentation process was
not understood—but the results were appreciated). Wine
was mysterious therefore and a "gift of the gods" in many cul-

tures long before the Bible was written. The Eucharist meal includes the taking of the cup of wine and the blessing of it in the memory of Jesus' Last Supper experience that the wine is Christ's blood.

A historian points out that in ancient times, in the cults of Dionysus and Bacchus, wine was encouraged

> not simply for intoxication, though that certainly happened, but for communion. Here the communion was less with one's fellows than with the earth—specifically with nature and nature's fertile power, a power literally felt in the heat of the wine one drank, a power far greater than anything fabricated by human beings.[32]

Thus Dionysus or Bacchus were not just the gods "of wine" but were also the gods "in wine." These gods did not come from the cities, but "from elsewhere—from the hinterland, from the vine, from nature. That nature—not the cultivated nature of the vinter or merchant, but the untamed nature of the vine itself, the nature of 'spontaneous wines'—was something that the city dweller both revered and feared."[33] In addition, Dionysus was honored for his seeming life, death, and resurrection—"corresponding neatly with the life cycle of the grapevine."[34] Thus there is immense richness in the phrase "I am the vine" that spoke to the persons of the late first century who first read these words in John's Gospel. The imagery is deeply panentheistic.

Paul too offers a panentheistic approach to the Christ when he speaks of believers being "in Christ" on numerous occasions. Indeed, this language lies at the very heart of Paul's mystical awareness, as Biblical scholar John Dominic Crossan points out:

Paul uses the phrase '*in* Christ' or '*in* Christ Jesus' or '*in* Christ Jesus our Lord' so often that you can hardly keep count. Even if we lose count, we must take it very seriously, because he intends that word more organically than we can ever imagine. For Paul, being '*in* Christ' is not just metaphorical trope, but mystical identity. It determines everything in his theology, so that Paul does not think that those '*in Christ*' need to be given ethical norms, legal rules, or communal instructions.....That *in* is the beating heart of Paul's theology, and everything else flows from it in life and in death. The character of Christ has been totally assumed by Paul, and Paul's own character has been totally subsumed by Christ.[35]

Paul is both the first theologian in the Christian movement and the first writer in the New Testament and his mysticism boasts a Christological panentheism. Biblical scholar Gustav Adolf Deissmann tells us what "in Christ" meant to Paul.

This primitive Pauline watch-word 'in Christ' is meant vividly and mystically, as is the corresponding 'Christ in me.' The formula 'in Christ' (or 'in the Lord') occurs 164 times in Paul's writing: it is really the characteristic expression of his Christianity.... The constitutive element in mysticism is immediacy of contact with the deity.[36]

This immediacy that panentheism names includes the suffering and darkness in life. Paul tells the Galatians, "It is no longer I who live, but it is Christ who lives in me" (Galatians 2:20) and he applies this relationship to his sufferings when he says that "my chains are in Christ" (Philippians 1:7, 13). Says

Crossan: Paul "experiences an immersion of his own sufferings under Rome at Ephesus *in* those of Jesus under Rome at Jerusalem."[37] The political implications of Christological panentheism are made clear: "In a world where identity was often shaped by one's relationship to Rome, by being, as it were, 'in Rome,' insisting on a self-definition exclusively by being 'in Christ' was subversive at best and treasonous at worst."[38] Panentheism can get one into severe imperial hot water.

Thus we see that Panentheism lies at the very origin of the Christian movement. How pitiful that anti-mystical biases of the Enlightenment and the academic theological training that followed right up to today have left the church as a whole so far behind the real mystics of the tradition and the very sources of the Christ path Christians claim as their own.

Of course, Jesus himself, steeped as he was in the Wisdom tradition of Israel, is also a panentheist and, as Everson insisted, a great shaman. He grew up close to the soil and seasons in Galilee and he came of age under the tutelage of John the Baptist in the wilderness of the desert and his parables are filled with the awareness of the nearness of the Kingdom/queendom of God within creation. He hastened to preach that sense of the sacred in all things in his parables, filled as they are with creation imagery. His message of the kingdom of God being "within and among you" suggests that our way of seeing the world needs to be altered—we need to see it in a panentheistic way. All things are already in God and God is already in all things. A change of consciousness—*metanoia*—is required. That is the demand that panentheism makes on us all.

New Testament scholar Bruce Chilton speaks of Jesus' consciousness being formed in the green and fertile landscape of Galilee and it is a deeply panentheistic awareness.

Here, in Galilee, the Kingdom was revealed in the weaving and stitching, planting and reaping, grape picking and pressing that assumed a full life, not merely survival. Those activities found their way into Jesus' parables as images of God's Kingdom in a way that contrasts with the far less organic imagery of the Essenes at Qumran and the rabbis in Talmud.

Galileans were enormously proud of the fertility of their land, which exceeded that of other regions in Palestine....The rich bounty of the green Galilean hills mirrored their hope for the Kingdom that God yearned to provide for his people....Then justice, compassion, and truth would rule....[39]

Crossan poses the following radical and challenging question: "Does Paul think, therefore, that only mystics can be Christians or that all Christians must be mystics? In a word, yes."[40] It follows then that *all Christians must be panentheistic* and that *only panentheists can be Christians*. If this be the case, a severe rewriting of prayers and liturgies and theological texts and of the very souls of our religious teachers is in order.

The Four Paths and Panentheism

The backbone to the creation spirituality path is the Four Paths. In what way is Panentheism integral to these paths?

1. The *Via Positiva*, or path of affirmation, is about the deep experience of awe, wonder, joy, delight and gratitude. If the Divine is present in all beings from the tiniest atom ("Christ is the light in all things" and every atom in the universe contains photons or light waves) to the galaxy as a whole, one is alerted

to the deeper experience of panentheism—God in nature and nature in God.

2. In the *Via Negativa*, or path of negation, panentheism, like the Cosmic Christ, is not just about God as Light but also about the wounds in all beings. God suffers along with the suffering of all beings. In panentheism we undergo the God presence within Darkness and Silence and Stillness; but at other times the God of suffering. In addition, the Via Negativa teaches us about the Apophatic Divinity, the God who is, in Eckhart's words, "Superessential darkness who has no name and will never be given a name." Divinity beyond all naming. The radically non-anthropocentric Divinity. To taste this dimension of Divinity, and the nothingness that accompanies it, is also part of the panentheistic experience.

3. In the *Via Creativa*, or path of creativity, we undergo co-creation with the creativity of the universe, a creativity that began with the original Fireball 13.8 billion years ago. A Panentheistic universe is a creating universe, or as Eckhart put it: "What does God do all day long? God lies on a maternity bed giving birth."

4. In the *Via Transformativa*, or path of transformation, the bringing about of a reign of Justice and Compassion is central. This is the work of Panentheism, for if all things are in God and God is in all things, and "God is Justice" (Aquinas) and "Compassion is the best name for God" (Eckhart), doesn't it follow that the work of inner and outer transformation is the outcome of a panentheistic consciousness?[41]

Thus we can see that the Four Paths work intersubjectively with the Panentheistic promise as does the reality of the Cosmic Christ archetype (known as the "Buddha Nature" in the East and the "image of God" in Judaism).[42]

There are four ways I know of to name our relationship to the Divine: 1) *Theism*—God is out there, we are here; 2) *Atheism*—a rejection of theism; 3) *Pantheism*—Everything is God; and 4) *Panentheism*—All is in God and God is in all. I, like mystics everywhere, opt for the latter.

Notes

1. I repeat these and other panentheistic stories in my autobiography, *Confessions: The Making of a Postdenominational Priest, Revised and Updated* (Berkeley, CA: North Atlantic Books, 2015).
2. Matthew Fox, "What is Prayer?", *Listening* (Winter, 1968):113.
3. Ibid., 112.
4. Ibid., 114.
5. Bede Griffiths, *Return to the Center* (Springfield, Il: Templegate Publishers, 1977), 105.
6. Matthew Fox, "Preface to Paperback Edition," in *On Becoming a Musical, Mystical Bear* (New York: Paulist Press, 1976), xx. The most recent edition is called simply: *Prayer: A Radical Response to Life* and is published by Jeremy Tarcher.
7. Matthew Fox, *Whee! We, Wee All the Way Home: A Guide to Sensual, Prophetic Spirituality* (Santa Fe, NM: Bear & Co., 1981), 119.
8. Ibid., 120.
9. Ibid.
10. Griffiths, *Return to the Center*, 86-87.
11. Fox, *Whee! We, Wee*, 121.
12. Ibid., 122.
13. Steven B. Herrmann, *Walt Whitman: Shamanism, Spiritual Democracy, and the World Soul* (Strategic Book Publishing and Rights Co., 2010), 230.
14. Steven Herrmann, *William Everson: Shaman's Call, Expanded Edition* (Strategic Book Publishing and Rights Co., 2015), 318. (Italics mine.)

15. Ibid., 318-319.

16. Cited in ibid., 327.

17. Cited in ibid., 329.

18. Ibid., 336.

19. Ibid., 350.

20. Matthew Fox, *A Spirituality Named Compassion: Uniting Mystical Awareness with Social Justice* (Rochester, VT: Inner Traditions, 1999), 51.

21. Cited in ibid., 52. See Thorleif Boman, *Hebrew Thought Compared with Greek* (New York: Norton, 1960).

22. References for Mechtild, Julian, Hildegard and Eckhart can be found in Matthew Fox, *Wrestling with the Prophets* (New York: Jeremy Tarcher, 1995), 91-93.

23. Cited in Matthew Fox, *Sheer Joy: Conversations with Thomas Aquinas on Creation Spirituality* (New York: Jeremy P. Tarcher, 2003), 67.

24. Ibid., 67-68.

25. Ibid., 70.

26. Ibid., 71.

27. Ibid., 73

28. Ibid.

29. Ibid., 72.

30. Ibid., 71.

31. Fox, *Wrestling with the Prophets*, 92.

32. Paul Lukacs, *Inventing Wine: A New History on One of the World's Most Ancient Pleasures* (New York: W.W. Norton & Co, 2012), 25f.

33. Ibid., 27.

34. Ibid.

35. John Dominic Crossan and Jonathan L. Reed, *In Search of Paul* (San Francisco: HarperSanFrancisco, 2004), 279. Italics his.

36. Cited in ibid.

37. Ibid.

38. Ibid., 280.

39. Bruce Chilton, *Rabbi Jesus: An Intimate Biography* (New York: Image Doubleday, 2000), 73-74.

40. Crossan, *In Search of Paul*, 280.

41. A fuller laying out of the Four Paths can be found in Matthew Fox, *Original Blessing* (New York: Jeremy P. Tarcher, 2000.)

42. For the latter archetype see David Mevorach Seidenberg, *Kabbalah and Ecology: God's Image in the More-Than-Human World* (New York: Cambridge University Press, 2015).

10. God: Autobiographical

Marjorie Hewitt Suchocki

I was born religious. My immediate family was not responsible for this anomaly—my father had rebelled against his father's stern Plymouth Brethren religiosity, and my mother's family was not given to religion. But there must have been something in my grandfather's DNA that transmogrified into my childhood soul, for I keenly remember regularly creeping out of bed to kneel by my window and pray, always wary lest someone catch me at it. If I heard a footstep on the stairs, I would quickly leap back into bed.

How did I pray? Despite his generally anti-religious fervor, my father taught me "Now I lay me down to sleep," concluding with blessings. And I would dutifully beseech the lady in the tree and the stars in the heavens to grant such blessings, always ending with the request that God bless God's own self—If God was always blessing others, who was there left to bless God? Not yet being a process theologian, it was always a bit of a perplexity to me.

I knew that the God to whom I prayed was not the lady in the tree, nor the stars in the heavens—but nonetheless, these were my icons, and I prayed through them. The stars are self-explanatory, I suppose—what child would not be filled with wonder at that beautiful display of light dancing across the sky? As for the lady in the tree—a great oak tree was not far from my bedroom window, and two large branches intertwined such that at their beginning they formed the outline of a head, and then they made a long flowing gown: my lady in the tree. These icons served me well; when my prayer was simply silence, I gazed at them; they were a kind of visible presence of a power I knew but could not see.

My parents did not attend church, but they sent my two brothers and me to the Congregational Sunday School not far from our home. In due time a child evangelist from Tennessee showed up in our town; she'd come to New England to convert all the little heathen children. She was given permission to start a Thursday afternoon Bible club at the church. The flannelgraph stories fascinated me; the "sword drill" contest of looking up Bible verses was fun, as was the Bible memorization and the singing. The difficult part was her message that God would be my friend if I said the right words: hadn't God been my friend all along? Only if I bowed my head, confessed I was a sinner, and invited Jesus into my heart, would God truly be my friend. So on December 16, 1943 at age 10, with "every head bowed and every eye closed," I dutifully raised my hand, stayed after club, and said the right words. Clearly my memory of the exact day indicates its significance for me; I remember my relief that God was once again my friend. My disillusionment came later, after our beloved dog Ginger died. "Do dogs go to heaven?" She told me that no, dogs did not go to heaven. "But they do," I thought.

By 1950 I was a teenager, and my childhood contact with God had receded in importance. Then a new kind of evangelist swept into New England, and my Nazarene friend invited me to go with her into Boston to hear Billy Graham. For several nights we sang in the vast choir, led by the charismatic Cliff Barrows, and of course I remembered that I had said the "right words" insuring God's continued friendship—but still? Hadn't I "backslid?" Could I get "unsaved?" So when, like my friends, I asked Cliff to autograph my Sunday School Bible, I asked the question: "Can a person get unsaved?" The pen stopped writing: "What is your name?" and "Has that been troubling you, Marjorie?" And so once again, I said the "right words." But this time—was it the fervor of the revival spirit? Teenage hormones?—this time it was as if I was swept through by a mighty wind; I hardly know how to describe it, save that an enormous joy encompassed me and continued for several days. And so I became an "evangelical," and began regularly attending Sunday evening services at the Nazarene church with my friend.

What was my notion of God at this time? It became somewhat more focused on Jesus, but in many respects Jesus was like that lady in the tree, an icon pointing beyond himself. God was the power and wonder of the universe, and also, miraculously, as our "friend," somehow mediated through Jesus.

My folks told me that people in families like ours didn't go to college, we went to work, so in high school I took the all-girl "commercial course," learning to be an office worker.

After graduation I found a job as stenographer, then a secretary, in Boston. But Park Street Church had a Tuesday evening School of the Bible; I could go after work. I enrolled, taking a class in Christian doctrine led by the pastor, Dr. Harold Ockenga. Our textbook was Louis Berkhof's *Systematic Theology*, a carefully reasoned tome in Calvinist theology. I drank it up, fascinated by it—until I reached the section on predestination. I was flabbergasted: how could such a grossly unfair doctrine be true? And if it were, who would dare be confident? That Tuesday night, in the great sanctuary of Park Street Church, Dr. Ockenga asked from his high-and-lifted-up pulpit whether we all agreed with the doctrine. In the silence that followed I horrified myself by saying in a loud, clear voice, "NO." I was becoming a theologian.

Two years later my hunger for college had only grown, whetted by my Tuesday evening studies. I decided that regardless of what people in families like mine did, I could work my way through school. But I wanted a "Christian college," far from home. So I applied, was accepted, and attended Houghton College, a school with Wesleyan Methodist roots in upstate New York. The school had what seemed to me to be a very peculiar policy that included strange dress codes (Arms and legs always covered? Whatever for?) and signing a pledge not to dance or go to movies while a student. I totally loved both activities, but was willing to sign the pledge if that's what it took to immerse myself in a Christian academic environment. I had just turned 20.

Because of that pledge, an event occurred that changed my life forever. Every Monday night my friend Vail and I took the bus to neighboring Lynn, where we attended a dance class. I loved that class! I loved losing myself in the music, moving to it and being moved by it. It was the Monday before I was to leave for college, where the pledge would take effect. And Vail was sick, she could not go. Normally, I just would have stayed home too, but it was my last chance before taking the pledge—I had to dance one last time! So by myself I took the bus to Lynn, which was where the bus turned around and waited a bit before making the return trip to Saugus. When I got to Lynn, I got off the bus—but had cold feet. Go to the class all alone, without Vail? How could I? So I got back on the bus; I would go home. The bus didn't leave. "Oh, I'm here—one last night to dance!" And I got off the bus and changed my life. I met John Suchocki at the dance.

John was smitten with this naïve young woman who was leaving a good job to get an education: he, the son of Polish immigrants, had done the same. We dated for the next four nights, and when I arrived at the college that weekend, I found his letter waiting for me. He visited me at the school, wrote frequently, listened to my pious religious beliefs, attended a revival service at the school, and got properly converted: he said the right words. But when he asked to marry me in February I said no: he "drank." My father had been a problem drinker; part of the safety of evangelical religion was its prohibition of alcohol. Amazingly, in April, John became "convicted" that drinking alcohol was sin. I knew it was a sign from the Lord, and I agreed to marry him after I graduated. But John promised that I could continue school after we married—so we married in December, 1954, and I did indeed attend a semester at Philips University in Enid, Oklahoma. However, early pregnancy and a course that involved dissecting pig fetuses wasn't a very good match—I finished the semester, and John finished his flight training; we moved to Fairchild Air Force Base in Washington, and our daughter was born in October. "You can go to school again when the kids are in school," said John.

Several months after the birth of my second child, a crack appeared in my strong evangelical conservatism. That morning I had heard on the radio that there were three billion (!!!) people in the world. I was suitably impressed, and meditated on this fact as I pushed the baby carriage with two little ones in it down the street. I remember thinking, smugly: "No, there are three billion and ONE! Here's Joan!" and then I started to laugh. How could it possibly be, that out of 3,000,000,001 people, I should know exactly who and what God was, let alone what God thought and did? How ludicrous! God was more than I could think; more than anyone could think. So all thoughts about God would be, in ways obvious or subtle, perspectival and inaccurate in ways unknown to the perceiver. Once, at a church supper, I looked at the rim of the thick coffee cup, and it seemed to me that it was as if in our search for greater understanding of God we were always like tiny, tiny creatures running toward the rim of the gigantic cup of all creation, never quite able to plunge into the depths we so desired and so loved.

In my evangelical zeal, I offered to lead a Bible study for the neighboring women on our small street back in Massachusetts, in Topsfield. I wrote to Campus Crusade for their study books, and handed them out to my neighbors. But the books were an insult to our intelligence—they simply asked a question, provided a blank space, and had us look up a Bible verse so that we could write in the answer! How idiotic! So we scrapped the books, and began meeting once a week where I, armed with Matthew Henry's commentary on the Bible, started in on Genesis 1, doing 10 chapters a week. I quickly found that my neighbors' questions were deeper and more important than my answers. One neighbor had lost a baby to infant death syndrome; another had an adult son in what was then called an insane asylum; another had recently been diagnosed with multiple sclerosis—as for me, I was dealing with my husband's increasing alcoholism. The questions were more important than the answers at my grasp. And I was learning that my faith was in God, not in my evangelical theology, let alone in the "right words." God *was*, and my ways of thinking about God were no longer adequate.

When our third child began kindergarten, I began attending evening courses at nearby Gordon College. My first course was in early Greek philosophy—what a strange and fascinating world I found! I could hardly get enough of it. When I encountered Plato's dialogues, I felt as if my mind had been in a tiny box, and Plato helped me break through it—but only to his larger box. Like Chinese nesting dolls, one worldview could be supplanted by another larger one.

In January of 1968 I learned that we were moving to California; I had just been accepted as a full-time day student at Gordon. "My college!" I exclaimed; "There's one out there," said John. "It's called Pomona; you can go to that." So on our corporation-sponsored house-hunting trip, I went immediately to the school. As it happened, the feminist movement had impacted the college's admission policies; they had opened up an office to help older women returning to school. And at age 34, I qualified! We were not many, to be sure—I had been preceded by one older woman the year before, and one other woman beside myself was entering in fall of 1968. It would be my junior year, and my major was, of course, philosophy, with a minor in English so that I could become a high school English teacher when I graduated.

The next two years were heady beyond my imagination, immersed in great philosophy and great literature. I would try philosophies on, like a garment; or rather, I felt as if I were crawling inside a philosopher's head to see what the world looked like. Sometimes it seemed as if the philosopher's head was too big for me as I rattled around attempting to see through "his" eyes (always his—it was as if there were a "no women philosophers allowed" sign posted somewhere). Other times the philosopher's head felt too crowded to me, his eyes were too small; too much was left out. My questions were tumbling out of me, working their way into the papers I wrote. In my senior year my advisor, Prof. Fred Sontag, took me to lunch and told me I should pursue a doctorate in philosophy of religion and philosophical theology at the graduate school. I was astonished! I could continue to study these things, forever?! But how could I do that? "I can't," said I, "I don't have enough brains!" "Nonsense," said Sontag, "all you need is perseverance, and you have plenty of that." I was late for my 19th-century philosophy class, and the hallway was empty; as I got to the bottom stair that led to the basement classroom I just sat down and hugged myself, rocking back and forth, back and forth. I had just been born.

A wonderful error occurred when I applied to Claremont Graduate School's Ph.D. program. I was admitted without qualification! The error? Because I only had the bachelor's degree, I should have been admitted to the three-year M.A./Ph.D. program. Had that occurred, I would not have been able to complete the program, because in May of my first year of course work I was told by John that we were moving again, this time to Kansas. It was 1971; my immersion in my wife/ mother/student roles meant that the great social movements of the time were peripheral to my intensely focused world. And while my evangelical world was crumbling around me, I was not emotionally capable of divorce at that time, despite the increasing problems created by John's alcoholism. My role was to stay in California with the children until the house sold, and for the only time in our moving history, the house did not immediately sell—not until I had completed my course work did a sale take place. I was able to take two independent studies and pass my second language exam in the summer of 1971, and take an overload of courses in the fall, so that by the end of my third semester I had finished the course work portion of the program. I could take my qualifying exams and write my dissertation from Kansas; I could earn the doctorate in philosophy of religion and philosophical theology, thanks to that admission error.

My understanding of God underwent profound changes because of my studies at Pomona College and Claremont Graduate School, and also, of course, through the steady dissolution of my marriage. "The family that prays together stays together" was false. To the depths of my being I was sure of God—how could I not be? I had so often experienced an unanticipated infusion of a sense of God's presence, and always this presence was, at the same time, a sense of irreducible love. God was certain; my thinking about God was inadequate to that sense of presence. Theology is provisional; God is not. Searching for a more adequate way to understand my experience of God and the world, I encountered Whitehead, first by a rather puzzled reading of the first hundred pages of *Process and Reality* in the summer of 1969, and then by the mentally explosive introduction to that book in graduate school under the tutelage of John B. Cobb, Jr. Finally, I had found a philosopher who seemed to look at the world through my eyes; he had crawled inside my head, instead of me crawling inside his. Whitehead's thought gave me "a local habitation and a name" for the way I felt and thought, providing a metaphysical basis for my developing theology.

Since that neighborhood Bible class with my neighbors, not to mention my own problems and my increasing awareness of social issues through the civil rights and feminist movements, I had puzzled over the issue of evil—not "Why do we have it" but "Does God do anything about it?" It seemed to me that in a finite world, all manner of things could and did go wrong—could broken things ever be made right? "Jesus died for your sins" did not seem to me to be a sufficient answer; how could that heal broken things? The evangelical answer that Jesus' crucifixion had cut the root of evil seemed palpably wrong. Evil hadn't grown less in the succeeding two thousand years; its roots seemed stronger than ever. Was brokenness just the way of the world, never to be satisfactorily answered?

I worked out my provisional answer in my dissertation, using Whitehead's metaphysics to develop a possible way out of my problem. Baldly stated, Whitehead's conception of God as a singular actual entity with a reversed polar structure necessitated that the world be taken into God at all moments of its multitudinous entities' completions. The dynamics also required that the received world must be integrated within the divine nature; therefore, the world would encounter its own transformation into the character of God within the divine life. This, of course, would entail judgment in various complex ways. The continuous results of this integration into God would affect the possibilities for temporal redemption that God could offer the world. Evil could be overcome; partially in the world, wholly in God.

Just before my graduation in 1974, we had moved again, this time to Cincinnati. During three troubled years there I worked my way toward divorce, and in 1977 took my first full-time academic job as assistant professor at Pittsburgh Theological Seminary. As a seminary professor I was invited to teach a class at a church, and I used the opportunity to work out the implications of Whitehead's metaphysics for a reframed Christian theology. This became the basis of my first book, *God Christ Church: A Practical Guide to Process Theology*, first published in 1982 and revised in 1989. In many respects, the positions worked out in that book remain as my Christian way of thinking, but with a provisional status.

Remember that baby-carriage moment, when it struck me as absurd that any finite mind, however great, could plummet the mind of God? On another occasion, while still in graduate school, I happened upon a very funny article on oxymoronism. The article concluded with the statement, "On the other hand, this may not be the case at all." And from then on it seemed to me that all theological statements or articles or books ought to conclude with that same sentence. But only once did I actually use it—even though I always mentally added it to every theology I wrote or read. A certain tentativeness belongs to all theological conclusions, even from great theological geniuses, but tentativeness is no excuse for not attempting to formulate just how and why we think as we do. We are driven to think, and to try to think better, critically using resources of philosophies, theologies, scriptures, traditions to inform us. Finally, it is God we worship, not any of our theologies.

As a process thinker, I was bemused by the three "Omnis" that have regularly been attributed to God throughout most of Christian history: omnipotence, omniscience, and omnipresence. By far the dominant category has been omnipotence, which was usually used to interpret both omniscience and omnipresence. Omnipotence implied omniscience, since a God who is source and chief exemplar of all power must know all things and ultimately control all things. The doctrine of predestination, so odious to my 18-year-old self, followed from the requirements omnipotence placed on God's manner of knowing. With regard to omnipresence, God was typically understood to be present to all things in the way a king's rule pervades his entire kingdom. In and through a king's absolute law, the king is virtually present. Thus presence, like knowledge, had been subsumed into omnipotence. With the possible exception of the mystics, God's omnipotence dominated philosophical and theological discussions of the nature of God.

But I had become a process theologian, with its basic supposition that God is present to all things, offering to each entity guidance toward its best contextual good. To the degree that an entity responds positively to this guidance, that influence from God is taken into the becoming entity, becoming thereby an internal presence. As each finite entity completes itself, its own relational influence is felt by its successors, and also by God. This presence of God, therefore, is the basis of God's knowledge: God knows all things relationally. It is also the source of divine power, and again, it is a relational power, an empowering power. Because God knows all circumstances affecting any becoming entity, both in terms of its possibilities and its probabilities, God is an influence toward what good is possible for every becoming occasion. It is a relative good and a persuasive good, neither an absolute nor a compelling good. God's power is relative, and is based on God's presence.

With these suppositions, it follows that God is incarnational and also revelational. Christianity clearly makes these qualities absolutely central in its understanding of God in Christ, and I surely concur in that. In Jesus we see the presence of God mediated through human presence. But I take this revelation generally as well as particularly: God is always incarnational, always revelational, according to what the context can bear of God. My assumption is that God works universally in all cultures, and that the holy men and women of those cultures become mediators of what good is possible within their contexts. Is there a goal, some sort of "Omega point" as Teilhard de Chardin suggested? Perhaps, but also, perhaps not. It's not really given us to know. But on a smaller scale, I like to think that there is a goal of increasing measures of kindness, and that religions and cultures expand insofar as their communal ideals of kindness toward one another expand to include kindness toward those outside their ordinary circles of care.

The technical name for these suppositions is "panentheism." "Theism" assumes that God vastly transcends the world, and is in no way dependent upon the world. Its opposite, "pantheism," assumes that God and the world are one, with distinctions being but matters of perspective, not substance. "God" and "nature" are synonyms. Panentheism is the "via media:" God is more than the world, but also immanent within the world. And the world is more than God, but also present within God. The "more than" is the realm of freedom, where God determines what to do with the world within the divine existence, and the world in its manyness decides what to do with the influences from God in its myriad instances of becoming. Interdependence exists between God and the world, each a necessary constituent of the other, like partially intersecting circles that both transcend each other, and continuously intersect with each other. This intersection is the dance and the dynamism of existence itself.

I do not know if process theology has it right. Its intricate metaphysical system, in its attempt to describe the world, may or may not concur with contemporary scientific understandings of the world. Certainly many process theologians argue vociferously that Whitehead's system holds up to scientific scrutiny in its various details, and perhaps it does. What matters to me is that its relational analysis of the world is consistent with the way the world is in a metaphorical way. Its metaphysics provide not a road map, but a metaphor for the fundamental nature of reality. And that fundamental nature is relational, through and through.

It's been many a long decade since I thought using the "right words" was required of us. Process convinces me that God is an incarnational God, whose nature is to reveal Godself for the sake of whatever form of well-being is possible in whatever circumstances. Insofar as we "know" God through Jesus, it seems to me that Jesus reveals the compassionate nature of God, boundless in its extent. The revelation is not through doctrine, but through story and action. And insofar as Jesus reveals God, then he reveals that God is by nature revelational. Therefore it must also be the case that God is revealed universally, in many times and places, adapting the revelation to that which works wellbeing in that context. Kindness, compassion, and a care for the wellbeing of those beyond one's own ordinary circles of care are the qualities by which doctrine is to be assessed.

To trust in God, then, is to trust what Paul Tillich once called "the God beyond God," which I take to mean to trust that reality who is more than our doctrines can fully express. Doctrines and theologies are after all a kind of "holy playfulness" as we work at the intellectual puzzles of the religious life. Clearly, God is more than our theologies.

I have known mystical experiences in my life both as a child and in my adult years. They have entailed an intense experience of the presence and encompassing love of God, a love not of my own making; it is sheer gift, sheer presence. And it has seemed to me that this intensity of love fills all things, albeit usually incognito. It does not particularly matter whether or not it is recognized; It is a love and presence that is simply always there, never absent, just at the other side of conscious experience; sometimes, occasionally, graciously invading conscious experience. We are called not necessarily to seek awareness of that presence, but just to assume God's presence, and get on with our lives in ways that are more or less congruent with that presence. "Congruence" requires commitment to an all-inclusive common good, to a society that "seeks justice, loves kindness," and walks humbly with its various notions of God.

And what of the icons of my childhood, the lady in the tree and the stars in the sky—what has happened to them? Perhaps it's simply the case that I've ended in my octogenarian years where I started: my deepest conviction is of the omnipresence of God, and the truest thing we can know about the omnipresent God is the mystery of an all-encompassing love that is beyond reduction to anything else. It's true: Charles

Wesley said it, "thy nature and thy name is Love." God is love, and present no matter what. The whole universe, in all its beauty, is a suitable icon through which we acknowledge the presence of a God whose beauty and whose love and whose presence is more than we mortals can ever fully comprehend. And it is enough.

11. Confusions About Pantheism

Richard Rohr, OFM

I think the reasons that Western Christians, both Catholic and Protestant, so easily and too readily make accusations of pantheism reflect our strong over-emphasis in the West on the utter distinction and even dissonance between Creator and creature. It is now very hard for many of us to "put Humpty Dumpty back together again" after the split and difference has been so emphasized in so many ways, for so many centuries, by so much moral theology, and by so many who thought they could and should promote God by demoting God's creatures.

My conviction is that the overcoming of this distinction and dissonance was precisely the Christian message of salvation, and the very meaning of Jesus. I also believe we probably need to overcome the split within ourselves to some degree before we are even capable of overcoming it out there, although

I am never precisely sure which comes first. Do split people always see division out there? Or does *perceived wholeness* out there, as in Jesus, allow me to trust wholeness in myself? For me it was surely the latter. Once I could fully trust that Jesus was both divine and human at the same time (all visible humanity not withstanding), this gave me the courage to believe the same about myself. But let's see how we get to this central and wonderful epiphany.

The word pantheism defines a belief that there is no critical distinction between God and "things"; God is somehow identical with the universe itself—as opposed to strict monotheism, which normally insists on a Creator God who is both separate and on a completely different plane than creation. Most monotheists would maintain a rather absolute difference, whereas a pantheist was thought to believe that "Everything is God" or "God is everything"—sometimes entirely erasing any distinction, it seemed.

Western theology in its attempt to preserve the transcendent end of the theological spectrum, invariably insisted on God as separate, almighty, and utterly beyond and different than creation, and this is true in different ways inside of all three monotheistic religions, Judaism, Christianity, and Islam. "Holy, Holy, Holy" Isaiah would put it (6:3) followed by his response "I am undone. I am a man of unclean lips" (6:5). This was surely the appropriate human response to Yahweh at that point in the evolution of spiritual consciousness. But soon the New Testament witness and later Christianity allowed two other manifestations of the Godhead to emerge— one we called the Christ, whom we saw as Isaiah's *Emmanuel* ("God With us" in 7:14)—and then another whom we called the (Holy) Spirit who was sequentially pictured as "descending," "abiding," and finally fully "indwelling." Jesus then significantly lessened the gap by calling this Jewish God "Father" in many settings, and by saying that God's Spirit *"was with you and is in you"* (John 14:17). So Trinitarian Christianity gave us a clear pathway out of the problem, by both preserving God's unknowable apartness ("Father") and God's immanent presence in two different manifestations ("Incarnate Christ" and "Holy Spirit").

So was Jesus his own kind of pantheist? He saw God from a third-person very immanent perspective, an "Indwelling Holy Spirit"; from a second-person perspective as a "Thou," a fully transcendent God or "Father"; and most daringly of all, in a first-person perspective when he spoke at least seven times in John's Gospel with the Great "I AM" as if he was fully God himself! This was, of course, the first daring revelation of what it then took us three centuries to unpack and finally name Trinity—a word not found in the Bible, probably because it would have been an affront to both monotheism and pantheism. This slowly emerging Trinitarian notion of God was supposed to keep the whole notion of Divinity in dynamic interaction with creation, but by and large it was only the mystics and those who went on inner journeys of prayer who were ever Trinitarian in any practical or pastoral way. They usually kept transcendence and immanence in a very creative balance, which is the key here.

Trinitarian theology overcomes the seeming problem, but most Christians had a rather static, substantial, inert notion of an unmovable mover of a God, and there was just no credible way to unite such "omnipotence" to a very vulnerable and always fluid humanity. They were two different planes of being. When orthodox Trinitarian theology fully emerges by the fourth century, what also emerges is a language of action, "procession," "filiation," inspiration, emanation, and many dynamic metaphors of movement and flow (wind, fire, bird, water, and *sending* itself). Now we see that these metaphors are fully compatible—and deeply intuitive—with the dynamic notion of reality we now have in this post-Einstein and quantum physics world. Once we have the language of flow instead of inert substances on utterly different planes, the whole problem begins to easily and quickly subside.

But I am jumping ahead of myself. We must recognize that a strong and seemingly unbridgeable gap still persisted between God and creation in the ordinary believer, despite Christian's central belief in the incarnation of God in Jesus (John 1:14), the Pauline doctrine of the Body of Christ (1 Corinthians 12), Jesus' promises about presence in the natural elements of bread and wine (John 6:51), and both Jesus and Paul speaking so much of a fully "indwelling Spirit" in persons (Romans 5:5 and throughout the Pauline corpus), and even in creation itself (Romans 8:21+). On the immanent-transcendent continuum, clerically-trained theologians felt it was their job to hold down the transcendent end, and protect God's awesomeness and majesty (much less so among lay and women mystics, however). Most clergy seem to think that God somehow needs our clerical and liturgical protection, and historically it was always the priestly class whose job it was to hide and protect all sacred objects from the invading barbarians.

True transcendence would never seem to need human protection or even promotion, in my opinion (which may be a proclamation!); but that is the way alienated humans think—as long as they are indeed "alienated" from their Source, or when the "branch is cut off from the Vine," as Jesus puts it (John 15:6). *In the practical order, I do suspect that most of us first need to experience the "Holy, Holy, Holy" before we can really honor and enjoy that this same transcendent God has also "leapt down from his Almighty throne"* (Wisdom 18:15). Maybe that is why such fear of pantheism persisted—most people felt that faith was to stay at that first experienced level of awe, fear, wonder, and transcendence. They felt they had no right to bridge the gap, not yet enjoying the fact that God had already bridged it in the Incarnation, and the generous and universal outpouring of the Spirit (Acts 2:1-13). We always have to allow the initiative from God's side, we call it grace.

Much pious Catholic and Protestant art, and sweet Sunday school stories and songs, did try to overcome the gap we presented, with some degree of success among sincere believers. But we well trained clergy still felt that it was our job to maintain God's "absolute otherness". What followed is the common "carrot on the stick" theology and spirituality, which kept the flock returning for *our* essential ministrations of sacraments and sermons—to overcome the gap that was not even there, according to the testimony of many Orthodox, Catholic, and Protestant mystics. Meanwhile most classic lay mystics like Catherine of Genoa just kept shouting without apology or explanation, "My deepest me is God!"

I am convinced that this practical split has largely contributed to the widespread agnosticism and even atheism that uniquely emerged in the countries inhabited by Western Christians. As someone once put it, "An absolutely alienated God alienates absolutely." Epistemologically, the problem was compounded by the lack of contemplative teaching given to the ordinary Catholic or Protestant in the pew. The non-dual or contemplative mind, does not overplay difference but in fact easily sees similarity and resonance—and thus allows similarity in its own inner experience. But this inner "prayer of quiet," or what they called the *Philokalia*, "the shedding of thought"—was largely the domain of early Eastern fathers and monastics, the Desert Fathers and Mothers, and in the West among a constantly recurring set of mystics at many levels of Christian society.

By mystics, I simply mean *experiential knowers* as opposed to textbook knowers. From the existing historical record that we share publicly, it seems they were often members of religious orders, hermits, anchoresses, monks, and members of contemplative communities who were more often encouraged, taught, and allowed to go to the Christian depths, where non-dual or contemplative thought could be appreciated. That pattern continued until very recently, when the deeper stream has finally opened up to the masses, like the spring flooding of the Nile River. Yet even now, many clergy warn their congregants against any deep inner journeys. Contemplative prayer is considered dangerous or even demonic by some! Mostly I fear because it will make their external ministrations less necessary and important. And they are right in one way—there is nothing more liberating and energizing than an actual life of deep prayer!

All the way back in Christian history, anyone who would be contemplative invariably had to go off to the deserts of Egypt and Syria, or later become aligned with a group like the Beguines or the Beghards or the Brethren of the Common Life, the latter of which produced Thomas à Kempis; or move to an anchor hold next to the kind of church that produced Lady Julian of Norwich and Nicholas von der Flue; or join a

"Third Order" group affiliated to a major religious order like both of the Catherines; or go off into the woods as a hermit or recluse, which was the choice of too many to count. The pattern was rather constant. *The church on the corner had real fear of depth because it looked like it led to pantheism to them.* And we had God fully localized in *our* church! Notice, for example, in Julian of Norwich's *Showings* how often she has to apologize or equivocate after she has just made an enormously non-dual or daring statement. And she kept herself protected inside those walls next to St. Julian's church for at least 20 years, always verbally deferring to the "Holy Church" and deprecating herself too often as a "mere woman" and "not educated."

The ordinary church-going Christian today has no idea how common this hermit or anchorite phenomenon was throughout the first 1,400 years after Jesus lived and announced what Owen Barfield called "full and final participation." Some kind of separation was the only way contemplatives could avoid detection and persecution for their outrageous and surely heretical belief that they learned and shared with Jesus, that "I and the Father are one" (John 10:30). They intuited the same for themselves, but seemed to know the ordinary parish priest or Sunday congregant would not understand. Just as with Jesus, it would be called blasphemy (John 10:31-33)—or perhaps "pantheism," presumption, or arrogance.

Do not assume that they were saying, nor am I saying, that an appropriate and real distinction between Creator and creature was completely denied either. More often than not, the statements of our tested mystics are very subtle and mysterious, holding a creative tension, but always pointing toward *objective relationship or* even *interbeing between God and the soul*—while also preserving essential difference—exactly as in the one life of the three persons of the Trinity. The Father is not the Son, and the Son is not the Father, and yet they are also ONE. Trinity is the code breaker!

If we had been more Trinitarian in our practical Christianity, we would have had the ideal and perfect template for preserving both clear diversity and absolute unity, but one needs a contemplative or non-dual mind to be at home with the mystery of Trinity, and most Christians were not taught the orthodox Christian shape of God in any pastoral or practical way. We just painted triangles and held up shamrocks. They were told about the life of the Trinity *ad intra* (from within), but really nothing about the Trinity *ad extra* (from without)! Thus we did not resolve the foundational philosophical and theological problem of "the one and *the* many" for the common Christian, which makes one think that it was not interiorly resolved for many theologians or clergy who did the teaching and preaching.

Academic and seminary theology had never perhaps heard what was attributed to at least five desert and early fathers of the church: "a theologian is one who prays." Theology itself was often practically split from spirituality, and remained a largely mental discipline, as was much of the preaching that followed from it. We ended up with a properly "transactional" Christianity much more than any real transformational Christianity. We are now forced to admit this humbly in midst of our postmodern, secular, materialistic, and individualistic world. We did not roundly transform either cultures or individuals with our distant, largely judgmental, and very "substantial" God who was more a noun than an active verb.

Pane_n_theism

Our truly orthodox Christian belief, directly implied and soon concluded from the incarnation of God in Jesus, what would best be called *panentheism*, or a belief that God is and can be found "in all things." This is the full meaning of the incarnation, of course, but most Western Christians had no cosmic notion of the incarnation; it was only a very personal notion limited and contained in Jesus, which unfortunately stole its transformative power for humanity. We ended up largely worshiping Jesus instead of following him or imitating him. It was mostly Eastern fathers like Irenaeus, Athanasius, Maximus the Confessor, and others who believed that the incarnation was a cosmic event, and Jesus was "merely" and wonderfully its perfect personification.[1]

There was always another and constant tradition, but to be sure it was usually the hidden or lower stream. In case you think this is some dangerous heresy, or this is just my opinion, consider this statement from Pope John Paul II in 1995: "The venerable and ancient tradition of the Eastern churches, that is the teaching of the Cappadocian Fathers on divinization (*theosis*), passed into the tradition of all the Eastern Churches and is part of their common heritage. This can be summarized in the thought already expressed by St. Irenaeus at the end of the second century: '*God passed into humanity so that humanity might pass over into God.*'"[2] Even a Pope could not dare to shout this too loudly in the West, for he knew the backlash that would come from the old antipathy between the Eastern and Western church, but he did affirm it in this Apostolic Letter to our Eastern brethren. Irenaeus, a Doctor of the Church honored in both East and West, who died in 202 AD, is a bridge figure here. He came from the East but was a bishop in what is now Lyon, France, where he is buried.

The Greek word *theosis,* often used in the Eastern churches, is probably best translated as "divinization"; this word usually sounds heretical and dangerous to most Western Christians. The shining and oft-quoted "proof text" here is, of course, 2 Peter 1:3-4, in which the inspired author writes, "Divine power has given us everything we need for life and godliness through our knowledge of God, who called us to *share in the divine glory and goodness.* In bestowing these gifts, God has given us the guarantee of something very great and wonderful to come. Through them you'll be able to *share the divine nature."*

I believe that every time the Christian church divided or separated, each group lost another "half" of the Gospel message. That seems to have been true in the Great Schism of 1054, when the patriarchs of East and West mutually excommunicated one another. The loss of Christian wholeness then continued after 1517 with the protesting and needed reformations of Martin Luther, John Calvin, John Knox, and Henry VIII, and then again with our split from science at the time of Galileo, and many times since, leading to modern and postmodern secularism. Despite the very important Marys in the Jesus story, we seem to have been split from the feminine from the very early period. (We made Peter the first apostle, for example, whereas the Gospel accounts clearly make Mary Magdalene the apostle to the apostles.) When revelation confronts culture, culture usually wins.

At any rate, whenever we split interiorly or externally, both sides lose something good and even necessary. This is the very sad result of dualistic thinking, which is incapable of comprehending, much less experiencing, the mystical, nonviolent, or non-dual level of anything ("not totally one but not two either"). The contemplative non-dual mind should and could be religion's unique gift to society. It provides a conveyor belt for all spiritual evolution and thought, as Ken Wilber rightly teaches.

So let's reintroduce "divinization," this Gospel "pearl of great price" to the Western Church, both Roman and Protestant, and to the secular seeker too.[3] Without it, we will continue to suffer from the seemingly low self-esteem and the "culture of death" that characterizes the postmodern world, along with seeking our identity in such superficial ways. We denied and rejected our own rock solid foundation for human dignity and human flourishing. The Gospel was just too democratic and inclusive, I am afraid. As one old story put it, when the young student asked the rabbi why no one saw God anymore, the rabbi answered, "Because nowadays no one is willing to stoop so low!"

The Winding Thread

Many of the early teachers of the Christian church deeply believed in a very real ontological, metaphysical, objective union between humanity and God, which allowed Jesus to take us "back with him" into the life of the Trinity (John 17:23-24, 14:3, 12:26). Jesus had ruptured the planes of being and "harrowed" the hell we had created. This was how many in the early church understood and experienced "full and final participation" to use Barfield's wonderful phrase. The Gospel proclaimed our *core identity as the crucial and necessary beginning point* (Ephesians 1:3-12)—and not just a later goal or ending point. We had thought our form was merely human, but Jesus came to tell us that our actual form is human-divine, just as his is.

Jesus was not much interested in proclaiming himself the exclusive or exclusionary Son of God, but he went out of his way to communicate an *inclusive* sonship and daughterhood to the crowds. We were to imitate and "follow" him more than worship him. Paul used words like "adopted" (Galatians 4:5) and "coheirs with Christ" (Romans 8:17) to make the same point. "Adoptionism" was much stronger in the early church than the later Catholic and Lutheran emphasis on individual "justification" of souls. We first localized salvation in creation and history itself, and not the later problem solving rescue for a few, or what Matthew Fox calls "Fall-Redemption" spirituality. We emphasized Genesis 3 as the starting point instead of the proactive "It was good" of Genesis 1.

In Genesis 1:27 we are told that we are "created in the *image and likeness* of God." Many tomes of theology have been written to clarify this single line. The consensus was that the word "image" describes our *objective* DNA that marks us as creatures of God from the very beginning. Whereas "likeness" is our personal appropriation and gradual realization of this utterly free gift of the *imago Dei*. This works. We all have the same objective gift, but how and whether we subjectively say yes to our implanted *imago Dei* is quite different. We all and already have image; we choose and allow likeness.

We were given the full courage to appropriate our "full and final participation" through and in Jesus, who clearly believed that God was not so much inviting us into a distant heaven, but inviting us into *Godself* as friends and co-participants already now. Remember, we are not talking about a perfect psychological or moral wholeness in humans, which is never the case, and probably this is why many dismiss the doctrine of divinization—or feel rightly incapable of it. I am talking about a freely and objectively implanted "sharing in the divine nature" as a gift from God to all that God created (2 Peter 1:4). This is the totally positive substratum on which we must and alone can ever build a civilization of love and inclusivity. Many have been predicting that the next century in Christian theology must be and will be a "turn toward participation" instead of walking around merely observing, critiquing, and analyzing, and calling that "belief."

The slowly unfolding goal and direction of the biblical revelation is a constant trajectory toward a mutual indwelling between Creator and creature, while still maintaining an important distinction between "I" and "Thou" or there can be no *relationship* as such, no choice for the other, no surrender, no real mutual love but only mechanical absorption. The movement toward union began with God walking in the garden with naked Adam and Eve, allowing them to admire and even name "all the array" of creation (Genesis 2:1); then the theme deepens through all the bookmarks of patriarchs, prophets, teachers, kings, and boring "secular" history of the Jewish Bible. The theme fully finds its shocking climax in the New Testament realization that Paul expresses as *"the mystery of Christ within you, your hope of glory"* (Colossians 1:27). Or as John excitedly puts it, *"You know him because he is with you and he is in you!"* (John 14:17). This is not Christian "supersessionism" but direct continuity with the original Jewish foundation and ground.

The eternal mystery of ongoing incarnation has finally met its mark, and "the marriage feast of the Lamb can begin" (Revelation 19:7-9). History is no longer a meaningless or random stab in the dark, ending with a "whimper," Apocalypse, or Armageddon; but history now has a positive and hopeful direction. There has to be a cosmic historical hope offered to people or it is very hard to heal individual people in the long term, as many of us have found in our ministries.[4]

Instead what we have today is what Ken Wilber sadly calls *"aperspectival madness"* and some even call a "post-truth world" as we have seen in the recent American election cycle. Christians have not deeply believed or proclaimed their own Good News up to now, and they ended up thinking the goal was to abandon or be allowed to destroy "the late great planet earth," which Pope Francis instead calls "our common home." *By a lack of a deep inner Christianity we have ended up not having a strong outer Christianity either.* In the world of religion, you either go deep or you slowly go dead.

Wedding Imagery

But back to the depths! If we could allow the panoramic view of the biblical revelation and also the natural history that we're a part of to really change us, we'd see how God is forever evolving human consciousness, making us ever more ready for divine union, love making, and what Jesus often refers to as a wedding banquet. We see this specific theme already in the prophets Isaiah (61:10, 62:5) and Hosea (2:18ff.), surely in the Song of Songs, in the school of Paul (Ephesians 5:25-32), and finally in the Book of Revelation (19:7-8, 21:2).

They all dare to speak of divine nuptials, or "preparing a bride to be ready for her husband." They intuit that the human soul is being gradually matured so mutual "espousal" and partnership with the Divine can be experienced both personally and historically. Maybe a major part of our resistance to such salvation is that we individualized the whole notion, and the imperfection of the normal individual just could not fully carry "the weight of glory." I really think that is true. Note that the early covenants were all with society and history and dynasties, with Israel as a whole, and even with creation but never about individuals "going to heaven." (To not see this is culpable ignorance at this point.) Israel, and then the Church, were meant to be the group of "called-out ones" (*ek-klesia*) who first bring this corporate salvation to conscious and visible possibility on the earth.

But isn't this just poetic exaggeration? If this is the divine agenda, why were most of us presented with an angry deity who largely needed to be feared, placated, and controlled by sacrifices? And why would God even want to "marry" this broken humanity? Yet Jesus' most common metaphor for the goal and end is a wedding banquet, where he is nothing less than "the bridegroom" (Matthew 9:15, Mark 2:19-20, John 3:29). Why would he choose such daring and unnecessary metaphors unless some kind of *interpenetration*, if I can use the word, was actually the goal and ideal? This seemingly impossible idea of real and objective union with God is still something we're so afraid of that most of us won't allow ourselves to think it, especially if we stay on the surface of cultural Christianity. Only God *in you* will allow you to imagine such a possibility, which is precisely the role of "the Holy Spirit planted in your heart" (Romans 8:11 and throughout Paul).

John's Gospel, of course, was quite direct about a very real union between God and the soul, but we largely read it as merely union between the Father and Jesus (exclusive sonship). Yet Jesus said "I pray not only for them, but also for those who will believe in me through their word, so that they may all be one, as you, Father, are in me and I in you, that they also may be in us, that the world may believe that you sent me" (John 17:20-21). For John, *Jesus came to give us the courage to trust and allow our inherent union with God,* and he comes to model this for us—so we can first dare to *imagine* it! It is surprising that most Christians would speak of heaven as "union with God" but they seem to tolerate a rather complete disjunction between the same situation in this world; here it is heresy and impossible, and there it is the entire goal and eternal prize! That is at the heart of our theological schizophrenia.

As the goal, what more fitting denouement could the second coming of Christ be if not that humanity collectively has become "a beautiful bride all dressed for her husband" (Revelation 21:2), with the Christ as the eternal stand-in for the Divine Bridegroom. Jesus, the Christ, trusted what we are afraid to trust, and became, as Paul calls in various places, the promise, the guarantee, the pledge, our victory, and "the first of many brothers and sisters."

Modern Witnesses

In Joseph Chilton Pearce's book, *The Biology of Transcendence,* he points to culture (and by implication the cultural entrapment of Christianity) as major blockages to potential growth toward overcoming our fear and denial of transcendence. Each stage of brain development provides a biological window to connect with higher levels. But if the child or teenager is threatened or shamed, these possibilities for higher connection die off and the connections to the lower primitive, reflexive, reptilian brain—which is hardwired for defense and survival—are strengthened. People stop developing and they even regress. Unfortunately, our culture's approach to childrearing and even the Church's teaching style have focused on shaming, punishing, and threatening, just the opposite of what Jesus actually modeled, but we refashioned Jesus in our image. Pearce points out that Jesus and other great spiritual teachers throughout history intended to awaken us to "the illusion of culture and the reality of our transcendent nature."[5] But we made God and Jesus into shamers and threateners too—the hard wiring and the fear was just too much in place.

Indeed, Christianity has not emphasized nor much taught our inherent transcendent nature for much of its mainline history. I fear that Christianity largely allowed itself to be co-opted by cultures for the purpose of social control and order. As Todd Wynward, a longtime and creative educator here in New Mexico, writes in his book *Rewilding the Way,* "We are the people God's been waiting for. Why is this so hard for modern Christians to believe and embrace? Because God's amazing expectations, and our divine potential, have been hijacked by empire-based Christendom and subverted by the framing stories of dominant culture.... Your native, indigenous character as a child of God has been distorted...."[6]

The Ultimate Template for All Orthodoxy

In summary, I must repeat that the ultimate Christian source and model for pan*en*theism is the central doctrine of the Trinity itself. God is "One," just as our Jewish ancestors taught us (Deuteronomy 6:4), and yet this perfect divine unity is precisely the self-emptying and outpouring between three distinct "persons" classically called Father, Son, and Holy Spirit. Divine unity protects both radical distinction and radical unity. God's love both unites and allows, and without God we normally do not know how to do both of these at the same time. *Divine union is not uniformity but precisely diversity loved and overcome! Only the contemplative, non-dual mind can process this, not the rational dualistic mind.* God is a mystery of relationship, an event of communion, a verb more than a noun, and so is everything God created "in his own image." *We are both distinct from God and yet one with God at the same time. This is precisely the mystery of divine relatedness and communion.*[7]

So Christianity is not offering some naïve "everything is one"; but instead it offers humanity what neither our religion nor our politics up to now have been able to achieve—the balancing act between protecting difference and achieving union—where the head is not the foot, and the eye is not the hand, yet all are part of the One Body of Christ (Corinthians 12:12-30). We must study, pray, wait, reconcile, and work to achieve this kind of unity—and never an impossible uniformity, which was the tragic mistake of both the early notion of Christendom, the later notion of Communism, and most "isms" in between. This is, in the end, a spiritual insight, grace, and possibility, which is why, for all of its weaknesses, I cannot give up on good and integral religion.

It is time for the lower stream to again become the upper stream. It was always there, and is now becoming visible so all can see and enjoy it, and make it impossible to deny or call heresy. Our job is not to discover it as if for the first time, but only to retrieve what has been discovered—and lost—and rediscovered again and again, in the mystics and seers, and prophets of all religions. Maybe that is the eternal pattern?

Maybe that is why so many of Jesus' parables are surprisingly about losing and finding?

Finally

In my own life, and according to teachers like the *Philokalia*, Dionysius, *The Cloud of Unknowing*, Bonaventure, St. John of the Cross, and St. Teresa of Avila, this knowing cannot be proven to anyone, or demonstrated by theological argument or made evident by any Scripture quote, although each of these will help us to know we are not arrogant, crazy, or misguided.

Our inherent union with God, what Julian of Norwich beautifully called "oneing," can only be known from the inside out—from inside of love, inside of prayer, and inside of God, *where the resonance between seer and what we can see is fully and finally enjoyed.*[8] It is known by participation or it is not known at all. This is the inherent vulnerability of a spiritual teacher. You can never prove it to anyone, you can only point to it, and hopefully to some small degree exemplify it.

But do remember this: *What we are looking for is what is doing the looking,* which is exactly why Jesus said we will always find it (Matthew 7:7-9); because we already have it.

Notes

1. Michael J. Christensen and Jeffrey A. Wittung (eds), *Partakers of the Divine Nature: The History and Development of Deification in the Christian Tradition* (Farleigh Dickinson University Press: 2007). This excellent collection will give you the history, loss, and development of the theme of "deification" in the Christian tradition. If you want to do your own research here, the fathers of the church to study are St. Clement of Alexandria, Origen, St. Basil, St. Athanasius, and St. Irenaeus in the West; and St. Gregory Nazianzen, St. Gregory of Nyssa, St. Maximus

the Confessor, Pseudo Macarius, Diadochus, and St. Gregory Palamas in the East. The primary texts are in the Philokalia collection and the teachings of the Hesychastic monks.

2. (St.) Pope John Paul II, "Orientale Lumen," Apostolic Letter of May 2, 1995, I:6.

3. Adapted from Richard Rohr, *Immortal Diamond: The Search for Our True Self* (San Francisco: Jossey-Bass: 2013), 117-119.

4. For more on earlier Christian hope, see David Burnfield, *Patristic Universalism: An Alternative to the Traditional View of Divine Judgment* (Universal Publishers: 2013). Christians deserve to know how many Fathers of the early Church, particularly in the East, understood cosmic salvation to be the whole point. This is just one more recent and well sourced example of a rediscovered theme in the Christian world.

5. Joseph Chilton Pearce, *The Biology of Transcendence: A Blueprint of the Human Spirit* (Rochester, VT: Park Street Press: 2004), 126-127.

6. Todd Wynward, *Rewilding the Way: Break Free to Follow an Untamed God* (Harrisonburg, VA: Herald Press: 2015), 26.

7. Richard Rohr, *The Divine Dance, The Trinity and Your Transformation* (New Kensington, PA: Whitaker House, 2016). Much of the point of this whole book.

8. Julian of Norwich, *Showings*, 51.

12. *The Seas Do Split: Dancing God's Liberation*

Rabbi Bradley Shavit Artson

How do you speak about a return to God when you don't remember having ever been with God in the first place? My life was the happy childhood of an atheist in San Francisco and, like most stories, this one won't proceed in a linear fashion. Instead, it will meander up and down main roads and byways, some of them reflecting what appeared to be dominant at the time and sometimes offering glimpses into a potential without precedent that would eventually open a portal leading to an entirely unanticipated possibility.

I am the product of those meanderings, those wanderings, not knowing where I was headed, and the consistent reality that my life thus far has turned out more beautiful and mysterious that I could have possibly scripted on my own. What follows is that story, my story.

It turns out that San Francisco was a perfect city in which to be an atheist. There was so much to do, to see, to participate in! I had the pleasure and the privilege of being from a family that allowed me to take full advantage of the city's many lures. My parents enrolled me in rigorous schools where I received a fine education. I was able to travel with my family, privileged to maintain wonderful friendships, and that happy rootedness is a gift that I carry with me everywhere. I have longed suspected that our origin stories (of having emerged from a pristine garden) really reflect the external narrative of each person's individual emergence from childhood, and subsequent expulsion into adulthood. My personal Eden was by the Bay.

Early Encounters

When I was almost 13, my father insisted that I become a Bar Mitzvah, as had every Jewish male in my family since time immemorial. Being a confirmed atheist and knowing that there was nothing (and no one) out there, I thought the preparation and ritual was a waste of time, so I resisted with everything I had. Ultimately, I consented to a pretty pro forma Bar Mitzvah, complete with two separate parties because my parents were embroiled in a really painful and hostile divorce procedure that was to last until I was 16. The Bar Mitzvah event didn't mean much to me, although I recognized that it meant something to my father. It didn't mean much to my mother, whose atheism runs deep to this day.

My spiritual autobiography really revs up after that opening salvo. You see, during the time that I was preparing for my Bar Mitzvah, I also developed an illness that has remained with me throughout my life. At the time I didn't know what it was; I just knew that it was both painful and humiliating. At 13, I was a boy emerging into my teen years and early manhood, yet I had these painful oozing lesions in a very private place; something I couldn't discuss and wouldn't share. The pain was so great that I would only defecate every three or four days which led to extremely painful intervals and a lot of bleeding every time I finally had to allow my bodily functions to transpire.

I don't know which was worse, the excruciating pain or the humiliation, but at some point I was caught (meaning, my stained garments revealed my condition to the adults in my home, forcing me to answer their probing questions). Those questions resulted in me being rushed to a Proctologist's office and having the worst two hours of my life until that moment. Strapped in the Proctologist's examination chair with my butt in the air, the doctor probing what were highly private parts, I was in incredible pain, and was mortified with a sense of shame and doom.

Vision Given by Spirit

Rabbi Abraham Joshua Heschel says that one must hit rock bottom before being able to let God in. I had descended as far as I could go, and there was God, just in time. In the middle of this two-hour medical exploration (one that was physically painful and felt personally degrading), I experienced a miraculous vision, meaning I saw not with my mind, but with my actual eyes. I *witnessed* Moses and the Children of Israel marching across the split sea to dry land! I *saw* the glory of God leading them in security to freedom, and I was among their throng! The vision was visual, clear, and experiential. Whereas in later years I continue to cherish that vision in my consciousness and my identity, at the time I had no way to relate to it. I had no intellectual or theological framework to think about God or visions, I had no emotional openness to the possibility of participating in miracles or liberation. After all, I had always assumed that being religious was synonymous with stupidity and ignorance. So I did what many of us do with aspects of reality that we don't have a framework to integrate: I just forgot about it and ignored it.

Within the week, the doctor had informed my mother that I had an inoperable terminal cancer. I was rushed to the hospital; my mother moved in with me, and we spent three weeks living in the hospital running a battery of inconclusive tests, until the specialist noticed that there were also small red bumps on my arms, chest, and legs. He linked those bumps to the more egregious wounds down below. After some deft reference checking, he declared that what I had was a disease called Histiocytosis X, a rare viral affliction which can be fatal if it strikes internal organs. Otherwise it is merely painful and disfiguring. Histiocytosis recurs in cycles every several years, with diminishing frequency and intensity until at some point it has either killed its victim or petered out entirely. This was my first round.

Not uncommonly, Histiocytosis X also accompanies a related illness called Diabetes Insipidus. This is not standard diabetes, it entails that the interior lobe of my pituitary gland no longer produces the hormone Vasopressin, one that causes the kidney to re-filter water. Consequently, I spent the early part of my teen years needing to drink voraciously and having to urinate every 15 or 20 minutes with a constant and unremitting sense of thirst. That cycle lent itself to teasing from other young teens because of my frequent visit to the men's room, and to my own sense of being marginal or, in some ways, not normal.

The dual diagnosis of Histiocytosis X and Diabetes Insipidus led to a series of medical interventions. I was subjected to rigorous radiotherapy and chemotherapy at the cancer ward of one of the local hospitals (although I didn't let myself notice that it was a cancer ward, the name emblazoned above the entrance notwithstanding). I didn't (at least consciously) notice that everyone in treatment there was a cancer patient. I just didn't allow myself to see it because I couldn't admit the reality of cancer to myself. As for the Diabetes Insipidus, the treatment was and is to take a dose of the hormone vasopressin twice daily, which allows my kidneys to refilter water normally.

In the rush of treatments, doctor's appointments, consultations, my stunning vision of the sea parting, of the children of Israel crossing to freedom, of God and I marching together evaporated. I had no way to internalize, no way to conceive of it. Like many American Jews, I embraced my identify as a Jew, but my Jewishness involved a sense of ethnicity, history, intellectual curiosity about the world, and prophetic morality. I had a keen sense that Judaism was adamant about social justice and human dignity, and that imperative constituted the primary legacy of my Jewish heritage. I did not engage in Jewish rituals; I did not engage in prayer or the study of traditional text, nor did I feel the need. I threw myself into my high school, surrounded by friends. High school was a time of blossoming on every possible level and I felt myself becoming popular, enjoying the company of my peers, loving the learning and sports that I finally could access.

First Fruits

In college the Histiocytosis X returned, and I again had to endure extensive treatments at the Stanly Farber Cancer Institute in Boston, still oblivious to the fact that I was there because I, too, was a cancer patient.

In college I became religious, and that transformation is worth dwelling upon for a moment. Two of my roommates were pious Christians, and I was puzzled on some level by this because I had grown up with the assumption that religion was a mental deficiency, yet these two people were smart enough to attend Harvard. Indeed, both of them have since gone on to enjoy illustrious careers in medicine, one of them in academic medicine. Even more striking to me, though, was that their sweetness and goodness was very much the harvest of their religiosity. One friend, in particular, was and remains among the most compassionate and decent people I have ever met, and that intrigued me. His decency inspired me to consider what it might be to explore taking on religious beliefs and religious commitments myself.

But having been a lifelong atheist, I had no idea how to begin. Here is where, according to some understandings of theology, what transpired might seem providential: the radio host Dennis Prager came to speak on campus, and he delivered an advocacy talk, the title of which was "Proving the Existence of God." Dennis claimed to be able to do just that. I attended his program, but not because I needed someone to prove the existence of God. All I needed was to know that you couldn't *disprove* it; I just didn't want to invest a lot of time and energy and then be shown to have been a complete fool.

There were two undergraduate philosophy students who shredded Prager's arguments, demonstrating conclusively that you simply can't prove the existence of God. But again, that wasn't what I sought. What I needed was to know that you can't *disprove* the existence of God, and they readily conceded that point. Their admission gave me the permission slip I needed to explore whether or not God had a role to play in my life. I scheduled an appointment to speak to the Hillel Rabbi, Ben-Zion Gold. Rabbi Gold was a Holocaust survivor whose entire family had been murdered in the Holocaust. He was a man of prophetic morality, passionate about human dignity and social justice. He was a great speaker and a deep, deep intellect, vastly literate in Jewish sacred sources and highly idiosyncratic.

I met Rabbi Gold in his book-lined study, and I told him that I was uncomfortable even having the conversation, but that I wanted to think about God. Rabbi Gold responded that there is no neutral place from which to think about God. He told me that being a believer involves certain implicit promises, and the only way to explore faith was from the inside: to give oneself to observance and belief, and then to see whether those promises ring true in one's own life.

Rabbi Gold gave me two challenges: He suggested I start attending synagogue services every Sabbath morning, stipulating that I had to attend for not less than two months. He explained that attending for less than two months would mean I would spend the whole time focusing on where I sat, who else was present, who people were, and what melodies we were using. He insisted that I needed to attend regularly for at least two months to be able to become sufficiently familiar with the community and the service to assess whether or not this religiosity was doing anything positive for me. The second challenge Rabbi Gold posed was an assignment: to read an anthology of the writings of Franz Rosenzweig.

So, a word about Rosenzweig: Franz Rosenzweig was a German Jew raised at the turn of the 20th century. He came from a prominent, wealthy, and assimilated family. His famous cousin had previously converted to Christianity, as had several of the assimilated Jews of Germany, exposed as they were to western culture, its beauty and depth. Rosenzweig decided, being of a philosophical bent, that he wanted to convert in the same way his cousin did: like Jesus, through Judaism. Rosenzweig resolved to enter Christianity through the Jewish religion, specifically by attending Yom Kippur services with his parents at their beautiful Berlin Temple and then, the next morning, proceeding to be baptized. His mother, in a remarkable display of religious courage, stood at the door of their temple dressed in her holiday best and refused to allow her son, Franz, into the synagogue. She said to him, "If you want to become a Christian, that's your business, but you can't do it through us."

She literally blocked his way into the synagogue and he found himself wandering the streets of Berlin. His grand drama caused him to feel frustrated by his mother's stubborn loyalty to her people and faith, and he wandered into a small Hasidic synagogue, simple, unadorned, not ornate in any way, but possessed of a deep authenticity and piety. He witnessed for the first time in his life people sobbing while they prayed. He witnessed people praying on their own with such depth and fervor as he had never previously seen, and he was utterly and completely transfixed. Rosenzweig resolved that very evening not to convert to Christianity, but instead to live a life of return, which he called "from the periphery to the center." He established programs and institutions to assist other assimilated Jews to return to the faith as well. He organized courses that were lay-led and lay-taught (by such luminaries as Martin Buber and Nahum Glatzer), that were conversational in nature, in which a text was set on the table and everybody had the right to offer their own responses and opinions, whether they were learned or not. In launching this bold kind of democratic learning, he created a model which is in use to this day, a hundred years later, allowing people to own their own heritage and to illumine its writings with their own authenticity.

But Rosenzweig's life is no less significant than his thought. He wrote an astonishing book of philosophy called the *Star of Redemption* that transformed Jewish and much of Christian thought in the 20th and 21st century, but he also developed Amyotrophic Lateral Sclerosis (also known as Lou Gehrig's Disease) and spent his last several years bedridden. By the end of his life, the only way he could write or communicate was by using a wire attached to his finger to point to a letter board held by his wife, Edith. He would indicate one letter at a time, and Edith would transcribe each and every letter, and in that way, he produced essays and short books up to his dying day. His example of that kind of courage, intellectual vision, and the ability to stand up against the dominant norms of one's culture and to live a life of meaning despite great challenge really captivated and inspired me, as did the community and synagogue services at Hillel. Everything was sung. Instead of a sermon, different congregants volunteered to teach, and those congregants were some of Harvard's best minds: Michael Walter from the political science department, Ben Schwartz from Chinese studies, Hilary Putnam and his wife Anna Putnam from the philosophy department. In those conversations, it was impossible to fear that religion forced a person to surrender either intellectual acuity or moral fervor.

That was my Semester of Love: the semester that I met God was also the season that I met Elana, who, 33 years later, remains my beloved wife. That magical period in my life launched a richness of mind and spirit, an openness of heart that altered my life's vector forever.

But the astute reader will have noticed that I haven't referred back to the cancer of my childhood or the miracle of the sea parting because I wasn't consciously aware of it yet. I finished college intending to be a politician. I was active in liberal and progressive causes and took a job as the legislative aide to the speaker of the California State Assembly, immediately after my college graduation. I was a legislative aide for two years and I loved the work building community and addressing possibilities for social change. But during those two years it also became clear to me that as a politician it was impossible to make new friendships, at least I couldn't figure out a way to do it. It was impossible to have real balance in my life, and it was impossible to honor my relationship with Elana yet also live the life of a successful politician. It took me about a year to realize I couldn't integrate the life I wanted and still pursue a career in politics, but I didn't have a fallback plan. I had previously mentioned to Elana that it was my intention, after retiring as the senator from California, after a long and glorious career in politics, to attend rabbinical school because of my growing love of Judaism and an attendant hunger to learn. Elana was and is a wise woman, and she responded that if I wanted to learn in rabbinical school I should not postpone it until the end of my life, because no one can know what life might to bring. She told me I should enroll at once.

Based on her sound advice, I spent a frenetic week applying to rabbinical school, was admitted, and found myself in enrolled New York. Elana attended Columbia Law School while I was attending rabbinical school nearby. The rabbinical school took five years to complete. I loved the learning; I made lifelong friendships there. Then I accepted a job at a congregation in Southern California.

All of this, you will soon see, set the stage for the most significant spiritual awakening thus far.

Harvesting Life; Pruning Faith

I entered the congregational rabbinate, as do most young clergy, I think: with a sense that if I smiled enough, loved enough, preached and taught enough, visited enough sickbeds, conducted enough lifecycle events, and was present and tireless, that I would be able to create a spiritual awakening in my congregation. I threw myself at the mission with the energy and the zeal of young clergy, and the first five years of my work in Mission Viejo, California, was beautiful and joyous. The congregation grew from 200 families to almost 600 families. There was an influx of young people and young children. We created a dynamism and an excitement in the community that lasted through the week and crescendoed on Sabbaths and holy days. I was offering adult education classes, teaching the teens, the kids, and the preschoolers, visiting the sick, and conversing with the elderly. It was nonstop work, but it was richly rewarding and my understanding of God powered me through. My theology was conventionally liberal, meaning I accepted a more or less Orthodox vision of God, except I didn't think that God sweated all the details. I was able to sustain that stance until Elana became pregnant with our twins. The twins were born prematurely after a difficult pregnancy fraught with peril. Then, at about two and a half years of age, Jacob was diagnosed with autism.

Hello, God: Hitting Rock Bottom (Again)

With that diagnosis, everything changed. I suppose that on an intellectual level I already knew that reality was messier, but emotionally I had an implicit confidence that, if I were a diligent rabbi and faithfully discharged my tasks, God would take care of me in the same way that, if I did my work, my congregants would take care of me. This didn't happen. Jacob's struggles were enormous and all-consuming. I could see that fear dominated a good part of his emotional life (and ours) and none of us knew where this was heading, or how to fashion a meaningful life with autism. My benign view of a God who was in control, a God who determined outcomes, a God who could shield the chosen and could change natural law to protect the favored ones; that vision shattered.

I spent two years largely not talking to God. It's not that I stopped believing in God's reality, it's just that I knew that it would be better for both of us if we didn't speak.

It turns out to be one of life's ironies, that among the best places to hide from God or from dealing with God is the American congregation. For two years I gave beautiful sermons about ethics and values, history and texts, and nobody noticed that I didn't talk about or to God. At least not publicly. In private, it was a bit more muddled. Even while not talking to God, I would find myself sneaking into my Jacob's room late at night when he was sleeping. I would lay hands on him and I would offer my version of Moses' prayer, *El na rafa na lo:* Please, God, heal him! I would utter these words yet if you had asked me if I believed in a God who heals autism, I would have said no. But I felt compelled to pray nonetheless.

From Where My Help Comes

This was my conundrum: I was not able to think or talk about (or to) God because my notion of God entailed an all-knowing, all-powerful deity who could control outcomes. That notion of God left me incapable of relationship without betraying my son.

My healing entered through the work of the mind, as I started to do doctoral work on science and religion, which I pursued for the most psychological of reasons. I knew I needed to get a handle on how it was possible in the universe to be a good person and yet to watch one's child struggle with such a life-changing challenge, and I wasn't willing to enlist psychotherapy to explore that question (my mother is an analyst, so you don't have to be Sigmund Freud to surmise why not!), and the only alternative path was to get a doctorate which would allow me to ask the really big existential questions.

I was fortunate to find a doctoral advisor who was really remarkable, both as a human being and as a scholar. Rabbi Dr. David Ellenson remains my role model in many, many ways. I began to work and the first step of learning about the universe was to read voraciously in science, an early love of mine from high school. I started reading about evolutionary theory, neurobiology and cognitive psychology, astronomy and cosmogony, all to try to get a handle on what constitutes this world we live in, and to then figure out what can religion legitimately offer by way of meaning and solace.

I joke that I invented process theology, although it is only partially a joke. Countless seekers in every generation discover that the cosmos is interactive, dynamic, and self-determining. Through my readings in science and philosophy, I came up with a distillation of a universe that is profoundly relational, in which all identities exist in their connections to each other, and modify each other by their own choices. I realized that this is a universe that is profoundly dynamic, not at all static; it is a universe of timeliness and not of timelessness. Then I picked-up an anthology on panentheism, and when I got to the chapter on process panentheism I realized that I had brothers and sisters in the world, that I was not the first to invent a process theology. Someone had beat me to the punch by about 100 years, and there was a blessed community of people of multiple generations who were already hard at work at articulating the implications of a dynamic relational world. I found a spiritual home with those people and turned to process theology with relish.

What process theology offers me in addition to extended community is a way to make sense of my son's struggles and triumphs. It allows me to affirm that Jacob isn't being judged or tested, that he in fact is like all of us, living with the random workings out of a natural order, and that meaning is to be fashioned by his response to life, not by happenstance. I realize that since God is self-surpassing and engaged in everything, every instant, every moment, that Jacob also can be self-surpassing. Indeed, he is! A few years ago, after a decade of hard work, Jacob marched across a graduation stage to receive an accredited high school diploma, and it was one of the proudest days of my life. But that day was far from the only proud moment because each and every day I see my Jacob surpassing the limits that the experts assume pertain to him. I see him surpassing his own sense of what is possible. I witness him thinking and writing and communicating; I see him mastering his anger and his fear; I see him creating friendships with people who are neurotypical and people who are on the autism spectrum. I see him bringing light and joy and meaning into the world, both for himself and for the rest of us.

But my daughter, who is neurotypical, is no less a miracle than is Jacob. In fact, every human being, every living entity, the whole of creation is eternally self-surpassing and dynamically interrelated, and that also means we are empowering to each other.

What that new understanding makes possible for me is that I am no longer afraid of an all-powerful, all-knowing bully in the sky. I no longer construe the world through the lens of a morality play in which there were winners and losers although there are beloved and outcast. Instead, divinity reveals itself as permeating all worlds. There is nothing, nothing in the world, no moment of time, no place, no created event, that is not marinating in God. That permeating Divinity is what gives each of us the capacity to reach out and to reach beyond ourselves, to grow in new and unprecedented ways, and to be capable of new achievements and new meanings that continue to make life rich and beautiful and worthy.

Those insights have shaped my professional work, my writing and my thinking, for the last decade. I have now produced books integrating Judaism and process thought because it turns out that among other advantages, a process metaphysics is also a great hermeneutical tool; a great way to interpret ancient texts and reveal their contemporary relevance. I no longer get tripped up by how tall was Adam and Eve at the moment of their creation? What color was Sarah's hair? How old was Isaac at the Akedah? Instead, I am able to understand these narratives as rooted in the Divine but blossoming through the

human, and therefore, their divinity is found not in historical accuracy (the facticity of the events they report) but in the
meaning that they reveal through the telling. The notion of
radical human equality and dignity is the insight that emerges
from the first and second chapters of Genesis. Whether or not
there was a first man named Adam and a first woman named
Eve becomes trivial because we stake our lives everyday on the
biblical insight that each and every person is a child of God.
The vitality of democracies vindicates this faith claim.

We stake our lives on the notion that we are each of us fac-
ing the imperative to love our neighbors as we love ourselves,
and that there are no exceptions to that Levitical rule.

All of us must love each other absolutely and we intuit
that justice is love with hands, so living a world in which the
biblical voice thundering "*tzedek tzedek tirdof,* you shall surely
pursue justice" shapes the way we walk in the world.

As a metaphysical perspective and a hermeneutical tool,
process allows me to focus on the deep ways that the bible reso-
nates: It's wisdom, it's compassion, it's morality, it's notion that
we are not alone, and never forsaken. An insistence that the
universe arcs toward justice and that Pharaohs will be brought
low. It's very realistic assessment that the fact that we are never
alone and won't be forsaken doesn't mean that we won't have
to endure terrible tragedy. All life is a mixture of delight and
suffering, and consciousness itself brings about the capacity to
delight and the capacity to mourn. We human *becomings* are
in some ways the articulate voice of the cosmos and we are the
voice of God in the world too, although not God's only voice.

"Panentheism" is the dry, technical term for the understanding that God isn't hermetically sealed from the world,
not reducible to some lifeless, platonic definition that stands

outside of space and time, which then creates a metaphysical impediment and an ethical catastrophe for those who would be devotees. Instead, panentheism articulates the insight that the very universe sings with the breath of God, that God is, as the ancient Hebrew author understood, *chei ha-olamim*, the very life of the cosmos. So we live and breathe and walk God; and we reach out and we celebrate God. In doing the work of social justice; and of binding the wounds; and of grieving together and rejoicing together, we do God in the world.

This new understanding allows me to walk and to breathe. It allows me to stand with my son. It provides me a mission each and every day of my life, for which I am profoundly grateful. So to the hearty band of process thinkers and theologians, who have taken me in and embraced me with such kindness and love, to them: resilient gratitude. To the One who is revealed, both in the unfolding tradition of Torah and in its younger nephew, process thought, I offer a lifetime of service and gratitude.

Conclusion: Returning to God After God

Andrew M. Davis

The story of my own Christian and spiritual journey thus involves the movement from supernatural theism through doubt and disbelief to panentheism.

–Marcus Borg[1]

In spirituality as in theology I find myself returning to the utterly personal panentheism of the God dwelling incognito at the heart of all things.

–John A.T. Robinson[2]

It was the German philosopher Ludwig Feuerbach who famously disrobed theology with his assertion that "Theology is anthropology."[3] Whereas the Book of Genesis envisioned humankind made in the "image of God," Feuerbach countered, declaring that God was actually fashioned in the image of humans. Lifting our desires to a vacant heaven, we see none other than our own exalted face looking back. In making God we only alienate ourselves from our own humanity, establishing our place as sinful earthen exiles, the lowly antitheses of our own divine creation. The "study of God," therefore, is really just the "study of humans."

There is much wisdom in Feuerbach's assertion and one need not subscribe to his atheism to see, as he did, something truly human in the pursuit of God. Far from being a challenge to theology, his statement can underscore the inherently anthropomorphic nature of this quest; for we are all *anthropos* (Greek for "human being"). This volume has born witness to this truth: the spiritual journey is intimately grounded in the human subject and as such, is intensely personal as it begins, continues, ends—and then begins again.

In this concluding chapter, my goal is to bring to together some of the central themes of this volume, as well as offer a deeper perspective of the dynamic theological vision that has emerged from its pages. To this end, my hope is not only to give a sense of *how* a "return to"—or continuation with—God is possible amid today's many challenges, but also *why* a "panentheistic" vision is integral to this path. This final chapter then offers yet another journey, one of wonder and seeking, dying and rising, and an open and imaginative theological future—*within* the divine.

God and the Human Endeavor

The spiritual or theological journey remains inherently human; its adventures and challenges express the restlessness of our inquiry into the mystery of existence and the mystery of God. Anyone who endeavors to think about God in a serious way knows that both patience and persistence are required. Beginning from the diversity of our experience, the questions of theology lead us upon a quest for coherence, meaning, and explanation. Theological questions meander; they evolve and even devolve as the years of our lives pass. Extending from the mysterious nature of existence, belief in God has always been at the very explanatory heart of the cosmos. We can agree with Feuerbach: theology is that discipline whereby God finds a good deal of creation through our human initiative. This need not be controversial. And yet, philosophers and theologians across the ages have been deeply convinced that our baffling residence in the universe finds ultimate coherence only if located in a larger divine initiative. Contrary to the popular opinions of some, talk of God need not (and should not) function without rhyme or reason. Rather, as we have seen, theology by its very nature is rooted in the unique experiential landscape of human existence, which itself contains many rhymes and plenty of reasons.[4]

From experiences of transcendence, awe, and an otherwise holy or sacred reality, people across time have developed religious conceptions. Coupled with the apprehension of values, beauty, and cosmic order and thus the distinctive rational, moral, and aesthetic faculties of human existence, God has had a foundational place throughout history. Indeed, if we are to speak of our intellectual past, God has usually been seen as that necessary postulate or condition that fully illuminates (and integrates) the puzzling realities of human life and ultimately the perennial question of why there should be something rather than nothing.[5] In a profound sense, many of us would echo the words of Howard J. Van Till:

It is remarkable enough that there is something rather than nothing. Far more remarkable...is that the something that exists would be a universe characterized by a robust formational economy—a universe that has all the "right stuff" to self-organize into atoms, molecules, planets, stars, galaxies, and a myriad forms of life. We are members of a remarkable universe. Even what we call "ordinary" or "natural" is deserving of our awe.[6]

Van Till points to the awe-invoking fact that the universe is not simply "something," but something utterly shocking in its formational potentiality. In a deep and bewildering sense, we are self-conscious and meaning-seeking actualizations of this potentiality. This astonishing thought alone leads one to consider something of the existential weight that has traditionally been assigned to the notion of "God." David A. Palin speaks rightly in this regard.

However limited may be human apprehension of the divine, in principle God is ontologically, valuatively, and rationally the final and proper answer to the questions of why there is something rather than nothing and of what that something—which is everything— is "for" or "about." Existentially theism finds in God that which answers the ultimate questions about life which haunt self-reflective human being[s].[7]

There was once a time when theology was understood as an all-inclusive discipline, the "Queen of the Sciences," upon which all avenues of life converged in a meaningful and sensible way. And it is no exaggeration to say that belief in God has been expounded by some of the most formative thinkers of the Western intellectual tradition as the most comprehensible way of understanding the world and our remarkable place within it. In truth, the notion of "God" is one of the major interpretations of reality that classical philosophers have actually accepted.[8]

But perhaps they were mistaken? It is no secret, after all, that this "interpretation" has fallen on hard, forgotten, and rather confused times. Many professional philosophers now subscribe to atheism, and common people too find that the viability of "God" is continually waning. Whitehead put it succinctly: "The modern world has lost God and is seeking him."[9]

A Challenging Milieu

Individuals who are seriously invested in questions about God must admit that doing theology is not an effortless task. It is difficult and often much is at stake. It seems fair to say that the spiritual journey has always been existentially demanding and fraught with disillusionment. Today, however, many believe that we face deeper challenges. Thinking and speaking about God is by no means a simple endeavor given what we now know about our world and its lumbering epochs of cosmic history. The questions emerging from this knowledge are, for many, quite serious. For me personally, it was challenges like those of the Scottish philosopher and skeptic David Hume, who pointed to the "faulty and imperfect" nature of the world as the "first rude essay of some infant deity" who was so "ashamed of his lame performance" that he abandoned it and moved on.[10] When confronted as I once was with the unimaginable and seemingly meaningless suffering and extinction that has characterized our evolutionary march—not to mention the ever-growing horrors perpetuated throughout history by human hands—many have found the idea of a benevolent and omnipotent "Being" who cares for our particular species, intervenes here and there, and has both a timeless plan and purpose, to be simply untenable.

Popular affirmations of a transcendent and "supernatural" God have long been met with a barrage of ridicule. Extending from the great legacies of the "masters of suspicion" (Marx, Nietzsche, Freud) and revamped—albeit less convincingly—in the works of the so-called "New Atheists" (Dawkins, Hitchens, Harris, Dennet), critics have diagnosed belief in God as a lamentable and laughable episode of human antiquity, a superfluous entity the world can readily do without. Indeed, the hammer blows of modernity have seen the "Queen" dethroned from her once esteemed position in the academy and culture. Many now agree with sociologist Phil Zuckerman that talk of God is not "theopoetics," but rather "theo-babble," or with H.L. Mencken, who once described God as the "immemorial refuge of the incompetent."[11]

What is more, the reigning paradigm of "Scientific Naturalism," being steeped in reductive materialism, is described by biologist Richard Lewontin as not allowing a "Divine Foot in the door."[12] This common conviction effectively leaves God to the archaic pages of scripture, forgotten within continually shrinking churches. At best, "theology" equates to what Steven J. Gould once referred to as "that great subject without a subject matter."[13] Echoing Nietzsche's Madman, Mencken too would ask, "Where is the grave-yard of dead gods? What lingering mourner waters their mounds?"[14] The Madman himself inquired, "What after all are these churches now if they are not the tombs and sepulchers of God?"[15] Bound together with the "presumption of atheism," many are singing the choruses of the requiem *aeternam Deo* ("eternal rest to God"). To those who continue to speak of God today, the haunting angels of modernity respond, "Why do you look for the living among the dead?" We certainly have seen the death of many gods throughout history. The Madman was correct: "Gods too decompose."[16] What he neglected to realize, however, is that gods also rise again.

Adventure and Decay

There is a sense in which the spiritual journey is adventurous by its very nature. Whitehead once insisted that "without adventure civilization is in full decay."[17] This is true of virtually every facet of the human quest; and it is no less true of our individual philosophical and theological pursuits that navigate the distinctive and often bewildering terrains of life. Essential to the adventure of human civilizations has always been religious and philosophical concepts that work to situate existence within a context wherein the numerous angles of life find both coherence and justification. According to John F. Haught, "At its normative best," religion "has been the most adventurous component in the historical evolution of human consciousness."[18] We must admit that as long as it is worthwhile to strive for comprehensive justification, the notion of "God" will retain an essential place in the adventure of ideas. I find myself in deep agreement with Anthony Kenny; no other idea has rivaled that of "God."

> After all, if there is no God, then God is incalculably the greatest single creation of the human imagination. No other creation of the imagination has been so fer-

tile of ideas, so great an inspiration to philosophy, to literature, to painting, sculpture, architecture, and drama; no other creation of the human imagination has done so much to stir human beings to deeds of horror and nobility, or set them to lives of austerity or endeavor.[19]

Throughout history conceptions of God or gods have been central in explaining the ambiguous nature of life. From its humble rudiments first considered in the hearts and minds of the ancients, to its diverse systematic elaborations in the Middle Ages, and its varied expressions of the modern and now postmodern world, theology has had quite the journey. Whitehead would agree: without adventure, theology too is in full decay. With its lasting questions of origin, meaning, morality and destiny and its assessment of life as something of supreme and intrinsic value, theology remains a journey for both the head and the heart—what the 13th century philosopher-mystic Bonaventure called the *itinerarium mentis ad Deum* ("the journey of the mind toward God"). The theological undertaking has always presupposed a certain willingness to enter into a very long and important conversation that has not yet ceased.

Many of us have witnessed, however, that one's theological or spiritual journey does come to an end. It often does so both personally and existentially. The sources of one's impasse remain distinctive—be they various challenges of science, or personal experiences of evil and suffering, or even a genuine sense that in our modern world, there is simply no need for any theological hypothesis. As a result, many have entered what Max Weber called the "disenchanted" world, a world deprived of any innate foundation for meaning and values. In the words of Catherine Keller, "the death of God has accompanied the slow deadening of the universe."[20]

Pointing to an apparent rationality behind the cosmos, theists of various stripes have often recited Einstein's famous remark that the most "incomprehensible thing about the universe is that it is comprehensible."[21] And yet, many agree with Steven Weinberg's modern sentiments that "the more the universe seems comprehensible, the more it also seems pointless."[22] Both Weber and Weinberg's diagnosis of the modern world fits squarely with the type of world Nietzsche's Madman foresaw, one that lacks both reason and direction and is plunging "backward, sideward, forward, in all directions" as though straying through an "infinite nothing."[23] Speaking prophetically of God's distant death the Madman asserts, "This tremendous event is still on its way."[24] But many now bear witness to this "event" and its arrival in their own lives.

Gods, then, do decompose and theological journeys do come to an end. But it is also true that the end of one theological adventure often makes way for the birth of another. Admittedly, we may assert "God is dead!" while also knowing that "God" by any serious definition cannot die. Nietzsche, of course, was not speaking of God's *literal* death, as if God was ever really alive. What assuredly can die, however (and Nietzsche knew it well), are certain *notions of God*. Indeed, we can agree with French philosopher Paul Ricoeur when he states that the affirmation "God is dead" need not be heard as a "triumphant thesis of atheism." To proclaim "God is dead," Ricoeur insists, has "nothing to do with" and "is not the same thing as" asserting "God does not exist"; rather it can be understood as its "total opposite."[25] I want to suggest that it deals instead with the need of arriving at a new (or renewed) understanding of God in light of the expiration of an old one. As one theological conception dies, therefore, another can rise to life, permitting the theological journey to begin anew. This is an integral part of the theological adventure, one that can happen again and again: a certain notion of God is increasingly met with various challenges which then open the way for a type of resolution and the possibility of charting new theological paths. So proceeds the dialectic of the theological journey, the structure of one's own spiritual revolutions. This is the adventurous process of the theological quest.

Anatheism: The Path of Return

Richard Kearney has recently introduced a term he calls *anatheism*. As the prefix *ana* indicates, the term anatheism involves a "repetition and return" to God; indeed, a "returning to God after God."[26] Anatheism, he says, is not an end, but a "way of returning to God beyond or beneath the God we thought we possessed."[27] It is a term I find helpful, one that denotes a path of return, a way of reencountering and rediscovering God that allows for the progression of one's spiritual journey in new and dynamic ways. It can indicate the distinctive path one has navigated from the death of one theological conception to the birth of another, and thus one's arrival back to a place of theological affirmation, now seen and understood anew. In this, Kearney stresses that the "*ana* of anatheism may be read as a departure as much as a repetition," and as an "odyssey that takes us away from home and back again."[28]

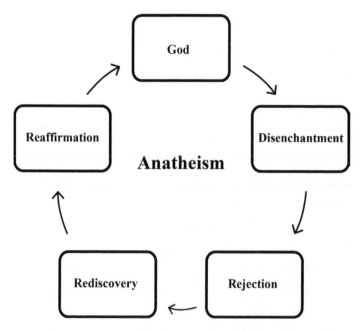

We can appreciate T.S. Eliot's well-known lines as a beautiful utterance of this anatheistic way: "We shall not cease from exploration, and the end of all our exploring will be to arrive where we started and know the place for the first time."[29] This is the heart of the anatheistic way, and the God that is discovered will be different from one's previous theological conception. What may result is a deeper affirmation of God, a more robust sense of the intimate reality that bears this name. Emerging from the variety of distinctive and often challenging avenues one's spiritual journey has traversed, God can be found again. We too can recite with the patriarch, "Surely God is in this place and I was not aware of it" (Genesis 28:16). It was such a God that Marcus Borg described as "the God we never knew."[30]

Finding God Again

The God many once knew was the transcendent and king-like monarch of supernatural theism. Popularly imagined to be outside the universe (or indeed, even a Zeus-like being within it), this God was filled with arbitrary commands and interventionist power, similar to a kind of cosmic landlord. Ignoring deeper visions of an intimate God of all-embracing love, Whitehead rightly states that God was assigned attributes belonging "exclusively to Caesar."[31] Such a vision of God or "Gawd"—as David Ray Griffin has recently argued—continues to be reinforced today.[32] In many ways this monarchial God captures the oddities of the human imagination which have long prioritized power and independence and thereby reinforced fear. Many would go as far as Rabbi Harold Kushner insisting "we can fear an all-powerful God, but we cannot love him..."[33] In a deep sense, it is no surprise that the rejection of this "God" remains at the forefront of so much of today's theological discontent. This is the "God" before whom the wisdom of atheism rages. Many have not known, however, that a deeper vision is (and always has been) available, one which has emerged variously from the pages of this volume.

Wider than Feuerbachian projections of independence, power, and fear, there had always remained the intimate and all-inclusive conception of God which silently staggered the heretical lines of both ancient and modern orthodoxies. "Is it not written...'I have said you are 'gods'" Jesus states, "Why then do you accuse me of blasphemy because I said, 'I am God's Son?'" (John 10:36). Indeed, the immediacy of such a vision was such that you were *in* this God and this God was also *in* you: "I am in the Father and the Father is in me" (John 14:11).

Although, ancient and even mystical in origin, it is this newly recovered spiritual vision that is re-emerging today in diverse and valuable ways for academics and common people alike.

Panentheism

First named by the idealist philosopher Karl Friedrich Krause, "panentheism" is a word that many are unfamiliar with.[34] As this volume has borne witness, however, it is also a word that a growing number of people are coming to know and also use in the context their own spiritual or theological journeys. We have seen that the "en" in the term pan*en*theism is its distinguishing factor. It is neither *pantheism* (Greek for "All-is-God") which insists upon God's radical imminence, even God's pure identification with the natural world itself; nor is it popular *theism,* which separates God from the world with a radical transcendence. Retaining the central insights of these two positions, panentheism (Greek for "All-in-God") maintains that God is the *all-inclusive locus of the universe* itself, at once both *transcendent ground* and *immanent participant.* The world finds its "place" *within* God even as God inhabits and actively animates all things. God is thus inclusive of and also immanent within all—what Marcus Borg described as "the beyond who is 'right here.'"[35]

Popular theism has often weighed the theological scales toward divine transcendence, imagining God as separate from and outside of the universe. By contrast, pantheism is commonly shown to weigh the theological scales toward the direction of divine immanence, eliminating any distinction between God and the world, and thus any individuality to the divine. Panentheism has emerged as a third option, often said to be a *via media* or middle way that holds onto the central commitments of both of these positions. "Divine transcendence," Elizabeth Johnson states, "is a wholeness that includes all parts, embracing the world rather than excluding it...while divine immanence is given as the world's inmost dynamism and goal. Transcendence and immanence are correlative rather than opposed."[36] John Cobb's words are also instructive in distinguishing panentheism from its popular alternatives.

> Theism denies both that God is the impersonal whole and that man is a subordinated part. The central concern of pantheism is to reject an external creator outside of and over against the world who manipulates or controls from without and to assert that God pervades the world and is manifest in all its parts. To both of these central concerns, panentheism says Yes, while providing a way conceptually to hold them together.[37]

Not only, therefore, are the valued aspects of theism and pantheism preserved in panentheism, the difficulties emerging out of either of their lopsided tendencies are also overcome. God remains *internal* to the universe and the universe remains *internal* to God, yet God always remains more than the universe as the very condition in which its possibility is grounded. There is then *a distinction* between God and the cosmos but not *a separation*, an otherness between God and creatures without any obstruction. As Johnson alluded to above, transcendence consists in God's all-inclusiveness, not in God's remoteness. The double "in" of panentheism is paramount as it indicates that the term itself can be read both forwards and backwards in a reciprocal fashion: *pan-en-theos* and *theos-en-pan* ("all in God" and "God in all").[38] Not only is God *immanent in the becoming of the world*, the world is *immanent in the becoming of God*. Contrary to many "classical" renderings, the world influences and affects God, impressing its own becoming reality upon that of the divine.

A simple and far too static diagram communicates the uniqueness of panentheism from common notions of both theism and pantheism. The broken line of the universe below represents the *mutual immanence* of both God and the universe. The locus of the universe is *in* God, but God also interpenetrates the universe as its dynamic and interactive ground.

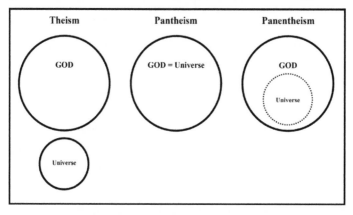

This basic visual portrayal allows one to see why panentheistic conceptions have not only viewed God as the "soul of the world," but also the world as "the body of God." "Just as the soul fills the body," Abraham Joshua Heschel states, "so God fills the world. Just as the soul carries the body so God carries the world."[39] In imagining the world to be God's body, one begins to see how deeply intimate and reciprocal this theological vision really is. For David Ray Griffin, the relation is one of mutual influence and sympathy.

> My body is the part of the universe that I directly influence and also the part that directly influences me,

being so intimately related to me that I feel its sufferings and enjoyments as my own. To call the world the
body of God is to say that God directly influences all
things, somewhat in the way that we directly influence our bodies, and also that God has the kind of
sympathy with all creatures that we have for our bodily members.[40]

Griffin echoes the influence of American philosopher
Charles Hartshorne who spoke of the panentheistic God as
one who "takes into his own life all the currents of feeling in
existence" and one who is "the most irresistible of influences
precisely because he is himself the most open to influence."[41]
In a reciprocal relation with the world, God both knows and
feels the ebb and flow, the joys and the sorrows of creaturely
experience. In the words of Whitehead (to whom Hartshorne
was an assistant), "God is the great companion—the fellow
sufferer who understands."[42]

Put differently, God does not have *knowledge* of the world
(as is popularly conceived) from an all-controlling position
external to the world, but *divine understanding*—extending
from the intimacy of *participation* in those very world processes that are interior to God's own life. In this way, God can
never be viewed as a divine chess master, pushing and pulling
the world; God is rather the "poet of the world," as Whitehead imagines, "with tender patience, leading it by his vision
of truth, beauty and goodness."[43]

History and Significance

Dialogues concerning God's relation to and interaction with
the world have been central throughout our religious and in-

tellectual traditions. A brief historical glance shows us that panentheism is by no means "new," but may be found (in various forms) among the deepest dimensions of the world's scriptures. As several authors of this volume have shown, anentheistic currents can be seen to flow, for example, out of the mystical springs of both the Upanishads and the New Testament. In the best of our intellectual traditions too, panentheistic insights have always been present, even to the extent that John W. Cooper calls panentheism "the other God of the philosophers."[44]

Limiting ourselves briefly to the Western intellectual tradition, the philosophical and religious journeys of thinkers like Herder, Schleiermacher, Fichte, Schelling, Hegel, Bergson, Teilhard, Whitehead, Hartshorne, and many others—not to mention pioneer thinkers that preceded them—all held to panentheistic understandings of the God-world relationship. Truly, the roots of panentheism run deep; these thinkers stand in the vast shadows of Plotinus, and before him Plato, whose insights surrounding the "World-Soul" prophetically invested the first rudiments of panentheism into the march of Western philosophy. Describing Plato's writings as "an inexhaustible mine of suggestion," Whitehead famously quipped that much of "European philosophy" can be characterized as "a series of footnotes to Plato."[45] Perhaps a panentheistic vision itself may be understood as yet another Platonic footnote.

Given its religious and intellectual antecedents, it is not surprising that panentheism is being "renewed" in the spiritual and theological journeys of many today. In addition to being formally named as a distinct theological position, the dialogues surrounding panentheism have received particular amplification in recent years. Philip Clayton has spoken of the "panentheistic turn" of modern theology. British theologian

Michael Brierley refers to panentheism as a "quiet revolution." David Ray Griffin even calls panentheism a "postmodern revelation."[46] And it is not just in academic circles.[47] On a lay level, the "panentheistic turn" is still happening and panentheism's ability to readdress and arguably resolve some of the most pressing challenges of thinking about God today, make it for many a viable path of return.

As one of its most celebrated advocates in recent decades, Marcus Borg candidly spoke to the significance of panentheism for his own Christian journey:

> Though I did not know about panentheism as another Christian option for thinking about God until I was in my 30s, it has since become of utmost importance. It resolved the central religious and intellectual problem of the first three decades of my life. Indeed, becoming aware of panentheism made it possible for me to be a Christian again.[48]

Borg insisted further that thinking about God panentheistically allows for a relational understanding of the spiritual life, which is "both true and profoundly life-giving." "Put very simply and directly," he states, "the course of my Christian journey from supernatural theism to panentheism has led me, experientially and intellectually, to three central convictions: God is real. The Christian life is about entering into a relationship with God as known in Jesus Christ. That relationship can—and will—change your life."[49]

With and Beyond Atheism

In contrast to the intellectual challenges posed by "supernatural theism," Borg maintained that one of the virtues of a panentheistic vision is its ability to keep the question of God *open* even when atheist critiques attempt to close it.

> [Panentheism] does genuinely resolve much of the intel-
> lectual difficulty posed by supernatural theism. For the
> most part, modern skepticism and atheism are a rejec-
> tion of supernatural theism, but if God is not thought
> of as a supernatural being separate from the universe,
> the persuasive force of much of modern atheism van-
> ishes. The resolution of this intellectual difficulty about
> God is no small matter, for it means that the "God ques-
> tion" becomes an open one rather than a closed one.[50]

To the extent that "God" is popularly conceived as a kind of separate super-Being "out there," many have felt fully jus-tified in giving a nod to atheism. There is, I think, wisdom here. Paul Tillich, one of the most influential Protestant theo-logians of the 20th century, remained adamant that "the first step to atheism is always a theology which drags God down to the level of doubtful things. The game of the atheist is then very easy. For he is perfectly justified in destroying such a phantom and all its ghostly qualities."[51] For Tillich, any the-ology that talks of being "outside of God" or that treats God as "an object beside other objects the existence and nature of which are matters of argument," rightly "supports the escape to atheism."[52] And yet, "genuine atheism," he contends, is not even possible, for "even the atheists stand in God—namely, the power out of which they live, the truth for which they grope, and the ultimate meaning of life in which they believe."[53] Til-lich, therefore, famously insists that God is not "a being" that may or may not exist, but the "Ground of all Being," which is existentially presupposed even if verbally denied.

Karl Rahner, Tillich's equally influential Catholic counterpart, spoke of God with similar conviction and similar results, both for the naïveté of much theism and the blindness of much atheism.

> For *that* God really does not exist who operates and functions as an individual existent alongside other existents, and who would thus as it were be a member of the larger household of all reality. Anyone in search of such a God is searching for a false God. Both atheism and a more naïve form of theism labor under the same false notion of God, only the former denies it while the latter believes that it can make sense of it. Both are basically false: the latter, the notion that naïve theism has, because this God does not exist; and the former, atheism, because God is the most radical, the most original, and in a certain sense the most self-evident reality.[54]

In truth, what these insights entail is that one is not able to argue against the existence of God without already assuming it. Atheism on this account would, of course, be a strange thing. The "supreme contradiction," said French theologian Henri De Lubac, "is to lean upon God in the very act of denying him." This, he insists "is a judgment which denies and destroys itself, not only where its content is concerned, in itself, but by undermining its own structure and refusing the condition of existence."[55] Perhaps it is this thought that lies behind the ancient utterance of the psalmist: "The fool says in his heart, 'There is no God'" (Psalm 14:1).

In light of these statements, there is a deep sense in which the common protest: "There is simply no evidence that God exists!" turns a blind eye to ontological wonder. This protest implicitly treats "God" as a localized existent (along others) somewhere in the universe, something that might be subjected to the scientific method. But this is certainly absurd. As the ontological condition without which nothing at all can be, God cannot be put under a microscope or found with a telescope. You cannot objectify what you are *within* any more than a fish can objectify the ocean in which it swims. It is rather the ocean of *existence as such* that is of profound evidential significance. And one should not protest against "lack of evidence" until they grasp the bewilderment of their own existence and whether or not they can actually admit that they alone are the source and ground of this existence. One does not, after all, bring oneself into existence, nor do beings by themselves constitute the fact that other beings also exist. Realizing this leads one to affirm one of the central convictions of the theological tradition: We are contingent beings with the divine source of existence transcending ourselves even as it is immanently instantiated in all things.

It remains far from absurd to infer from the *fact of existence itself* to an all-inclusive reality which grounds this existence. This point has been made in different ways by great minds throughout the Western intellectual tradition, from Aquinas through Tillich, to Rahner, Hartshorne, and beyond: "God must coincide with Being as such; for he cannot be without existence, and therefore equally existence cannot be without him, so that the very meaning of 'exist' must be [panen]theistic..."[56]

Much of today's atheism, although helpful in its denial of a false God, has stopped rather short of the real ontological question. It is not enough to assume that a defeat of supernatural theism constitutes the validity of atheism. In fact, such a jump is hasty, as deeper panentheistic understandings, such as those in this volume, continue to rise to the forefront of the discussion. Speaking as an agnostic, J. Angelo Corlett has nonetheless boldly insisted that, despite its many reasons, as long as atheism fails to address novel panentheistic visions, it remains "guilty of a kind of epistemic irresponsibility." Unless this stage of the argument is reached, he states "the scientific and rationalistic enterprise of atheism remains incomplete, and thus found wanting in a serious way."[57]

Much more of course could (and perhaps should) be said. For now, however, we realized that it would indeed be absurd to deny *existence* or *reality as such*. To question after "God" for panentheism then, is not a matter of trying to "prove" whether there is or is not some being "out there" with a the proper name "God"; it is rather a question about the *deepest nature and character of the reality we already inhabit and participate in now*. It was in this way that Heschel declared that we cannot be "noncommittal about a reality upon which the meaning and manner" of our existence depend. Rather we are driven "toward some sort of affirmation." In whatever decision we make, he states, we implicitly accept "either the presence of God or the absurdity of denying it."[58]

In drawing our attention to our own experience as exemplifications of reality, panentheism can help make sense of these profoundly existential themes. As Corlett strongly insists, panentheism is a kind of theism that may well "defeat atheism once and for all."[59] I want to emphasize, however, that the point is not to "defeat" a particular worldview, but rather, to see it within the wider perspectives the spiritual journey might offer. Atheism is perhaps one important stop along the *anatheistic* way; but one can nevertheless pass through its purifying fires to theological renewal and reenchantment.

Why Panentheism?

In a time when reflective people can find so many spiritual alternatives to any theism, why does this term, this concept of all-in-God, have resonance for a growing public?

—*Catherine Keller*[60]

Through their respective writings, authors both lay and academic have offered a number of reasons for why panentheism has been attracting attention in recent years. These reasons can be found in many of the personal narratives of this volume. Depending on the origin and context of one's spiritual journey, there are a variety of motives behind a return to God through panentheism. Undoubtedly, a prime reason panentheism arises in the return to God (anatheism) is because it appears to address some of today's most pressing theological challenges with a more adequate framework than any of its theological competitors. As Griffin comments, "...although people have often been lead to believe that they must choose from among only three options—traditional theism, pantheism, and atheism—there is a fully distinct fourth alternative, panentheism, which an increasing number of thinkers are finding more satisfactory."[61] For this reason, I want stress that panentheism is not just *an anatheistic path*, but increasingly *the anatheistic path* that individuals are navigating in order to return to God and deepen their spiritual journeys. Like that of Marcus Borg and others, many journeys have involved a move from supernatural theism through doubt and disbelief to the inclusive and immanent vision of panentheism.

What then are some of the concrete reasons individuals are adopting panentheism as a more suitable vision of God?

In the words of Catherine Keller, "What is the lure of panentheism?"[62] Advocates have identified at least seven central arenas through which one may draw near to panentheism as a spiritual or theological model. While one or more of these arenas may be of more personal consequence to one's theological narrative, they can certainly overlap and intersect. Indeed, in a certain sense, to affirm one arena may be seen as an implicit affirmation of the rest. And, when taken together, I believe these arenas construct a cumulative case for *why* individual theological journeys are making a "panenthistic turn." Consider the following diagram expressing the interconnected nature of what I shall call the *panentheistic arenas of return.*[63]

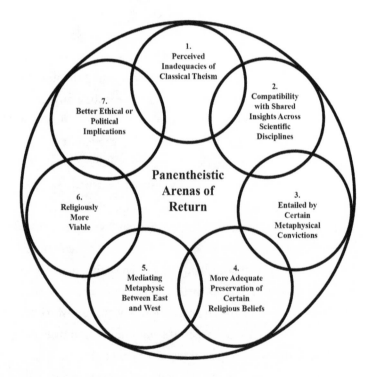

It will be helpful for us to briefly consider each arena in turn before drawing this volume to a close.

1. For a variety of reasons, many have become convinced that "classical" or "supernatural" theism is simply no longer a viable option. For them, atheism has largely become the more convincing answer. Panentheism, however, offers a compelling vision of the divine without the deep problems raised by naïve forms of theism or shortsighted proclamations of atheism.

2. An increasing number of individuals view panentheism as being more compatible with particular results in physics or biology, or with common features shared across the scientific disciplines, such as the dynamic structures of evolutionary emergence. Indeed, panentheism continues to be at the center of discussions surrounding the relationship between religion and science, theistic evolution and quantum physics.

3. A commitment to the truth of a particular metaphysical framework (that is, a way of viewing the nature of reality) may be near to if not inherently panentheistic in orientation. Schools of thought such as German idealism or process philosophy/theology, for example, both involve a panentheistic inclusion of the world within the divine. From Fichte, Schelling, and Hegel to both Whitehead and Hartshorne, God is variously conceived as the dynamic and all-encompassing Mind. For these thinkers and those like them, God is intimately involved with the world. Although eternal in nature, God develops in and through the evolution of history as the world develops in and through the ubiquity of the divine life.

4. Others have insisted that panentheism does a better job preserving core religious beliefs such as revelation, incarnation, sacramental awareness and religious or mystical experience.[64] A vision of the world *within* the divine also allows for the de-

velopment of more adequate notions of divine action without insisting upon supernatural "interventions." For panentheism, the notion of divine interruption from the "outside" is non-sensical; nothing is (or can be) outside of God. Divine activity, therefore, is better understood as radiating from *within*. God's working with the world is not fundamentally external to the world but rather finds its efficacy among the internal workings of the world itself. In this way, advocates have roundly argued that panentheism can be understood as a "naturalistic theism."

5. Panentheism has also been recognized as a mediating metaphysical bridge between Western and Eastern religious systems. Not only is panentheism more conducive as a model for interreligious dialogue and spiritual practices, it also allows for a pluralistic outlook regarding the diversity of the world's traditions and religious figures. The various experiences of religious founders, for example, might be viewed as diverse and partial glimpses of the all-inclusive and multifaceted nature of divinity. Panentheism also offers a position of common ground between religions as panentheistic dimensions can be found within the tapestries of all the major religions of the world. Whether one belongs to a single tradition, multiple traditions, or no tradition at all, panentheism offers a spiritual framework that is thought to include rather than exclude the diversity and depth of world's religions expressions.

6. Panenthesim is also seen to be more religiously viable. The omnipotence, omniscience, and omni-benevolence of traditional theism, for example, have long raised the barricade of the problem of evil. For many, however, the *inclusion* and *immanence* of panentheism can avoid and even offer compelling responses to the infamous problem; for God too is a suffering participant—a victim—of the world's evils. This deep *internal-*

ism expressed by panentheism is also religiously significant: one need not seek a divine being beyond space and time with which to have religious communion; for nothing can be external to the panoramic presence of a God in, with, and under all things.

7. Finally, many insist that popular theism has unacceptable ethical or political implications. Historically, this has been expressed in the "divine right of kings," or more recently perhaps, with the notion that God has a preferential option for one "great" country, thereby giving it license to invade and coerce another. Panentheism, however, cannot be modeled after a divine monarch, but rather a divine companion, as Whitehead suggested above. What is more, passivity regarding the ecological crisis has also been linked to a belief in a supernatural God who controls and governs all things. For panentheism, however, likening the world to the *divine body* means that it cannot be "left behind." Rather, it is God's sacred dwelling place and as such demands respect and proper stewardship. Far from waiting for an omnipotent "Gawd" to bring the world to an apocalyptic end, panentheism insists that God works in and through human creatures to sustain the environment. In this way, it is a vision that necessitates human action.

For these and a variety of other reasons, panentheism is increasingly seen to offer a more satisfying and viable means of conceiving and returning to God today.

The Journey Continues...

In this concluding chapter I have briefly considered the inherently human nature of theological and spiritual journeys. The adventures of the quest to understand the divine bring deep challenges and express the restlessness of our human inquiry. I have stressed the value of panentheism as a way of returning to God *after* God (anatheism), which allows for the continuation of one's spiritual journey even across the challenging terrains of the postmodern world. I have also briefly reflected upon some of the prime arenas through which one might return to God through panentheism.

Recent writings on panentheism, being often scholarly and overly academic in nature, have focused principally on the *why* question. They debate its strengths as a theological framework, its compatibility with the sciences, its promise and value as an interreligious and pluralistic platform, and its importance as a historical phenomenon from Plato to present.[65] And yet, for those less interested in academic debates (which is most people), the message is simple: *for many today, the spiritual journey has led to a shift in orientation toward a divine reality they actually inhabit—one which both includes them and is immanent within them.* This, anyway, is one of the key messages arising from the diverse narratives of this volume.

In the spirit of Borg, we should remember that it has never been enough to simply ask the impersonal question of *what* one affirms about the divine. Rather, I have sought in this volume the more personal—and far more interesting question—of *how* they have found their way. As we have seen, every journey involves different landscapes—rivers, valleys, and mountains—that one navigates on their way to their destination. To ask the *how* question of one's spiritual journey is to ready oneself to hear a tale.

For many, complicated theological arguments may not be necessary in this regard. After all, most people don't wake up one morning only to proclaim, "Ah, now I'm a panentheist!" Rather, over many years and all variety of terrains, they find themselves drawn into a spiritual vision which they believe escapes traditional designations such as "theism," "pantheism" or "atheism." While Carol P. Christ and others may be right that "panentheism" is not a word that will "likely slip into everyday language," the term, nevertheless, remains for many an eminently helpful means of moving beyond these views to a more satisfying spiritual and theological home.[66] And while others dislike the term, or have wished to use another (perhaps "cosmotheandric"), they are nonetheless lured to the dynamic, participatory, and *mutually immanent* vision such language attempts to express. In the end, perhaps we can be glad that the exactness of language fails to fully name "That" which encompasses us all.

The authors of this volume by no means agree on everything, but they certainly do share the conviction that there is deep value in charting one's internal spiritual journey. It is not easy—if it ever was. Many of our journeys have limped under the burden of modern criticisms and existential angst. It helps, however, to have access to the spiritual journeys of those who have gone before us and to see the resonances between them. After all, the God they have discovered we may have never known. What good is a journey, after all, if it cannot be shared?

In making these spiritual and theological narratives pubic, Philip Clayton and I have sought to unveil their various visions of the return to—or continuation with—God. To see how others have navigated this path is an ideal way to chart one's own spiritual journey and to find renewal and reenchantment. The meanderings of the spiritual journey will continue to lead individuals to a variety of theological destinations; but the collective visions of this volume reveal how the interiority of God's own life can be one of them. One can indeed return to God *after* God; and one does so from the *inside*.

Notes

1. Marcus J. Borg, *The God We Never Knew: Beyond Dogmatic Religion to a More Contemporary Faith* (New York: HarperOne, 1997), 12.
2. John A. T. Robinson, *Exploration Into God* (Stanford: Stanford University Press, 1967), 141.
3. See Ludwig Feuerbach, *The Essence of Christianity* (Amherst, NY: Prometheus Books, 1989).
4. See for example John F. Haught's treatment of experiences of depth, future, freedom, beauty and truth in *What Is God?: How To Think About the Divine* (New York: Paulist Press, 1986).
5. For a dizzying array of possible approaches to this wonderful question see John Leslie and Robert Lawrence Kuhn, *The Mystery of Existence: Why is There Anything at All* (West Sussex, UK: Wiley-Blackwell, 2013).
6. Howard J. Van Till, "From Calvinism to Claremont: Now That's Evolution! Or, From Calvin's Supernaturalism to Griffin's Theistic Naturalism," in John B. Cobb Jr. (Ed.) *Back to Darwin: A Richer Account of Evolution* (Grand Rapids: William B. Eerdmans Publishing Group, 2008), 355-356.
7. David A. Palin, *God and the Processes of Reality: Foundations of a Credible Theism* (New York: Routledge, 1989), 40.
8. See for example Keith Ward, *God and the Philosophers* (Minneapolis: Fortress Press, 2009) and *God: A Guide For the Perplexed* (London: Oneworld, 2002).
9. Alfred North Whitehead, *Religion in the Making* (Cambridge: Cambridge University Press, 1926), 62.
10. David Hume, *Dialogues Concerning Natural Religion*, Richard H. Popkin (Ed.) (USA: Hackett Publishing Company, 1998), 37.
11. H.L. Mencken, *Minority Report* (Baltimore: Johns Hopkins University Press, 2006).
12. Richard Lewontin, "Billions and Billions of Demons," *The New York Review*, January 9 (1997): 31.
13. Steven J. Gould, *The Panda's Thumb: More Reflections in*

Natural History (New York: W. W. Norton & Co., 1982), 225. Quoted in David Ray Griffin, *God and Religion In The Postmodern World: Essays in Postmodern Theology* (New York: State University of New York Press, 1989), 1.

14. Quoted in John F. Haught, *What Is God?*, 43.

15. Friedrich Nietzsche and Walter Kaufmann (Trans.), *The Gay Science* (New York: Vintage Books, 1974), 182.

16. Ibid., 181.

17. Alfred North Whitehead, *Adventures of Ideas* (New York: The Free Press, 1933), 279.

18. Haught, *What Is God?*, 91. For Haught's most recent statement of the significance of religion in an "unfinished universe," see *The New Cosmic Story: Inside Our Awakening Universe* (New Haven: Yale University Press, 2017.)

19. Anthony Kenny, *The Metaphysics of Mind* (Oxford: Oxford University Press, 1989), 121.

20. Catherine Keller, "The Body of Panentheism," in Loriliai Biernacki and Philip Clayton (Eds.), *Panentheism Across the World's Traditions* (New York: Oxford University Press, 2014), 73.

21. Albert Einstein, *Ideas and Opinions* (New York: Bonanza, 1954), 292.

22. Steven Weinberg, *The First Three Minutes* (New York: Basic Books, 1977), 144.

23. Nietzsche, *Gay Science*, 181.

24. Ibid., 182.

25. Paul Ricoeur, "The Non-Religious Interpretation of Christianity" in Brian Gregor and Jens Zimmerman (Eds.), *Bonhoeffer and Continental Thought: Cruciform Philosophy* (Bloomington: Indian University Press, 2009), 164-165.

26. Richard Kearney, *Anatheism: Returning to God After God* (New York: Columbia University Press, 2010), 6.

27. Ibid., 3.

28. Ibid., 13

29. In "Little Gidding" (No. 4 of "Four Quartets").

30. See Marcus J. Borg, *The God We Never Knew: Beyond Dogmatic*

Religion to a More Authentic Contemporary Faith (New York: HarperCollins, 1997).

31. Alfred North Whitehead, *Process and Reality*, (Eds.) David Ray Griffin and Donald W. Sherburne (New York: The Free Press, 1978), 342.

32. See David Ray Griffin, *God Exists But Gawd Does Not: From Evil to New Atheism to Fine-Tuning* (Anoka, MN: Process Century Press, 2016).

33. Harold S. Kushner, "Would an All-Powerful God Be Worthy of Worship?" in Sandra B. Lubarsky and David Ray Griffin, *Jewish Theology and Process Thought* (Albany: State University of New York Press, 1996), 90.

34. While Krause (and perhaps Schelling) had used the term in the early 19th century, "panentheism" was largely popularized by Charles Hartshorne in the mid-20th century. See for example Charles Hartshorne and William L. Reese, *Philosophers Speak of God* (Amherst, NY: Humanity Books, 2000).

35. Borg, *The God We Never Knew*, 51.

36. Elizabeth A. Johnson, *She Who Is: The Mystery of God in Feminist Theological Discourse* (New York: Crossroad, 1992), 231.

37. John B. Cobb Jr., *God and the World* (Philadelphia: The Westminster Press, 1965), 80.

38. Corresponding to both the transcendence and immanence of God, the double "in" expressed here is widely used as a generic definition of panentheism. While we need not go beyond this broad meaning of the term, it is important to also note that "panentheism" can be used as an umbrella term, corresponding to a diversity of nuanced positions like those expressed in this volume. Although various, these include the core convictions that the divine is dynamically inclusive of and also immanent within (but not reducible to) the world. There are thus a variety of forms of panentheism and not just one. Marcus Borg rightly states, "One may thus speak of a process panentheism [A.N. Whitehead], a primordial panentheism [Huston Smith], a Tillichian panentheism [Paul Tillich], and so forth." Borg, *The God We Never Knew*, 51, n. 4. I

39. Abraham Joshua Heschel, *Man is Not Alone: A Philosophy of Religion* (New York: The Noonday Press, 1976), 122.

40. David Ray Griffin, P*anentheism and Scientific Naturalism: Rethinking Evil, Morality, Religious Experience, Religious Pluralism and the Academic Study of Religion* (Claremont: Process Century Press, 2014), 28.

41. Charles Hartshorne, *The Divine Relativity: A Social Conception of God* (New Haven: Yale University Press, 1948), xvii.

42. Whitehead, *Process and Reality*, 351.

43. Ibid., 346.

44. John W. Cooper, *Panentheism: The Other God of the Philosophers – From Plato to the Present* (Grand Rapids, MN: Baker Academic, 2006).

45. Whitehead, *Process and Reality*, 39.

46. See the respective chapters by Brierley, Clayton and Griffin in Philip Clayton and Arthur Peacocke, *In Whom We Live and Move and Have Our Being: Panetheistic Reflections on God's Presence in a Scientific World* (Grand Rapids, MN: Wm. B. Eerdmans, 2004).

47. A search for "panentheism" on YouTube, Google or Amazon, for example, has yielded increasingly more results even in the last five years. Panentheism has also appeared as the subject of Robert Lawrence Kuhn's many popular interviews and T.V. episodes on *Closer to Truth*. (See https://www.closertotruth.com/episodes/panentheism-the-world-god.)

48. Borg, *The God We Never Knew*, 12.

49. Ibid, 51.

50. Ibid., 33-34.

51. Paul Tillich, *Shaking the Foundations* (Eugene: Wipf and Stock Publishers, 1948), 45.

52. Ibid., 45, 127.

53. Ibid., 127-128.

54. Karl Rahner, *Foundations of Christian Faith: An Introduction to the Idea of Chrstianity*, William V. Dych (Trans.) (London: Darton, Longman and Todd, 1978), 63.

55. Henri de Lubac, *The Discovery of God: The Roads that Run from*

God to Man and from Man to God, Alexander Dru (Trans.) (New York: P.J. Kenedy & Sons, 1960), 40.

56. Hartshorne and Reese, *Philosophers Speak of God*, 8.

57. J. Angelo Corlett, *Errors of Atheism* (New York: Continuum, 2010), 63.

58. Heschel, *Man is Not Alone*, 81-82.

59. Ibid., xiii.

60. Keller, "The Body of Panentheism," 63.

61. Griffin, *Panentheism and Scientific Naturalism*, 14.

62. Keller, "The Body of Panentheism," 63.

63. This diagram re-fashions what Philip Clayton has called a "rational reconstruction of some of the central options" involved in one's adoption of panentheism. See Clayton and Peacocke, *In Whom we Live*, 73-74.

64. It was a series of profound mystical experiences that ultimately lead Marcus Borg to embrace panentheism. Borg rightly insisted that the reality of mystical experience must affect the way we think about God:

> "A theology that takes mystical experiences seriously leads to a very different understanding of the referent of the word 'God.' The word no longer refers to a being separate from the universe, but to a reality, a 'more,' a radiant and luminous presence that permeates everything that is. This way of thinking about God is now most often called 'panentheism.'"

In Marcus Borg, *Convictions: How I learned What Matters Most* (New York: HarperOne, 2014), 45. Borg offers personal accounts of these experiences in this last book. See chapter three specifically, "God is Real and Is a Mystery."

65. See for example, Clayton and Peacocke, *In Whom We Live*; Griffin, *Panentheism and Scientific Naturalism*; Biernacki and Clayton, *Panentheism Across the World's Traditions*; and Cooper, *Panentheism: The Other God of the Philosophers*.

66. Color P. Christ, *She Who Changes* (New York: Palgrave Macmillan, 2003), 209.

Contributor Bios

Rabbi Dr. Bradley Shavit Artson is the Abner and Goldstine Dean's Chair of the Ziegler School of Rabbinic Studies and a vice president at American Jewish University. He is also the founding dean of the Zacharias Frankel College at the University of Potsdam, Germany, ordaining Masorti rabbis for Europe. His many books include *God of Becoming and Relationship: The Dynamic Nature of Process Theology* and *Renewing the Process of Creation: A Jewish Integration of Science and Spirit*.

Loriliai Biernacki is an associate professor in the Department of Religious Studies at the University of Colorado at Boulder. Her research interests include Hinduism, gender, and the interface between religion and science. Her first book, *Renowned Goddess of Desire: Women, Sex and Speech in Tantra*, won the Kayden Award in 2008. She is coeditor of *Panentheism across the World's Religious Traditions* (2013), and is currently working on a study of the 11th-century Indian philosopher

Abhinavagupta within the framework of wonder, the New Materialisms, and conceptions of the body-mind interface.

Cynthia Bourgeault is a modern-day mystic, Episcopal priest, writer, and internationally-reknowned retreat leader. She divides her time between solitude at her seaside hermitage in Maine and a demanding schedule of traveling globally to teach and spread the recovery of the Christian contemplative and Wisdom paths. She is a core faculty member at the Center for Action and Contemplation, alongside fellow teachers and colleagues James Finley and Richard Rohr, and is the author of nine books, including *The Wisdom Jesus: Transforming Heart and Mind—A New Perspective on Christ and His Message, The Holy Trinity and the Law of Three: Discovering the Radical Truth at the Heart of Christianity,* and *The Heart of Centering Prayer: Nondual Christianity in Theory and Practice.*

Deepak Chopra, MD, FACP, is a world-renowned pioneer in integrative medicine and personal transformation. He is the founder of the Chopra Foundation and cofounder of Jiyo.com and the Chopra Center for Wellbeing. *TIME* magazine has described him as "one of the top 100 heroes and icons of the century." He is board certified in internal medicine, endocrinology and metabolism; a fellow of the American College of Physicians; a clinical professor in medicine at the University of California, San Diego; an adjunct professor at Kellogg School of Executive Management at Northwestern University; an adjunct professor at Columbia Business School, Columbia University; and a professor of consciousness studies at Sofia University in Palo Alto, California. *The World Post* and *The Huffington Post* global internet survey ranked "Chopra #17 influential thinker in the world and #1 in Medicine." In conjunction with his medical achievements, Dr. Chopra is recognized as a prolific author of more than 85 books, translated into over 43 languages; 25 of his books have achieved the status of *New York Times* Bestsellers. His latest national bestseller, *The Healing Self*, was coauthored with Dr. Rudolph Tanzi. Dr. Chopra is also a contributing columnist for the *San Francisco Chronicle*.

Philip Clayton is the Ingraham Professor at Claremont School of Theology in Claremont, California. He has taught or held research professorships at Williams College, Harvard University, Cambridge University, and the University of Munich. His research focuses on biological emergence, religion and science, process studies, and contemporary issues in ecology, religion, and ethics. He is the recipient of multiple research grants and international lectureships, as well as the author of numerous books, including *The Predicament of Belief: Science, Philosophy, Faith* (2011), *Religion and Science: The Basics* (2011), *Transforming Christian Theology: For Church and Society* (2009), and *In Quest of Freedom: The Emergence of Spirit in the Natural World* (2009). He also edited *The Oxford Handbook of Religion and Science* (2006). Over the last 20 years he has written extensively on "the world in God," and worked to defend panentheism within the academic community in such works as *Adventures in the Spirit* (2008) and *In Whom We Live and Move and Have Our Being* (2004).

John B. Cobb Jr. is an American theologian, philosopher, environmentalist and preeminent scholar in the field of process philosophy and process theology. He is a founding co-director for the Center for Process Studies and professor emeritus of Claremont School of Theology and Claremont Graduate University. He is the author of numerous articles and books, including *God and the World, Christ in a Pluralistic Age, A Christian Natural Theology, Is It Too Late? A Theology of Ecology, Beyond Dialogue: A Mutual Transformation of Buddhism and Christianity,* and *Jesus' Abba: The God Who Has Not Failed.* In 2014, he was elected to the American Academy of Arts and Sciences.

Andrew M. Davis is a philosopher, theologian and scholar of world religions. He holds degrees in philosophy/theology and interreligious studies, and is currently a doctoral candidate in Religion at Claremont School of Theology. His research interests include metaphysics and philosophical theology, philosophy of religion, natural theology, comparative religion, and applied spirituality. His studies have led him to India, Israel-Palestine, and Europe. In 2013, he received Claremont's Award for Excellence in Biblical Studies and in 2017 he was awarded a fellowship with FASPE (Fellowships at Auschwitz for the Study of Professional Ethics).

Ilia Delio, OSF, holds the Josephine C. Connelly Endowed Chair in Theology at Villanova University and has authored or co-authored many books, including *Care for Creation,* which won two Catholic Press Book Awards in 2009. Her recent books include *A Hunger for Wholeness: Soul, Space and Transcendence* (2018), *Making All Things New* (2015), and *The Unbearable Wholeness of Being: God, Evolution and the Power of Love,* which received the 2014 Silver Nautilus Book Award. She lectures nationally and internationally in the areas of science, religion, and culture, and is the general editor for the series *Catholicity in an Evolving Universe,* published by Orbis Books.

Matthew Fox is an activist and spiritual theologian who has written numerous books on mysticism, spirituality, and culture, including *Original Blessing, The Coming of the Cosmic Christ, The Reinvention of Work, A Spirituality Named Compassion, Hildegard of Bingen: A Saint for Our Times, Meister Eckhart: A Mystic-Warrior for Our Times, A Way to God: Thomas Merton's Creation Spirituality Journey, Naming the Unnameable: 89 Wonderful and Useful Names for God,* and, most recently, *Order of the Sacred Earth* (2018). His books have been translated into 69 languages and received many awards. As an activist, he has designed a pedagogy for teaching spirituality that has proven dynamic in many schools, most recently at the Fox Institute for Creation Spirituality in Boulder, Colorado.

Richard Rohr is a globally-recognized ecumenical teacher, bearing witness to the universal awakening within Christian mysticism and the Perennial Tradition. He is a Franciscan priest of the New Mexico Province and founder of the Center for Action and Contemplation (CAC) in Albuquerque. His teaching is grounded in the Franciscan alternative orthodoxy—practices of contemplation and self-emptying, expressing itself in radical compassion, particularly for the socially marginalized. He is academic dean of the Living School for Action and Contemplation and the author of numerous books, including *Everything Belongs, Adam's Return, The Naked Now, Breathing Under Water, Falling Upward, Immortal Diamond, Eager to Love: The Alternative Way of Francis of Assisi,* and *The Divine Dance: The Trinity and Your Transformation.*

Rupert Sheldrake is a biologist and the author of more than 85 scientific papers and 12 books, including *The Presence of the Past, Science Set Free* and *Science and Spiritual Practices.*

He has been a Fellow of Clare College, Cambridge University, a Frank Know Fellow at Harvard University, and a Research Fellow of the Royal Society. From 2005 to 2010, he was the director of the Perrott-Warrick Project for research on unexplained human and animal abilities, funded by Trinity College, Cambridge. He is currently a fellow of the Institute of Noetic Sciences in Petaluma, California, as well as of Schumacher College in Devon, England.

Marjorie H. Suchocki is professor emerita at Claremont School of Theology, where she held the Ingraham Chair in Theology for 12 years. She is also the faculty co-director emerita of the Center for Process Studies and the director of the Common Good International Film Festival. She is widely recognized as a leader in process thought, and has written many articles and books in philosophy, theology, and religion, including *God Christ Church: A Practical Guide to Process Theology, The End of Evil: Process Eschatology in Historical Context, The Fall to Violence: Original Sin in Relational Theology, Divinity and Diversity: A Christian Affirmation of Religious Pluralism,* and *Through a Lens Darkly: Tracing Redemption in Film.*

Keith Ward is professor of religion at Roehampton University, London. He is a former professor of the history and philosophy of religion at London University; dean of Trinity Hall, Cambridge University; and Regius Professor of Divinity at Oxford University. He is a fellow of the British Academy, and has written numerous books, including *God: a Guide for the Perplexed, Christ and the Cosmos, The Christian Idea of God,* and *The Big Questions in Science and Religion.* He is a priest of the Church of England, and a Canon of Christ Church, Oxford.

260